Imagining the Mulatta

Imagining the Mulatta

Blackness in U.S. and Brazilian Media

JASMINE MITCHELL

UNIVERSITY OF ILLINOIS PRESS
Urbana, Chicago, and Springfield

Library of Congress Cataloging-in-Publication Data
Names: Mitchell, Jasmine, 1981- author.
Title: Imagining the Mulatta : blackness in U.S. and
    Brazilian media / Jasmine Mitchell.
Other titles: Blackness in U.S. and Brazilian media
Description: Urbana : University of Illinois Press, [2020]
    | Includes bibliographical references and index.
Identifiers: LCCN 2019052065 (print) | LCCN 2019052066
    (ebook) | ISBN 9780252043284 (cloth) | ISBN
    9780252085208 (paperback) | ISBN 9780252052163
    (ebook)
Subjects: LCSH: Mass media and race relations—United
    States. | Mass media and race relations—Brazil. |
    Women in mass media—United States. | Women in
    mass media—Brazil. | Celebrities in mass media—
    United States. | Celebrities in mass media—Brazil.
    | Racially mixed women—Race identity—United
    States. | Racially mixed women—Race identity—
    Brazil.
Classification: LCC P94.5.M552 U663 2020 (print) | LCC
    P94.5.M552 (ebook) | ddc 305.48/80509096—dc23
LC record available at https://lccn.loc.gov/2019052065
LC ebook record available at https://lccn.loc.gov/
    2019052066

Contents

Preface

Crossing uneven geographies of oceans and rivers, the ground on which descendants of Black survivors of the Middle Passage, European colonizers, and Indigenous peoples dwell, this book threads an embodied architecture of the Americas. Whether haunted, romanticized, or illegible, the underpinnings of racial mixture go beyond static national borders. The directions of this book, just as the directions of my journey and the passages of my ancestors, slides along multiple constellations. The hemispheric routes of traversing through, within, and in relation to the Americas inform the genesis of this project. Like many women who do not fit into the imagined U.S. racial landscape of Black–white binaries, I am often asked "where are you from?" or "what are you?" With the U.S. fascination of mixed race as the advent of a new special group, people seldom believe me when I reply that my family has been in the United States for hundreds of years. When I travel outside of the United States, I often receive the same questions as the ingrained U.S.-exported media images largely erase my visibility of U.S. national belonging. Growing up in the 1980s, I rarely saw images of interracial families on television or in film. Mistaken for everything from Moroccan to Colombian to Filipino to Hawaiian, these interactions map race, ethnicity, and nationality onto my own body. My working-class parents—an African American mother from Philadelphia and a white father from semirural Pennsylvania—recognized this potential illegibility when they purposefully selected our diverse Brooklyn neighborhood because they thought we would be accepted. Growing up alongside Puerto Ricans, community members often assumed that my brother and I were also Puerto Rican and that my father was a light-skinned Puerto Rican man. In white neighborhoods, my mother, just as I now experience with my own two children, was often assumed to be the nanny. At an early age when we would go out as a family beyond our neighborhood, I became accustomed to stares. The notion of racial mixture as also African American often evoked surprise.

My understanding of mixed race and Blackness have evolved over the course of my adulthood, and I now identify as a mixed-Black woman. In college, I created an organization called Students of Mixed Heritage to give students like me at Williams College a space for discussions about race and ethnicity. We did not think of ourselves as separatists but as working in conjunction with other minority groups such as the Black Student Union. However, by the mid-2000s, I was wary of the idea that mixed-race heritage is special. Seeing the influx of multiracial images and the rhetoric of mixed-race people as a new development within U.S. culture, I became skeptical of the political stakes of the "discovery" of mixed-race people as new phenomena.

Like many descendants of enslaved African Americans, my mother's side of the family runs the gamut of skin tones. Our family histories illustrate the terrain of how racial mixing is not new and has not created racial paradise thus far. My earliest known ancestor on both maternal and paternal sides, Amanda, was a light-skinned African American woman who was born into U.S. chattel slavery. The photograph of her that my relatives discovered in the late 2000s reveals a body that could be read as white. The recovery of Amanda's photograph is also a re-membering of mixture within Blackness. She, like many other relatives, reflects African American and hemispheric histories of racial mixing interwoven within the legacies of slavery and colonization in the Americas. For Amanda, descended from my maternal grandfather's side, the written historical narratives are incomplete, and the family stories and imagined futures are what we have left. Like much of the fabric of African American histories, the relatives on my grandfather's side have been registered as negro, mulatto, colored, and Black. Like many of my relatives, my grandmother's side of the family had light-skinned members from my great-grandmother and dark-skinned members from my great-grandfather. Stories of Indigenous kinship and mixture also wove into larger family narratives. Within this larger family of variant skin and eye colors, hair textures, and sprinkled freckles, everyone belonged.

As a child, I spent many summers at my grandparents' house in West Philadelphia. While surrounded by generations of extended family, I loved hearing of familial farmland stories in the Carolinas, urban migration to the Northeast, and journeys beyond the geographical bounds of the United States. The Love and Reeder clans were proud of their achievements. Nestled within these enclaves, my racial identity was part of larger stories of the mixedness within Blackness. Along with our own histories as models, my grandparents, great-uncles and -aunts shared books and conversations of Black histories and traditions evidencing a sense of Black diasporic pride. Yet, some family members often commented on my fairer skin and my hairline, which curls on the underside but could be tussled until straight on the top. Like much of Latin America in which phrases of "Black behind the ears" are commonplace, the privileges attuned to the proximities of whiteness reverberate down generations through the very structures and intimacies of our families. Immense Black pride alongside the valuing of slim, light-skinned, wavy-haired bodies, illuminates the messy imperfections of Black histories. While I also spent parts of summers with my father's sides of the family in rural and semirural settings and enjoyed the loving and nurturing connections, I knew that I belonged *in* the family but *not* to whiteness. Embarked with a scholarship to Phillips Academy Andover in Massachusetts, I navigated multiple environs of white upper-class privileges alongside national, racial, ethnic, and socioeconomic diversity within the school. I had learned from childhood to move between many worlds. But, I would not be considered white in any of these worlds. While my racial ambiguity positioned a flexibility that many Blacks in the United States do not have, the constant questioning, policing, and fascination of my racial background revealed a national obsession with managing and categorizing Blackness.

A stay in Havana in 2000 introduced me to national distinctions of racial mixing and the entangled transnational manifestations of mixed women of African descent. I was already accustomed to piropos, the practice of catcalling, in Cuba when I heard two Cuban men holler "*mulata!*" at me. I was taken aback by the term, which I considered an antiquated denigration loaded with slavery connotations. But I heard this term repeatedly in Cuba and then during my travels to Brazil for work and this research. The ebb and flow of the mulatta/*mulata* in popular vernacular, discourse, and imagery has continually perplexed me.

Friends explained to me that in Latin America *mulata* is a compliment. Yet, these loaded raced and gendered terms carried political commitments, practices, and tools of race making. On that same trip to Havana, I was barred from entering a tourist hotel in 2000 because my phenotypical characteristics led personnel to assume I was a sex worker. In the same year on a trip to Managua, Nicaragua, two Nicaraguan men asked me if I was Cuban or Panamanian. When I signaled my disinterest in their sexual advances, they called me a nigger and physically threatened me. The next year as I studied in Buenos Aires, the *mulata* comment continued and I was frequently asked if I was Brazilian as Argentine men propositioned me on the street and groped and threw condoms at me in bars. It is an understatement to assert that the supposed flattery of the term *mulata* carried forth racialized sexualization. It signaled the expectation that I perform a certain kind of identity and certain kinds of behavior, especially that of being sexually available. I saw that the hypersexual *mulata* circulates transnationally throughout Cuba, Argentina, Nicaragua, and beyond.

Yet I thought Brazil might be different for two reasons: first, it styles itself a racial paradise where race has no meaning; second, I thought the hypersexual Brazilian *mulata* trope could hardly hold as intensely in Brazil itself. However, I soon faced my own disillusionment with a Brazilian racial utopia. My students mistook me for cleaning staff on my first day at an elite international private school with an almost uniformly white faculty, despite my professional attire. Brazilians often told me I was not Black but *morena*, a vague term for brown. A woman in Rio de Janeiro told me at a social engagement that she did not like having Blacks in her house. When I mentioned that my own mother was Black, she said that African Americans were different than Afro-Brazilians—cleaner, better looking, and smarter. I also befriended Brazilians of varying skin tones in both São Paulo and Rio de Janeiro who chose to identity as Black, expressed solidarity with African Americans, and also recognized me as Black.

When conducting research for this book at the Universidade de São Paulo, which is both one of the most prestigious and one of the whitest universities in Brazil, I found that many professors often avoided discussions of race by saying that I saw race when it did not exist in Brazil because of my U.S. mindset. The few professors who were willing to discuss race often closed their office doors so their colleagues could not overhear our conversations. Starting with my first trip to Brazil in 2001, I had been approached for sex by multiple white male European and U.S. tourists as well as African American tourists. I soon realized that my physical appearance coincided with international images of *mulata* sexual availability. On a 2010 trip to Rio, my white U.S.-born husband and I attended a workshop tour of a luxury jewelry store. After the tour, the sales representative took me for a girlfriend for hire; indeed, he confided with my husband in English that he did not need to spend a large amount of money on a woman like me. In turn, I replied in English, mortifying him. His immediate apology was prompted by my U.S. privileged position authenticated by my use of English. Now that he was able to see and hear me differently, my body represented the United States and eclipsed his racism and sexism. It was clear that he would not have apologized to a Brazilian who looked like me.

I share these experiences not to indulge my own indignation; they are in fact the tip of the iceberg. Rather, I wish to illuminate the genesis of this work and the guiding questions that led me to explore these hemispheric routes of white patriarchy and the controlling of mixed-Black women's bodies. Experiencing firsthand how the idea of the hypersexual mulatta/*mulata* for consumption circulates transnationally exposed me to the phenomena this book examines. I piece together these personal points of reference to help illustrate the practices and processes of managing Blackness. The inspiration for this book has been this personal landscape of negotiating race, gender, sexuality, class, and nationality and hope for further solidarity between the United States and Brazil in struggles for social justice.

Acknowledgments

Writers often describe the book process as one of isolation, yet the seeds of this work were sprouted far beyond my own two hands. I am grateful to the many family members, friends, colleagues, and comrades who helped mold this book and support me in the process through life and scholarly experiences of intense joy, grief, exhaustion, and hope. This book has been sustained by rich communities across multiple geographies. This list is not exhaustive but a mere sampling of the debts to whom I owe.

Long before the writing and research that this book entailed, I have been grateful for the cultivation of research, teaching, and writing for social change as embodied in De La Salle Academy, the Oliver Scholars Program, and Phillips Academy Andover. This book would not be possible had I not been encouraged, while a sophomore at Williams College, to consider a career in the academy through the Mellon Mays Fellowship. I received immense support from the program coordinator, Molly Magavern. In graduate school to the tenure track, the Mellon Mays Program has faithfully encouraged this project. There are numerous individuals to name, but I would like to thank my friends, teachers, professors, and staff at these schools and programs as a whole for the visions of empowering students of color to transform our worlds.

The seeds of the research of this book began in graduate school. Bianet Castellanos (once a Mellon, always a Mellon) encouraged and prodded the hemispheric lens toward race in this book, provided crucial mentorship and strategizing, and modeled how to be a professional academic. Erika Lee offered guidance, advice, and encouragement as I pulled together multiple archives, languages, and locations. Beyond furthering my Portuguese and understandings of Lusophone and African Diaspora, Fernando Arenas exemplified the kind, generous spirit that I hope I can also transmit to my students. Jigna Desai helped me realize my contributions to feminist and cultural studies. I thank her for the critical insights, thoughtful feedback, and questions. Roderick Ferguson helped me unpack the stakes of racialization and sexuality. Their encouragement sustained me as I traveled back and forth between Minneapolis, New York City, São Paulo, and Rio de Janeiro.

In Brazil, I am grateful for the kindness and graciousness shown as numerous people opened up their homes to me, pointed out archives, drove me around the maddening traffic of São Paulo, introduced me to gatekeepers, and conversed with me over numerous cafés and caipirinhas. Cristina Mungioli of the Universidade de São Paulo helped introduce me to the world of telenovelas, secure a visa, carry out a research agenda, and has provided years of support. Cristina, along with Maria Immacolata Lopes, helped integrate me into the Centro de Estudos de Telenovela. The numerous conversations and poring over archives with professors and students there helped fuel this project. I am also particularly indebted to Aline and Camila Barbieri, Luna Chino, Nixon Alves, Carlos Martin, Paola Prandini, João Feres, and Débora Almeida for their social and intellectual exchange.

Support from the Woodrow Wilson Career Enhancement Fellowship for Junior Faculty and Andrew W. Mellon Mays Fellowship Program provided critical time for completing the manuscript as well as financial and mentorship resources. Mary Beltrán's mentorship during my Woodrow Wilson Career Enhancement Fellowship was invaluable. Her commitment, thoughtful comments on a manuscript draft, and kindhearted encouragement helped steer this project along. I also appreciate Alisha Knight's professional mentorship as I navigated junior faculty terrain. I am also grateful for fellowships from the Graduate School at the University of Minnesota and the Interdisciplinary Center for the Study of Global Change during the course of the research in graduate school.

The State University of New York–Old Westbury provided a supportive environment to develop this book. I am fortunate enough to have landed in the American Studies and Media and Communications Department that is simultaneously welcoming, collegial, and supportive. I am thankful especially for the advocacy of Jermaine Archer, Amanda Frisken, and Andrew Mattson during their time as department chairs. Carol Quirke, Samara Smith, Llana Barber, Laura Chipley, John Friedman, Karl Grossman, Aubrey Bonnett, Lisa

Payton, Denton Watson, and Joe Manfredi have made departmental citizenship pleasurable. At a university with a mission for social justice, numerous faculty, administration, and students offered support and key questions in the framing of the stakes of this book.

I would be remiss if I did not thank Dawn Durante of the University of Illinois Press. Her enthusiasm, patience, wise counsel, and acumen helped me re-envision this book over the years. Thanks to the anonymous reviewers who dedicated their time and attention to providing comments and critiques for pushing this book forward. Much gratitude to Deborah Oliver for polishing my words. Special thanks to Sika Dagbovie-Mullins, Alvaro Jarrín, Rachel Quinn, Frank Guridy, and Habiba Ibrahim, who read portions of the manuscript and offered thoughtful feedback to clarify the book's arguments. Tanya Hernández, Reighan Gillam, and Gladys Mitchell-Walthour helped shaped this book through conversations and conferences. I am also grateful for fellow conference panelists and attendees at the Critical Mixed Race Studies Association, American Studies Association, Brazilian Studies Association, and National Women's Studies Association for sharpening the analysis in this book.

To my husband, Travis Batty. I promised life would never be boring! Thank you for your immense faith in my intellectual and social justice pursuits as we have journeyed near and far from each other. Thank you for always believing that I am a rock star even when I don't feel like one. Thanks for your sense of humor with me on this adventure with life! Our two children, Indiana and Violet, light up my world with their smiles, curiosity, and laughter. I thank all of the caregivers who have provided love for our children as I wrote this book. Violet and Indiana, you remind me that I stand on the shoulders of our ancestors as well as those of future generations. You both inspire me to illuminate the paths of freedom for those to come.

My first teachers were my family members. My parents, Bill and Janise Mitchell, fostered my intellectual curiosity, provided unwavering support as my journeys took me far from home. To my mother, I am grateful for your love of history and teaching, and for always stepping in to help as I learn to nurture my own children as you have done for me. My father's integrity, advocacy, and sense of humor inspire me and so many other generations that he illuminates. My brother, Ben Mitchell, has always evinced his pride and support while reminding me to slow down and enjoy. My grandparents were my first intellectual models. James (Pop Pop) and Margaret (Mom Mom) Reeder regaled me with narratives of our family's histories, encouraged me to write down my stories and seek connections across the globe. My paternal grandmother, Patricia Mitchell, like my maternal grandparents, always fed my curiosity, encouraging me to read as much as possible, to question everything, and to pursue my research with humility and an adventurous spirit. Even without doctorate degrees they have been very much my most important professors. My family's compassion inspires the kind of scholarship I want to do and the life I want to lead. I hope my family can see in this book the manifestation of love.

Imagining the Mulatta

Introduction

The April 2018 cover of *National Geographic* featured two mixed-race twin girls of African and European descent, one light-skinned with blue eyes and the other dark-skinned, to promote the headline, "Black and White: These twin sisters make us rethink everything we know about race." In the same issue, pairing four thousand portraits with Pantone color cards, Brazilian photographer Angélica Dass "shows us there is no such thing as black and white."[1] Although the issue was conceived as an apology for *National Geographic*'s past racism, the magazine nonetheless formulated race and racism as individual rather than structural, ignoring the ongoing and historically determined social processes that media culture constructs and reinforces. The issue follows a pattern of exoticizing mixed-race bodies and fetishization of light-skinned racial ambiguity.

National Geographic is not alone in its recasting of mixed-race bodies as foreign, far off in the future, or else a rare and extraordinary object of curiosity. In the 1990s and 2000s, numerous other U.S. magazines such as *Time* and *Newsweek* repeated descriptors like "beautiful," "unexpected," "striking," and "remarkable" to imagine the mixed-race women they predict will populate a new racial utopia.[2] A 1993 cover of *Time* magazine envisioned the "new face of America," a computer-generated image of a slightly tanned woman embodying the nation's racially mixed future. Twenty years later, a 2013 article in *National Geographic* magazine similarly announced that "we're becoming a country where race is no longer so black and white."[3] Projecting the multiracial woman as a global

SPECIAL ISSUE

NATIONAL GEOGRAPHIC

Black and White

These twin sisters make us rethink everything we know about race

APRIL 2018

WHAT'S YOUR STORY? #IDefineMe

The April 2018 issue on the subject of race featured fraternal mixed-race twins on its cover. Courtesy of *National Geographic*.

political ideal, these representations nevertheless blot out histories of racial violence and national and hemispheric conditions of anti-Blackness. In the imagined future that transcends race, Blackness becomes archaic, a barrier to actualizing these visions of utopia.

Paralleling what is happening in the United States, Brazilian visions and anxieties of hybridity also take up the inclusion of Blackness. Ideas about race are enhanced if Brazil and the United States are placed together in a hemispheric framework rather than viewing them as wholly isolated and separate. In this book, "hemispheric" refers to a relational understanding of interconnected histories, narratives, ideas, and social structures in the Americas. The United States and Brazil each have specific manifestations of larger configurations of racial regimes rooted in colonization, slavery, and capitalism. Beyond discrete national boundaries, this hemispheric approach is a way of engaging the racial, gender, and sexual dynamics through the prism of the mixed-black female figure. As did the United States, Brazil used media representations of racial mixture as evidence that race and hence racism are fictions. In 2007, the Brazilian magazine *Veja* also featured twins on its cover with the headline "Raça Não Existe" (Race doesn't exist). A bold-faced headline reading "Branco e Negro" (Black and White) topped a story that presented one identical twin classified as Black under university racial quotas while the other was classified as white.[4] In the same year, BBC Brazil premiered "Afro-Brazilian Roots," a documentary in which nine celebrities underwent genetic ancestry tests. Sérgio Pena, a prominent Brazilian geneticist, led the testing, asserting that the results reinforced Brazilian racial mixture, which emphasized a feeble relationship between ancestry and skin color, thereby undermining the idea of any biological basis for race.[5]

In both countries, the juxtaposition of racial mixture and ambiguity of Blackness have triggered larger debates about racial policies, identity narratives, and the future of the nation within global orders. Both nations position themselves as global leaders and hence set forth paradigms of racial thought and practice. Although racial categories are not static, whiteness has remained central to racial hierarchies in the Americas. Blackness, as a social and political formation, encompasses mixture and accounts for the varied lived experiences, histories, and subjectivities of people of African descent. However, not all forms of Blackness are valued in the same way. Mixed-Black bodies illustrate the tension between an acceptable Blackness that can be incorporated into the nation and an abject Blackness, imagined as racial and sexual excess, impropriety and immorality. As women of mixed European and African descent, the mulatta in the United States and the *mulata* in Brazil stand in for these anxieties over the place of Blackness in the Americas. In a post–civil rights United States, mixed-Black bodies elicit the discordance and overlapping nature of multiculturalism, neoliberalism, the eradication of race, and abject Blackness. Brazil's racial management strategies rely on discourses and performances of racial diversity while disavowing race through the denial of racialized structures of inequality. Neither the United States nor Brazil is normative nor exceptional in the way that race operates, but rather they function along shifting contours of the strategies rather than the premise of race itself. While anti-Blackness is a transnational phenomenon, different nations have divergent strategies for managing Blackness.

Imagining the Mulatta: Blackness in U.S. and Brazilian Media shows how Brazil and the United States have used the image of the mixed-Black female body as an instrument to buttress white supremacy and discipline people of African descent. Exposing national and transnational logics of racial management that center on gender and sexuality, it looks at how popular media representations of the mulatta/*mulata* manage Blackness through its erasure, its sexual regulation, and/or the presentation of an acceptable Blackness with the potential to whiten the population. The mulatta/*mulata* as constitutive of nation-building projects in the United States and Brazil ruptures linear racial progress narratives and reveals the suturing of colonial legacies to the millennium.

Piecing together the media representations of the mulatta/*mulata* in and across two nations, this book maps how dominant ideologies of whiteness remain entrenched in the organization of racial hierarchies. These media narratives extend a political project in the Americas to erase undesirable Blackness physically while managing Blackness as a form of sexual pleasure and labor. Encountering these media representations forces the unveiling of new and old structures that manage Blackness with the ultimate goal of its expunging. This book centers on particular media texts as objects of analysis to chart the processes and means of racialization. Exploring a range of popular media texts from Brazilian telenovelas (serial melodramas) to U.S. hip-hop music videos, from films set in Brazil to film and television set in the United States, this book conveys how popular culture helps reflect and create an ideology of Black containment through the contested symbol of the mixed-race woman. Largely drawing from the cultural imaginaries attached to key celebrity figures, Jennifer Beals and Halle Berry in the United States and Camila Pitanga in Brazil, this book accounts for how mixed-Black women embody fantasies of interracial desire while manifesting racial hierarchies. These celebrities and their works hold resonating functions of historical narratives, future hopes, and evidence of national racial exceptionalisms. These widely consumed cultural forms serve as platforms for the management of Blackness and articulate formations of mixedness.

In both the United States and Brazil, these cultural productions share the goal of shoring up whiteness through the maintenance of an ongoing racial hierarchy. Importantly, this book examines the constitution of these racial hierarchies through the management of Blackness specifically, rather than looking at the management of Indigeneity or of Asian-descended peoples. The book examines the specific cultural, social, and political function of Black–white mixture representations in this context. *Imagining the Mulatta* embraces the racial ambiguities and continuous reimaginings of mixedness in order to manage Blackness.

A hemispheric framework that views the United States and Brazil together helps elucidate how much Brazil and the United States have in common. The two nations utilize racial mixing as evidence of simultaneous racial progress and racial crisis. Both have large populations of African descent; legacies of slavery and manumission; large film, television, and music industries; and a widespread Indigenous presence that complicates Black identities. Both countries are undergoing shifts in discourse as they grapple with the challenges of racial classification, inequality, and demographic change alongside the continuing devaluation of Black life through police violence, anti-Black criminalization, ongoing social inequality, abuse, poverty, and the fetishization and disposability of Black bodies in the public sphere. Since the early twentieth century, scholars and cultural producers have been engaged in a long-standing dialogue around racial understanding in Brazil and the United States.[6] Scholars like Micol Seigel have demonstrated that intellectuals construct the very categories of race and nation and employed these comparisons to portray national racial depictions to support particular political projects.[7] Yet the plethora of works comparing understandings of race and race relations in Brazil and the United States often tends to depict rigid biological ideas of race in the United States and flexible concepts of race in Brazil. Indeed, much of this comparative work relies on the legibility of Blackness to U.S. or Brazilian audiences rather than placing the construction of Blackness itself under question.

Using a hemispheric framework that places Brazil and the United States together, *Imagining the Mulatta* contributes to understanding national and transnational logics of racial management. With a focus on how racialization occurs through gender and sexuality in popular media, the book demonstrates how mixed-race women represent racial anxieties and desires in Brazil and the United States. With global racial formations that determine who is human and that have been influenced by colonialism, slavery, and imperialism, the book provides multiple scales in which to understand this phenomenon.[8] Unraveling the figure of the mulatta as a national symbol and as a hemispheric icon becomes the opening to contesting racialized gendered projects of containing Blackness.

Symbolic Value of the Mulatta and *Mulata*

In this book, I use "mulatta" as the term for women of mixed African and European descent in the United States and "*mulata*" in italics as the sexualized term for women of mixed African and European descent in Brazil. While both identifiers are often considered impolite or offensive, I use these terms to highlight the historicity of these figures, especially from nineteenth-century popular culture onward, and their inextricability from contemporary discussions of race, gender, and sexuality in the Americas. These categories do not describe racial difference, but rather racial *and* sexual differences, and stand apart from terms like "mixed-race" and "biracial," which neither specify Black–white mixture nor hold the same historical or ideological symbolism. This terminology foregrounds the ghostly presence of these figures and the persistency of the gendered, classed, and sexualized nature of racial taxonomies.

Furthermore, the mulatta/*mulata* figure is distinctly gendered. I employ these terms to evoke the gendered, racialized, and sexualized tropes that have framed her existence in the imaginary of the Americas. The gendering of mixed Blackness relies on practices that continue to subsume the mulatta/*mulata* as sensually exotic and desirable. Presented as attractively hybridized, the logics undergirding the mulatta/*mulata* are linked to the premise of sexual availability and sensuality as a site of racial difference. As bell hooks and Celine Parreñas Shimizu point out, visual mediums often reduce women of color to the locus of an exotic, sexually consumable, and fetishized body.[9] The mulatta and *mulata* often stand in for a racialized sexuality that stands in for interracial sexual desire, fear, and violence. Thus, the feminization and exotification of mixed Blackness highlight the mulatta/*mulata* as sexual creations and her important role as an object of desire, instrument of reproduction, and/or reminder of Black difference. Contemporary iterations of the mulatta and *mulata* signify this mixed-race sexual history. In both the United States and Brazil, the figure of the contemporary mulatta embodies the contradictions inherent in these racial histories and present legacies; she functions as a symbol of multiracial harmony in the United States and Brazil while simultaneously masking anti-Blackness in the Americas.

Managing Race in a Hemispheric Framework

A hemispheric framework allows a relational view of national and transnational processes of race making at the same time. Understanding how representations of the mulatta in both countries facilitate social control requires a conceptual apparatus that examines the intersection of race, sexuality, gender, and class. The mechanisms and ideologies that govern social control encompass various forms of containment, subjugation, force, and discipline. These representations also show how media can operate as a technology that facilitates the management of Blackness. This book theorizes how representations, performances, and practices of the mulatta/*mulata* become tools of social control. Managing Blackness entails continuing the biopolitical project of engendering a whiter population. Thus, the mixed-race body nonetheless corresponds to a racial ordering in which the ideal of whiteness remains supreme.

Long-standing debates in history, anthropology, and political sciences have contested the role of mixed race in the differing racial trajectories of Brazil and the United States. In the 1930s, Brazilian anthropologist Gilberto Freyre's seminal comparisons between the United States and Brazil situated racial mixing as an essential component of Brazilian identity, a vision of harmonious race relations, and set forward decades of research on comparative scholarship on the United States and Brazil. In the 1970s, historians such as Carl Degler argued that a key difference with the United States was the Brazilian "mulatto escape hatch," which corresponded with whitening ideologies and provided a way for individuals of mixed race to disassociate from Blacks, marry upward in the racial order, and hence, also whiten their progeny.[10] Nonetheless, this historiography and these debates presume that Brazil and the United States have been fundamentally different from their origins. This is why these discussions often revolve around questions of racial fluidity and better or worse racial inequalities rather than framing Brazil and the United States as both undergirded by white supremacy and strategies to control the Black population.

Through a hemispheric framework that takes up gender and sexuality as key analytics, this book demonstrates that both Brazil and the United States regulate race with mass media as a central instrument of managing Blackness. The mixed-race body becomes a means of generating an ongoing project of eventual whiteness. Meanwhile, this same project arranges Blackness as a threat to be subdued and continued. As Christen Smith argues, the Brazilian state's espousal of racial democracy goes hand in hand with state-sponsored violence against Black bodies.[11] In both the United States and Brazil, the continual devaluing and diminution of Blackness also functions to bolster the whiteness project. Espoused color blindness combined with multiculturalism in the United States juxtaposed with Brazilian racial democracy disavows the salience of racism and justifies attacks on policies such as affirmative action. Media representations parallel this devaluation of Black life.

Mixed bodies have fluctuated between being regarded as good and redeemable versus bad and deviant—either way, Blackness is subordinated and reduced to an Otherness. Meanwhile, the disavowal of racism combined with racialized stigma demarcates inclusion and exclusion in both national and global social orders. The incorporation and legitimization of mixed-race bodies are nonetheless based on the violence, devaluation, and social death of Blackness. This mode of social control relies on practices and performances that produce intersecting norms of race, gender, sexuality, and class. In order to unveil how the management of Blackness intersects with the management of gender, sexuality, and class, I examine the interlocking ways that the mixed-race female body circulates in popular culture. For example, Camila Pitanga, a Brazilian actor who publicly identifies as Black, is often marked in newspapers and magazines with other racial identifiers such as *mulata* and *morena* (a vague term encompassing anything from brunette to dark-skinned). Despite her Black political identity, her star text collides within this redeemable or deviant narrative of the mixed woman. In telenovelas, she is frequently cast in the role of upwardly mobile feminine respectable domestics who marry into whiteness and citizenship. Alternatively, she also plays sensual uninhibited seductresses unworthy of national inclusion. Pitanga embodies these multiple spaces of Black femininity and points to the stakes of how Blackness is managed.

Imagining the Mulatta also seeks an understanding of race outside the bounds of the nation-state. In the Americas, while the strategies of racial management might differ, the undergirding racial thought relies on the actual necessity of diluting and containing Blackness to restricted spheres of sexual pleasure or a remnant of the past. Hemispheric racial logics allow us to see attitudes, practices, and relations of race that are not sutured by national borders but are pertinent to the Americas due to their common history of conquest, colonization, and slavery. The premise of racialization of Blackness connects the Americas, but the discourse and memory of racial mixing differs in that Brazil, along with other Latin American nations such as Mexico and Cuba, has long capitalized on racial mixing as the foundation of new hybrid societies.[12] The U.S. myth of the melting pot is likewise a positivist narrative of U.S. diversity, yet at the same time this notion largely deemphasizes histories of racial mixing. These myths rest on the erasure or removal of non-whites in the United States and the gradual dilution of Blackness in Latin America. Despite distinct histories, Brazil and the United States have utilized related images and discourses of racial mixing as proof of both racial progress and racial danger. Mixed-race women's bodies embody the anxieties, tensions, and desires of these racial projects.

This hemispheric approach reveals that discussions and anxieties over the management of Blackness are not just solely national discourses. Examining the interrelationships between the United States and Brazil and transnational processes of racialization, colonialism, imperialism, and neoliberalism furthers understandings of how operations of power manifest. The hemispheric framework strives to release the constraints of a rigid adherence to the nation-state, the prioritization of U.S. perspectives, and the homogenization of racial identities and formations. The transnational and the comparative methodologies do not work separately but offer different perspectives on how the management of Blackness occurs through mixed female bodies. Therefore, some chapters in the book are explicitly transnational, examining how Brazil and the United States speak through each other, and other chapters place Brazil and the United States side by side to demonstrate the particular national articulation of these strategies of Black management.

The idea of race has transnational and national components and movements. Numerous scholars have noted the tension of comparative and transnational frameworks in which comparative frameworks invariably inscribe national differences without accounting for the ways nations influence each other, whereas transnational approaches account for the ideological, material, and social flows that influence the constitution of both.[13] This book both reaps the flows from transnational methodologies while discarding assumptions of stable and rigid racial national categories that comparative methodologies often reinforce. A hemispheric framework allows a relational view of both the national and transnational at the same time. This relational analysis connects common discourses of racial progress among continuing practices of anti-Blackness. For example, juxtaposing readings of the celebrity personas of U.S. actor Jennifer Beals alongside Brazilian actor Camila Pitanga points to the political valence of self-consciously asserting a racial identity that negates national racial norms, yet also illustrates the fetishization of light-skinned racial ambiguity as a form of sexual allure in the Americas. For example, the emphasis in the U.S. television series *The L Word* on the mulatta as exemplar of sexual desire and threat parallels the nonconformity and deviance of the *mulata* in the Brazilian telenovela *Paraíso Tropical*. Meanwhile, the circulation of the Brazilian *mulata* as a sensual object of desire within U.S. hip-hop music videos illustrates how cultural products and media technologies transmit ideas of race and sexuality, the expansion of global capital, and the transnational movements of racialized sexuality. The book lays out a hemispheric conversation to bring together U.S. and Brazilian manifestations of mulatta/*mulata* imagery. This management of the mulatta/*mulata* highlights redeeming whiteness as a path toward citizenship while containing Blackness as sexually nonreproductive pleasure that furthers marginalization.

While the histories and experiences of mixed-race people of African and European descent in the United States and Brazil are distinctive and historically specific, overlapping histories and experiences rooted in slavery, emancipation, and debates over the incorporation and/or erasure of mixed-race people point to anxieties over the place of mixed-race people within and beyond the nation. A hemispheric lens highlights tropes, genealogies, identity formations, and cultural productions of the mixed-race figure that historical experiences and legacies of colonialism, slavery, and nation-state formation shape. Hemispheric study of the mixed-race female figure illuminates connected practices of the management of Blackness. Framing the management and containment of Blackness in a hemispheric context allows for an identification of the specificities of race in the United States and Brazil while also exploring the transnational dimensions of race making and whitening projects. Rather than reproducing a north-south binary, this book places Brazil and the United States in conversation together. Both the national and transnational significances of the mixed-race figure are linked to hemispheric practices of anti-Blackness and practices of potential resistance. While this book does not take on social movements, contemporary practices of anti-Blackness such as state-sponsored violence in both the United States and Brazil are also met with activist resistance demonstrated by the Black Lives Matter movement and Afro-Brazilian organizing. Thus, while the apparatuses of anti-Blackness are hemispheric and interconnected, decolonial struggles and visions also are inherently linked. A hemispheric approach does not jettison dissonance, asymmetry, and untranslatability, but rather holds them in fruitful tension.

Imagining the Mulatta takes up the mulatta (U.S.) and *mulata* (Brazil) figures instead of other mixed-racial figures in order to grapple with the enduring traumatic histories of slavery, racism, and its structural inequalities. Fantasies of interracial intimacies as inversions of oppression obfuscate deeply ingrained relations of domination and histories of sexual violence. The understandings of colonization and slavery as hemispheric processes of racialization also require a comprehension of the role of eroticized racial intimacies. These eroticized racial intimacies function as a form of sexual labor through the reproduction of a whitening project or the containment of Blackness and sexual pleasure.

When using the word "erotic," I refer to desire, pleasure, and repulsion associated with carnality and feeling. The questions of procreation and the conditions of Black erotic life are essential for accounting for the contours of racism. This book deploys how racial intimacies function as tools of colonial and postcolonial management of sex along with the racial intimacies of affect and feeling. Ann Stoler explicates how colonial authorities implemented the management of racial difference through sex, domesticity, and sentiments and desires with social formations such as the family. These intimate ties operate as technologies of race.[14] As such, intimacy also demonstrates the affective desires and attachments between racialized subjects. Through an analysis of cultural production, this book extends a form of reading that takes into account racial intimacies and elucidates the exotic mulatta/*mulata* body commodified in national and hemispheric imaginaries.

Racial difference is produced through a reiteration of histories of intimate encounters. Embodied enactments of racialized and sexualized identities work through spaces of desire and affect to produce the figures of the mulatta and *mulata*. The eroticization of mixed women also encompasses objectification. Contemporary media representations of Black sexual labor situate the national and transnational dimensions of erotic politics and pleasures. This book eschews binaries of the positive representation of the respectable wife and the negative representation of the lascivious mistress in order to highlight the ways in which these forms both highlight eroticism, desire, and sex as a form of labor and commodification. Exploring the multiple deployments of mixed-Black female sexuality shatters binary oppositions of normal and respectable versus deviant and lascivious. Emphasizing a reading that focuses only on representations as damaging to a sense of Black feminine progress limits the complexity and ambiguities of Black pleasure.[15] While Black sexuality has often been considered inherently nonnormative, the mixed-Black woman often inhabits the heart and the threat of hemispheric imaginaries.

Restricting the framing of Black female sexuality to histories of violence, abuse, and exploitation limits ways of thinking about how racialization, in particular the slave trade, structures sexuality in the Americas for all subjects. As Sharon Holland argues, the erotic has been utilized to reinforce and ingrain difference. She places "the erotic—the personal and political dimensions of desire at the threshold of ideas about quotidian racist practice."[16] Racist practices configure sites of intimacy, pleasure, and desire. The fetishizing and renouncement of white intimate contact with racialized Blackness signifies how desire is not raceless. Moreover, this erotic life of racism descends from the afterlife of slavery. Within this larger historical context of systemic oppression, the imagining of the erotic must also contend with the arousal and fear related to interracial mixing and the creation of the mulatta/*mulata* herself. The pervasive legacy of sexual violence—from the coercions of slavery's reproduction to the commodification of Black female sexuality to the invisibility of rape in political legal systems to cultural imaginings of Black hypersexuality as justification for racist fantasies—inform contemporary media texts. Thus, sexual violence as a physical, structural, juridical, and cultural framing situates the mixed female body. These legacies of sexual violence inform but do not necessarily determine mixed-Black sexuality. Despite discourse circulating in the United States and Brazil that proposes that racial intimacies can create conditions to overpower racist practices, racial differences are instead expressed, upheld, and reproduced through racial intimacies. The preponderance of interracial relationships is not inherently a symbol of the disassembling of white supremacist patriarchal logics. Rather, racial and sexual grammars are diffused, not just challenged through these intimate relationships. I build on Holland's theorizations to show how media texts convey this yearning of racial eroticism and the intertwinement of identity categories.

These racial eroticisms are wrapped up in citizenship, consumerism, and commodification. The commodification of racialized sexuality is central to colonial legacies involved in media industrialization. Media industries in the United States and Brazil mobilize the sexual labor of the mulatta as part and parcel of a racialized system of desire. Through the binding up of the mixed body as a consumable commodity through marriage, sex work, domestic sexual relations, and the reproduction of the family, mulatta labor participates within a sexual economy. Thus, some of these mixed figures embody racial and sexual capital yet depart from African American middle-class modes of respectability and Brazilian bourgeois aspirations of racial whitening as avenues to mobility and citizenship.

With the intertwining of popular culture and mass media, media representation also facilitates belonging and exclusion based on the ideological processes of race, gender, sexuality, and class. Within capitalist frameworks, the mulatta/*mulata*'s consumption of goods becomes a means of upward mobility. Hence, the commodification of mulatta sexuality, which then enables the mulatta to become a consumer who operates within a system of exploitation. Yet, this same self-commodification present in media texts also confers the agency to participate in a capitalist economy. While this agency should not be overlooked in these media texts, it must also be noted that the majority of these media texts nonetheless operate on the premise of sexual trade and white sexual desire in order to achieve advancement. From Hollywood's *Monster's Ball* to the Brazilian telenovela *Paraíso Tropical*, the ample display of naked physicality stirs the sexual desire of white men, who buy nonessential goods and secure essential housing or cars for these women to survive.

Through the commodification of racialized and sexualized difference in both national contexts and as part of global capitalism, the media industries operate as technologies enabling the logics of multiculturalism and racial democracy in which the visibility of nonwhite bodies are valued for consumption and the collapsing of media representation with sociopolitical power. Media representations of racialized sexualized differences reinforce national imaginaries to obscure the entrenchment of inequalities. As consumption and citizenship have increasingly merged in an age of globalization, citizenship is performed through consumerist logics to enter the national imaginary and a global order.[17] Notions of citizenship, a sense of belonging politically, culturally, and economically, are connected to the media industries. These media texts that I examine then delineate the production of a particular type of citizenship that permits a limited number of acceptable Blacks with social, cultural, and political access while excluding the vast majority of Blacks. Media representations of mixed Blackness both legitimizes celebratory diversity and requires the dissolution of Blackness as a path toward citizenship.

Unearthing Strategies of Racial Exclusion in the United States and Brazil

To unweave these complex hemispheric strategies of Black containment, I focus on the uses of mulatta and *mulata* in the United States and Brazil as points of departure for explanations of the co-emergence of these interlinked racial projects in the 2000s. Alternating between the United States and Brazil throughout the book, I concentrate primarily on the first decade of the 2000s due to transformations in racial discourse in both nations in these years. While the 1990s were characterized by an emphasis on color blindness, in the early 2000s the United States sought to present itself as the global exemplar of multiculturalism even as it grappled with racial inequality and political marginalization, both legacies of a long history of colonization and slavery. This articulation of race recognized and privileged some racial subjects conforming to assimilated capitalist values while repudiating others. By the mid-2000s, the ascendance of Barack Obama, the increased popularity of mixed and racially ambiguous celebrities, and the census report detailing the rise of the self-identified multiracial population were deployed by many to usher in a postracial era emphasizing racial progress through the declining significance of race.

Following *Loving v. Virginia*, the 1967 Supreme Court decision that repealed antimiscegenation laws nationwide, the growth of the mixed-race population brought about an increase in a self-identification among multiracial people. In 2000, the federal census began to allow individuals to check more than one racial-identification box, resulting in 6.8 million Americans—2.4 percent of the population—identifying themselves that year as multiracial, a figure that grew to 9 million people (2.9 percent) in 2010, and is expected to triple by 2060.[18] In comparison to other minority groups, the percentage of self-reporting multiracial Blacks is relatively low and the rate of intermarriage among African Americans is significantly smaller.[19] Yet, mixed-race individuals of Black and white descent have continued to garner fascination and anxiety and hold symbolic value within the vision of national identity and race relations. By 2017, the fiftieth anniversary of *Loving v. Virginia*, fantasies of racial harmony hoisted interracial love and mixed-race children as emblems of racial progress. The resurgence of stories such as the critically acclaimed film *Loving* (2016) marked the reemergence of the redeemable mulatta as a tool to regulate race and sex in visions of family and nation. Such narratives of racial progress rely on mixed-race female figures and interracial heterosexual intimacies. While the optimism of a postracial or multicultural project has now unraveled, the nonwhite population will nevertheless comprise over 50 percent of the U.S. population by 2042.

Media hopes of a postracial future were often channeled through mixed-race bodies beginning in the early 2000s. The fetishizing of mixed-Black bodies also parallels and coincides with the fascination with Latina celebrities such as Jennifer Lopez, Zoe Saldana, and Shakira. Many of these Latina star texts rely on sexualized constructions of Otherness while also allowing for a malleable performance of race. Into this environment, the tragic mulatta, a figure of mixed African and European descent that frequently appeared in the cultural productions of the nineteenth and early twentieth centuries, reemerged, symbolizing the moral and social cataclysm resulting from racial mixing and the threat to whiteness. The reinscription of the tragic mulatta onto twenty-first century media texts directs attention away from racial inequality and social structures by focusing on the tragic mulatta as the root of social debacle. Such framing allows for the conversion of this figure to align with color-blind, neoliberal, and postracial ideologies. The erotic mulatta of nineteenth- and twentieth-century myths, who ensnares white lovers and endangers social order, resurfaced in the 2000s. The sexual desirability of the erotic mulatta relies on her sexual deviance and the imposition of interracial fantasies projected upon her body. Such symbolism reinforces power structures that surveil and regulate mixed-Black female sexuality. The morphing of these mulatta figures into celebratory symbols of racial hybridity and harmony in the 1990s and 2000s belies the fraught histories of racial mixing.

The book aims to explore the hauntings of the mulatta figure tethered to legacies of U.S.-based slavery and futuristic optimisms. For example, the 2003 *New York Times* article "Generation E.A.: Ethnically Ambiguous" explored this fascination with examples from media, fashion, and advertising.[20] In line with what Jodi Melamed terms "neoliberal multiculturalism in which neoliberalism and multiculturalism become the solutions to racism," mixed bodies serve as emblems possessing cultural value or as commodities rather than as vehicles of exploitation.[21] These visions of the "cool" mulatta repress her origins in the sexual exploitation of enslaved women, which continue to haunt the United States. These legacies of the tragic and erotic mulatta nonetheless haunt postracial ambitions and continue the dehumanization of Black women's bodies within contemporary conditions.

In 2008, President Obama's mixed-race Black and white ancestry was a key component of media postracial discourse that foresaw a national transformation beyond racial identities, racial difference, and racial discrimination. However, over the course of his administration, Obama's opponents "blackened" him through race baiting and demonization and by association also African Americans, as evidenced by a rise of white-supremacist hate crimes. Indeed, by 2013, bringing up race outside of predetermined liberal norms garnered accusations of racism as these same norms helped justify inequalities. For example, former New York City mayor Michael Bloomberg labeled then candidate Bill de Blasio's campaign as racist on the basis of his usage of pictures and videos of his mixed-race family.[22] In the 2000s, universities across the country had already begun dismantling affirmative action programs. Racial pay and health care inequities, high levels of Black incarceration, and police violence against African Americans persist. Thus, racism is neither a vestige of the past nor an exception but rather an ongoing presence. The very existence of the contemporary Black Lives Matter movements attests to these contemporary manifestations of anti-Blackness. With continuing Black deaths, vulnerability to state surveillance, and mass incarceration, mixed-Black media representations might seem tangential. Yet, it is precisely the sensational media circulation of such representations that bolster claims of the irrelevancy of race while reinforcing racial inequalities.

By 2016, the conservative white nationalisms spanning the hemisphere following liberal hopes of inclusion and progress in the mid-2000s are not aberrations, but rather part of enduring dynamics of tension. As biopolitical technologies, media texts from the 2000s embed and normalize the regulation and disciplining of Blackness while deploying mixed bodies as instruments of U.S. exceptionalism and racial progress. *Imagining the Mulatta* reveals how the mulatta figure became a key conduit for the management of Blackness and how she facilitated the emergence of multicultural and postracial discourses. Further, this book illustrates how her symbolism ultimately served a much longer project of Black containment.

With the rise of self-identified multiracial populations and predictions of a majority-minority United States, the vision of Brazil as a future mirror of biopolitical projects looms large. A range of scholars predict that continued racial mixing will bring the countries closer together, as when noted African American studies scholar Henry Louis Gates Jr. stated that "no-one is pure in Brazil. That's why the country has the face of the future" and ecology scholar Stephen Stearns proclaimed that "a few centuries from now, we're all going to look like Brazilians."[23] These limited essentialist views of race reinforce notions of racial purity versus racial mixture and also displace the vast racial mixing and variance within African American communities. Thus, utopian visions of a racially mixed and harmonious society are presented as an expectation that the future racially mixed society will render racial distinctions meaningless. Hence, Brazil is key for understanding U.S. postracial fantasies and myths of racial mixing.

By the early 2000s, the provocation of the Latin Americanization of racial politics emerged. For example, Eduardo Bonilla-Silva hypothesized that by the late twentieth century, the United States became more like Latin America in the espousal of color-blind racism that disavowed the existence of race while maintaining white supremacy and racial inequities, evidenced by the discarding of race in public policy. The thesis includes a move from a binary Black–white to a tertiary system of racial stratification.[24] However, this thesis again presumes that the United States and Latin America have been different but are now becoming more similar. Instead of emphasizing the construction of Blackness and whiteness as both national and hemispheric projects, this thesis also assumes that racial politics are fixed. However, if we view the United States and Brazil in a hemispheric context rather than separately, we can uncover a panorama of white supremacy and anti-Blackness that interplays across national borders. The dismantling of these racial regimes and the mediated use of mixed-race women for political projects also encompass a hemispheric vision. Thus, the transformation of white supremacy into racial inclusion also requires a hemispheric analysis.

While the United States has a history of maintaining a strictly enforced color line, Brazil has often been regarded in the transnational imagination as a mulatto nation. Postcards portray caramel and honey-colored *mulata* samba dancers and scantily clad beachgoers, advertising a racially mixed paradise that suggests a self-conception of Brazil as having achieved a racial utopia. For Brazil, the *mulata* is a symbol of national identity. Samba lyrics, novels, Carnival pageantry, and other forms of cultural expression celebrate her as a sexual object and physical and symbolic proof of Brazilian racial democracy. Racial mixture itself is not a form of racial hegemony, although the uses of racial mixture to posit mixing as a path toward the dilution of Blackness are.

Yet public acknowledgment of massive racial inequality and the need for Black identification has been increasing since the early 1990s. Afro-Brazilian social and political mobilization, the introduction of affirmative action and racial quotas, and the gradual opening of spaces for Afro-Brazilian actors on mainstream television have heightened debates around race. In 2002, affirmative action began in Brazil and in 2012, then President Dilma Rousseff passed legislation mandating all federal public universities to adopt the policy. Public debates—over racist representations of Afro-Brazilians in Monteiro Lobato's classic Brazilian literature; the 2003 passage of Law 10–639, requiring the inclusion of African and Afro-Brazilian history and culture in public school curriculums; and controversy over affirmative action and racial quotas in public universities—all pointed to a disruption of Brazil's self-image as a racial democracy.[25] Yet, racial inequalities, particularly in political and economic exclusion, did not disappear, and the dominant discourses of racial democracy and *mestiçagem* (racial mixing) remained fiercely entrenched in notions of Brazilian identity.

Long before the United States fixated on postracial ideologies, Brazilian dominant discourse depoliticized race through an emphasis on the transcendence of race through mixing. Similar to U.S. exceptionalism, Brazilians also operationalize an exceptionalist view depicting Brazil's historical *mestiçagem* as mitigating racial difference. The comparisons to the United States both bolster and suppress racial policies based on notions of racial mixing in both countries. Opposition to race-based policies is often framed as an importation of U.S. policies that are inappropriate in a Brazilian context. Hence, the United States is presented as possessing distinct races, and the highlighting of its image of racial segregation and strife are juxtaposed with Brazilian racial mixture and cordiality. Afro-Brazilian activists, meanwhile, have pointed to U.S. racial policies as progressive in comparison to Brazil by emphasizing a more robust African American middle class and the election of President Obama despite racialized state violence and a lack of political power. The perception of the

United States pushes both countries into exceptionalist logics that present a hierarchy of which country is better or worse in terms of race relations.

While the Brazilian racial system is rooted in white supremacy, a shift in understandings of racial identity toward an embracement of African descent is also currently taking place. The Brazilian census provides the racial categories of *branco* (white), *pardo* (brown), *preto* (Black), *amarelo* (yellow), and *indígena* (Indigenous).[26] Brazilian discourses of *mestiçagem* urge respondents to select the lightest category they plausibly can, but a 1991 Instituto Brasileiro de Análises Sociais e Econômicas (Brazilian Institute of Social and Economic Analysis) publicity campaign for the census encouraged respondents to embrace Blackness through the slogan, "Não deixe sua côr passar em branco. Responda com bom c/senso" (Don't let your color pass off as white. Respond with good sense/census), which encouraged embracing Blackness and selecting a darker rather than a lighter color.[27] A Brazilian governmental television campaign for the 2010 census in Brazil doubled down on this message, enlisting Taís Araújo, a famous telenovela actor who has coffee-colored skin and phenotypical features similar to white actors. Traditional Brazilian classification might have described her as "parda."[28] She told viewers, "Eu sou negra e a côr da minha pele é preta" (I am Black and the color of my skin is Black), encouraging them to select the darkest classification that might suit them.[29] The politics of Black consciousness and racial mixture were evident as she continued: "só sabendo quem você é, o Brasil vai pode atender às suas necessidades e ser um país cada vez melhor" (only by knowing who you are can Brazil attend to your needs and become a better nation).[30]

For the first time in 2010, the population classified as preto, pardo, amarelo, or indígena was larger than the population classified as branco. While the branco population was still the largest group overall, it was also the only group to diminish in size in comparison to past years.[31] The campaigns mark not only the visibility in affirming Blackness, but also the articulation of Black identities in which racial mixture does not lead to whitening. In both the United States and Brazil, racial policies, such as affirmative action and the census, reflect continuing struggles over recognition, resources, and definitions of race.

Just as the hope of progress represented by President Obama's election was quickly replaced by the authoritarian white populist tendencies of Donald Trump's presidency, a coalition of white male conservatives organized the impeachment of President Dilma Rousseff in August 2016. Both former President Lula's and former President Rousseff's governments led to greater inclusion through their social and racial policies. These progressive policies directly countered the common ideology that Black people are neither fit for positions of power nor should they be fully included in society. The quick reversing of these policies, largely secured through Afro-Brazilian activism, harkens to the repression and exclusion of Black communities. The persistence of de facto segregation and ongoing police violence against Afro-Brazilians belied the idea of a racial utopia. This state terrorism against Black bodies is juxtaposed against the uses of these Black bodies to package an exotic racial democracy for domestic and foreign consumption.[32] The March 2018 assassination of Marielle Franco, a prominent queer Afro-Brazilian feminist activist, exemplified the dismal state of patriarchal anti-Blackness. By October 2018, extreme-right former military officer Jair Bolsonaro won the Brazilian presidential election. His stances on race, gender, and sexuality exemplify the constellation of whitening and Black devaluation. After a visit to a *quilombo*, an Afro-descendant community, he characterized the residents as lazy, obese, and dirty and remarked on their unsuitability for procreation. In other remarks, he encouraged sterilization of low-income recipients of the Bolsa Familia, a cash transfer program that supplies a stipend on the condition that children attend school and receive medical checkups on a regular basis.[33] As the vast majority of Bolsa Familia recipients are Afro-Brazilian and the program has facilitated the entrance of millions into the lower middle class, his remarks recall notions of eugenics and racial improvement tinged with fears of disintegrating racial hierarchies.[34] During an interview, Preta Gil, an Afro-Brazilian singer and actor, asked Bolsonaro how he would react if his son fell in love with a Black woman. Bolsonaro responded that he would not discuss promiscuity and proceeded to rationalize that since his sons were raised well and do not live in a lamentable environment like Preta, he would never encounter such a "risk."[35] His comments evoke tropes of Black female promiscuity as well as how representations of women's bodies shape visions of the idealized racial nation. Despite his own history of racist remarks and policies, Bolsonaro claimed in May 2019 that racism is rare in Brazil and thereby he disregards structural racism.[36] The racial hegemony of anti-Blackness coinciding with the denial of racism is thus enacted through practices of the state and non-state institutions, such as the media industries.

Media Archive

While acclaimed books have compared race in Brazil and the United States in recent years, these texts predominantly hail from the fields of history, sociology, and political science.[37] This book provides interdisciplinary and hemispheric methodologies, joining the growing body of literature that relates how Brazil and the United States have shaped each other's racialization processes and how transnational activities inform racial meaning and thought in both countries.[38] Most scholars have not positioned the range of images, discourses, and practices of mixed race within a larger hemispheric framework that encapsulates the management of Blackness intersecting across the Americas. This book does so by specifically addressing cultural production and the roles of gender and sexuality in racial formation and performance. Thus, it joins the growing media studies work on representations of mixed-race characters and performers in the United States.[39] By considering Brazil and the United States together, the book bridges comparative work on race in Brazil and the United States—which largely excludes the role of media texts—with the emerging field of critical mixed-race studies. *Imagining the Mulatta* positions the mixed-race figure into a hemispheric conversation on the intersection of race, gender, and sexuality.

To produce this conversation, I juxtapose various popular Brazilian and U.S. media texts that range from television programs to Hollywood films to hip-hop music videos to newspapers and magazines. Stamped with laden racial, gendered, and sexual meaning, I primarily examine the star texts and works of U.S. actors Jennifer Beals and Halle Berry and Brazilian actor Camila Pitanga. Celebrity figures often serve as lightning rods for discussions of race, gender, sexuality, and class. By attending to these celebrities and how their work intersects with hemispheric racial projects, the book reveals the centrality of the mixed-Black female body to anxieties around Blackness. The star texts of Beals, Berry, and Pitanga facilitate the production and circulation of racial narratives and fantasies. Their media careers facilitate narratives and contestations of neoliberal multiculturalism, racial democracy, and postracial ideologies. Their incarnations as mulattas and *mulatas* are subjected to racial regimes of anti-Blackness while also acting as reminders of Black subjectivities. Rather than breadth, I have chosen to offer close readings of few texts that illustrate racial and sexual myths, at times amplifying or contesting them. The media texts I have chosen are not necessarily critically acclaimed, but possess mass following and audiences. By bringing these media texts into conversation with one another, the premise of racial thought that requires a management of Blackness is unveiled. Furthermore, even when presented in their national contexts, these media texts actually go beyond conceptual geopolitical trappings to demonstrate hemispheric logics of race as they reify mixed bodies as vehicles for disciplining or expunging Blackness.

As such, media texts act as a form of biopower. *Imagining the Mulatta* reveals how popular media demonstrate the ideological structures for producing and managing racial difference. In this analysis, the book goes beyond notions of "positive" or "negative" representation and instead considers how representations of women of mixed African descent negotiate structures of race, gender, and sexuality. The limited incorporation of mixed-race women relies on ascribing social value only insofar as they have the potential for whitening or containing Blackness by seeing it in reference to sexual pleasure. These logics of race operate far beyond the bounds of any one nation-state in the Americas. Yet, media, both as national and global projects, are vital for neoliberal formations of race. U.S. and Brazilian media deploy Black racial difference to manage contradictions emerging from espoused racial democracy and multiculturalism with inequalities.

These media texts show hemispheric racial systems intended to manage Blackness as well as national strands of racial thought that morph in the 2000s. Brazilian sociopolitical developments in the early 2000s set the stage for a revision of the dominant nationalism valorizing racial democracy and mixed-racial inheritance. Despite the rise of the Partido dos Trabalhadores (Workers' Party) and the creation of policies designed to advocate for the poor and people of African descent, the attack on the leftist Brazilian government signaled an assault on racial equity. The selected Brazilian media texts illustrate the underlying influence of white supremacy as well as the transnational influences in Brazil's own self-definition. Meanwhile, in the United States, the rise of Barack Obama's presidency and his hallmark campaign slogan, "Change," a general desire to look beyond race, and an affirmation of racial progress all heralded a destabilization of race. His mixed-racial ancestry, along with increasing intermarriage and immigration among the populace, hinted at the development of a new age. Yet, his presidency elicited the formation and strengthening of the right and an uptick in hate speech while police violence and inequality continued unabated. In a post-Lula, post-Dilma, post-Obama age, this particular period of hopefulness can be seen more clearly along with the foundations of white supremacy. The development of media representations of mixed-Black women and persistent Brazilian and U.S. racial politics are a continuation of managing Blackness. Thus, examining media representations of the early to mid-2000s illuminates the 2016 presidential election of Donald Trump, the 2016 impeachment of Dilma Rousseff, and the 2018 presidential election of Jair Bolsonaro.

While both nations have distinct histories and strategies of managing Blackness, the central premise remains that Blackness is a threat that must be diluted and contained in ways that largely subsume Blackness as solely for sexual pleasure or entertainment. While G. Reginald Daniel argues that Brazil and the United States are on converging paths, this book argues that the two nations are not inherently different.[40] Yet, by the 2000s, the media representations of mixed-Black women do converge in order to support similar ideas of racial progress alongside contradictory disavowals of racism and acknowledgment that diversity is being satisfied in the public sphere. Such diversity in the public sphere is a mirage, however, because U.S. neoliberal multiculturalism is a system that closely manages difference and the inclusion of multiraciality in public discourse; mixed-Black bodies are quite deliberately utilized in the media to project the United States as progressive and exceptional. Thus, this book examines the period right before and immediately after the heightened discourse of postrace coinciding with the U.S. 2008 election of Barack Obama, whose own multiracial Blackness signaled a "more perfect union." In Brazil, I focus largely on the period of President Lula's administration (2003–11), during which major policy shifts provoked debates about racial inequality. Further, Brazil experienced an economic boom from 2003 before it fell into a recession in 2015. During that economic boom, Afro-Brazilians held greater economic purchasing power and heightened media visibility than in previous periods. The book proceeds prior to the 2013 mass protests and the 2014 World Cup and 2016 Olympics, during which Brazil experienced increased international attention and a further questioning of racial inequalities.

In both countries, conversations around racial progress and inclusion moved to the forefront of national concerns. This book takes up the mediated terrain of a hemispheric liberal telos alongside racial violence. Contemporary discussions of the Americas as postracial necessitate how popular cultural discourses of mixed-race women have been used as a strategy for the management of Blackness. In the United States, this approach led to the striking down of civil rights policies, the dismantling of affirmative action programs, the stripping of voting protections, and the rise of racial inequalities. In Brazil, on the other hand, the promotion of affirmative action programs to stem pervasive racial inequalities contends with continuous attempts to demolish these recent racial policies on the grounds that such policies are antithetical to the nature of the nation. Given the postracial debates following President Obama's historic election, the Black Lives Matter movement, and Donald Trump's election alongside President Lula da Silva's progressive policies, Afro-Brazilian activist movements, President Dilma Rousseff's impeachment, and Jair Bolsonaro's presidential win, this book presents a trajectory to grapple with these contradictions. Examining the media productions in the 2000s unravels how white supremacy was not a relic of the past, as evidenced by the political and social shifts in both countries in 2016 and 2017. The book utilizes the media productions of the 2000s to illustrate how Blackness was nonetheless managed through the mixed-Black female figure.

When I began my research in Brazil in 2008, I believed that I would study Brazilian film. However, I soon realized that telenovelas, not film, largely captured the public imagination. As telenovelas largely dominate the Brazilian mediascape, TV Globo is a principal producer of Brazilian televisual fiction and one of the largest networks in the world, with the telenovela as its major export. Between 2009 and 2011, I spent a total of eleven months in Brazil at the Centro de Estudos de Telenovela at the Universidade de São Paulo, which afforded me opportunities to not only conduct research on archival telenovelas (serial television melodramas) and on the press but also to build relationships with Brazilian researchers. In Brazil, I also conducted archival research and site visits at Cinemateca Brasileira and Brazil's largest media company through visits to TV Globo's archives and TV Globo's production campus. Between 2011 and 2013, I conducted U.S. film, television, and press archival research at the Academy of Motion Picture Arts and Sciences Margaret Herrick Library, the University of California Los Angeles Film and Television Archive, the New York Public Library for the Performing Arts, and the Paley Center for Media.

Studying representations of the mulatta and *mulata* in a hemispheric context requires an engaging of these primary texts through interdisciplinary theoretical frameworks and approaches, including critical race studies, feminist theory, postcolonial theory, cultural studies, and African diaspora studies. In particular, taking up an intersectional framework from Black feminist critique assembles this book as a way to advance past binary notions of identity and static borders in favor of a mode that explores hemispheric processes while remaining aware of specific local and national contexts. As such, this feminist reading practice also resists focusing on fixed meanings in media texts, but rather accounts for how power is articulated in terms of race, gender, sexuality, class, and nation. An array of figures, practices, texts, and relationships interweaves to provide a critical space for investigating how Blackness is managed in the United States and Brazil.

Charting the Conversation on the Mulatta/*Mulata*

In chapter 1 I lay out the historical foundation for understanding mixed-race identities and representations in the United States and Brazil. As the chapter outlines, constructions of mixed race in the United States and Brazil date from the development of slavery to debates over the census and affirmative action in the 1990s and 2000s. Along the way, the chapter unravels racial intimacies under heteropatriarchy and the subsequent violence on mulatta/*mulata* subjectivities. This chapter presents ways of thinking about the continuities between colonialism and slavery and contemporary racial regimes labeled as new, multicultural, or postracial. The chapter provides a framework for an exploration of how dominant popular media draws on legacies of slavery or relegates the legacies of slavery to the past to produce narratives of racial progress, racial democracy, multiculturalism, and postracial visions.

Contemporary popular culture of the 2000s draws from the images of the hypersexual mulatta/*mulata* and the tragic mulatta. Exploring how historical narratives and future routes of the racial state pivot on celebrity, Chapter 2 focuses specifically on newspaper and magazine depictions of figures like Jennifer Beals and Halle Berry in the United States and Camila Pitanga in Brazil. These celebrities epitomize embodiments of the mulatta/*mulata* in the early 2000s and set the stage for later iterations of mulatta/*mulata* celebrity star texts. As post–civil rights era celebrities, Beals and Berry became instruments facilitating the trade of racialized and eroticized allurement and imagination that relied on the tropes of the U.S. mulatta figure and produced meanings of racial progress. Pitanga symbolizes celebrated Brazilian *mulata* iconicity, yet her celebrity also reveals a refusal to conform to racial and gender expectations under this trope. I read the celebrities as texts on which political and social discourses around race are negotiated and how these celebrity personas both identify and challenge normative articulations of Blackness. These star texts reveal a constant negotiation of feminized exotification and commodification.

Like mixed-race female celebrities, mixed-race film and television characters are often key sites of social, political, and cultural debates, anxieties, and desires regarding mixed-race people and race-relations in Brazil and the United States. The cultural commodification and sexualization of mixed female figures function here as strategies of gendered Black containment. Chapters 3 and 4 use case studies from Brazilian telenovelas and U.S. film and television to compare mixed-race figures in the two nations. The chapters utilize the same actors from chapter 2—Pitanga, Beals, and Berry—to further elucidate how mixed-Black women's bodies are entrenched in the disciplining of Blackness. Although chapters 3 and 4 each adopt a national frame, these chapters are intended to be read side by side in order to provide a hemispheric understanding of the role of fictional media narratives and racial management.

The ubiquitous Brazilian telenovela comprises the subject of chapter 3, which examines the Brazilian telenovelas *Belíssima* (2005) and *Paraíso Tropical* (2007). These television programs represent dominant metanarratives of race, gender, sexuality, class, and nation in Brazil that mandate compulsory heterosexuality. Given the important role of Brazilian telenovelas in both articulating and reflecting social issues, the wide demographics of their viewing audiences, their broad domestic and foreign consumption, and their narrative structure, telenovelas reveal much about Brazil's relationship to the *mulata* figure and the dissemination of ideologies of nation, race, sexuality, gender, and class.

As visual representations are not the sole source of racialization, the same actor can be racialized differently based on how her sexuality is framed. In these stories, mixed-race women of African descent can gradually be uplifted and, hence, whitened if they adhere to expectations of purity, respectability, and reproductive labor. In contrast, the hypersexual mixed-race figure can also occupy the role of excessive sexuality and sensual pleasure in the national imagination. Sexual activity and marriage, therefore, also become racial projects through the whitening of the population or the containment of Blackness through the desirable nonreproductive sexuality of the *mulata* figure. Chapter 3 examines *Porto dos Milagres* (2001) and *Duas Caras* (2007–8) as possible alternatives to these narratives.

Despite different geopolitical locations and the asymmetrical flow and exchange of media products, chapters 3 and 4 have similar overlapping preoccupations with race. U.S. television and film productions manage Blackness through the mulatta figure as well. Chapter 4 illustrates how understandings of mixed-race sexuality function as part of national racial narratives, and how concern over the place of Blackness is inscribed on mixed-race characters. The U.S. film *Monster's Ball* (2001) and the U.S. television series *The L Word* (2004–9) ground a discussion of U.S. national identity and offer a comparison point to Brazilian telenovelas and the mediation of race, gender, sexuality, class, and nation. Here, the tensions of the racial past and the optimisms of the future reside in Leticia of *Monster's Ball* as a tragic poor southern woman searching for solace with a white man and *The L Word*'s Bette as the polished, educated Los Angeles professional searching for familial and career success with a white woman. Yet, both reveal how the idea of the mixed-race figure of European and African descent is hemispherically circulated, such that similar indicators of sexual availability are signified in both the United States and Brazil.

Chapter 5 explores the transnational dimensions of racial imaginings through the vision of Brazil as a mixed-race tropical paradise in both U.S. and Brazilian productions. This chapter looks at contemporary hip-hop music videos and Hollywood films produced in the United States but set in Brazil. As an object of desire, the transnational popular imaginings of Brazil become a central node of a promised racial sexual paradise unburdened by U.S. racism. These U.S. productions use Brazil to mediate contemporary anxieties and desires surrounding mixed-race women and a mixed-race future in the United States. The idea of Brazil as a multiracial nation without the racial conflict of the United States is key to this imagery. Like Brazil itself, the *mulata* figure becomes reconfigured in U.S. imaginings of Brazil as a site of racialized sexual pleasure and freedom, and symbolically mediates between the exotic and the familiar. Chapter 5 concludes with a consideration of the materials promoting Rio's successful bid for the 2016 Olympic Games and the 2012 London hand-off ceremony, which demonstrated Brazil's representation of itself racially to the world, and contrasts that with how it managed Blackness at home. These hemispheric forms of racial management illustrate the lack of transformations in the social structure, despite the politics of racial inclusion and multiculturalism.

A Note on Language

A challenging aspect of interdisciplinary work in Brazil and the United States is striving to attain consistency in language while also honoring intellectual and political genealogies of different communities. Describing and theorizing mixed-Black women is difficult for many reasons, but among them is the incommensurability or impossibility in translating racial terms. When specifically using the U.S. context, I often describe these women as African American, despite my recognition that the U.S. nomenclature of "American" obscures the majority of the Americas. In the early 2000s, Brazilian activists adopted the term *afrodescendente* (Afro-descendant) to refer to African ancestry rather than color, and to express collectivity with other Latin Americans of African descent. Afro-Brazilian and Afro-descendant are thus used interchangeably in this book. When I use the term "Afro-Brazilian," I am also including "Black" and "brown" in this nomenclature. Like the term "Black" in the United States, "negro" in Portuguese became a politicized racial category associated with pride and empowerment. I capitalize "Black" as part of decolonial practices to signify political and cultural conditions, identities, and communities. "Black" here is inclusive to encompass multiple subjects and locations. Quotations preserve the capitalization use of the source. I do not capitalize specific Brazilian racial terms in Portuguese, as common practice uses lowercase when denoting nationalities, ethnicities, and racial groups.

The multiple categories in Brazil based on phenotype such as morena, *mulata,* and negra are quite different from the United States rules of hypo-descent. In Brazil, "morena" is a vague term that can refer to anything from a brunette to dark-brown skin. Brazil thus has a great deal of racial ambiguity that is further shaped by expectations of gender and class. I am cognizant of how these color categories complicate self-identification and how an individual can be viewed in different color categories depending on the viewer and context. I am also aware of the differences between U.S. and Brazilian understandings of race and consciously try not to impose a U.S. point of view. I realize that racial and color categories are highly contested in Brazil.

Most often, I use the terms "mulatta" and *"mulata"* as these terms usually best encapsulate the type of sexualized figure that this work explores. I also use these terms in order to evoke the historical images of the mulatta and *mulata* figure in the United States and Brazil. As I explain in chapter 3, I differentiate the morena from the *mulata* in a way that is grounded in the historical use of the two terms, which both describe an intermediate racial category. Mulatta is left in roman font and *mulata* is italicized as a Portuguese word. From this point onwards, I do not italicize other terms besides *"mulata"* in order to not further barriers and power imbalances between languages and nations. While italicizing words can reinforce uneven power dynamics between the United States and Brazil, this choice to italicize *mulata* is for the sake of clarity and the ability of readers to comprehend rather than overlook these different national contexts. It is difficult to develop a vocabulary that can convey and translate racialized forms of ambiguity and racialized histories without reifying the idea of race as biological in itself. I use the terms *"mulata"* and "mulatta" to highlight the enduring legacies of race. Rather than doing away with the mulatta and *mulata*, I utilize these terms to turn not toward racelessness, but to foreground processes of anti-Blackness.

What's in a Name?

Uttering the word "mulatta" or *"mulata"* induces cringing lingering remains of the past wrapped up in the present and the imagined trappings of racial sexual allure. The mulatta/*mulata* has its own visual and linguistic grammar that does not denote exact taxonomic obsessions of fractions of racial mixture, but rather how the palpability of Blackness remains intact. From the visual imagery from Beyoncé's haunting visual album *Lemonade*—light-skinned women in bustiers and bustles lounging and fanning themselves in New Orleans octoroon bordellos—to Rio de Janeiro tourism advertisements splashed with "show de mulata" imagery promising a spectacle of scantily clad high-heeled samba-dancing *mulatas*, all evoke these illusions of racial fantasies and desires. The fluctuation of mulatta, octoroon, *mulata*, and morena are nonetheless all categories that bind together a concern over Blackness. These terms matter and hold within them sagas of exploitation and desire.

Rather than expunge or dismiss these signifying terms, this book uses the fluctuating discomfort and appeal these words engender in order to elucidate the management of Blackness. Juxtaposing multiple cultural productions that conjure iterations of the mulatta and *mulata* avoids the totalizing frame of anti-Blackness flanked by U.S.-focused histories and conditions. Reading Brazilian and U.S. media archives within networked relationships accounts for a range of strategies that maintain white supremacist structures. As the two most-populated former slaveholding nations, both the United States and Brazil have touted multiculturalism and racial mixture as models to the world despite entrenched racial disparities. Spanning spatial temporalities and languages, the chapters that follow expose how reconfigurations of mixed-Black women evoke deep racial ambivalences. The mulatta and *mulata*—haunting lingering presences and retooled figures of racial reconciliation—cannot be forgotten, cannot be left alone, and cannot be settled.

Foundations of the *Mulata* and Mulatta in the United States and Brazil

She is an honorable and strikingly beautiful woman with predominantly European features, whose taint of Black blood can lead only to tragic endings. She is sensual, voluptuous, insatiable, and available to fulfill any sexual desire. She is a persistent reminder of slavery and sexual violence. She is a lovely beacon of hope and upward mobility. She is an exuberant and attractive embodiment of racial harmony and utopia. As race, gender, and sexuality intertwine, the mulatta/*mulata* embodies all these varying images and contradictions.

Shaped by the simultaneous celebration and denial of racial mixing, the images of the mulatta in the United States and the *mulata* in Brazil are embedded within the histories of hemispheric colonialism and slavery. The construction of the concept of racial classification relied on "scientific," philosophical, and moral justification to mark differences with the goal of justifying slavery and Indigenous oppression. Throughout the Americas, Europeans invented racial categories based on phenotypical characteristics and imposed these on bodies as a means of social and organizational management. However, the mixed-race body challenged the very idea of rigidly bounded, stable racial categories. Representations of these mixed-race bodies, particularly women's mixed-race bodies, make them the focus of racialized intimacies. As the starting point of whitening processes and as the key vessel of Black containment, the body is in constant tension. It is a sign of both the presence and invisibility of Blackness, and both the fear and desire of racial mixing. By examining the historical contours of the mixed-race woman, this chapter explicates the mixed-race figure and the ways in which historical legacies still plague these bodies in the 2000s.

As phenotypical racial indicators for the mixed-race body are ambiguous, sexuality and gender serve as clarifiers and are therefore central to the invention of race. The mulatta/*mulata* is also a sexual invention, born from colonial legacies of sexual violence while also embodying the eroticism of Black and white mixing. As this chapter shows, in the United States and Brazil the mulatta/*mulata* crystallized a particular kind of Black womanhood in which sexuality is the primary form of labor. While dominant culture often exalts her for her sensual appeal, it excludes her from political and economic power. Her hypersexuality is justification for colonial racialized sexual violence. Through the sexual control of nonwhite women's bodies, patriarchal dominance played a central role in constructing the nation and in a hemispheric investment in whiteness. While both the United States and Brazil underwent parallel processes of European colonialism, national independence, slavery, and manumission, U.S. and Brazilian racial categories and ideas of race differ. Nonetheless, the two nations have in common a vision of racial hierarchies that privileges whiteness.

In both the United States and Brazil, the mulatta/*mulata* provided a theoretical tie between legacies of slavery and the prospect of racial harmony. This chapter begins with slavery to understand how contemporary representations of the mixed-race figure serve as an enduring investment of Black containment, justifying dehumanization and fetishization of Black bodies. Embedded within the sexual and racial economies of slavery, the mulatta and *mulata* figure reinforced white supremacy yet also exposed the tenuous foundations of whiteness itself. In the United States, the figure emerged in a context of the establishment of racial boundaries between the free and unfree within a Black-white dichotomy. In contrast, the *mulata* in Brazil inhabited a Black-white continuum. Brazil was the largest slaveholding society in the Americas, and the United States was the second largest. Brazil's population of African descent is much larger, both in raw numbers and as a proportion of the population, than that of the United States.[1] African Americans are an excluded minority; Afro-Brazilians a marginalized majority.

Hemispheric Legacies of Slavery: The Mulatta/*Mulata* and Divisions of Race

In the United States, the definitions and boundaries of race have been under constant negotiation since British colonization and have largely centered on delineations of Blackness and the maintenance of these boundaries through sexual control. Over the course of the seventeenth and eighteenth centuries, the capitalist expansion of the North American British colonies relied on forced labor, and racial boundaries emerged as a way to distinguish free subjects and enslaved people. The North American colonies initially employed the British patrilineal system. In Maryland, for example, by 1664, the mixed-race children of white women inherited their fathers' condition, and white women who married enslaved men had to serve their husbands' masters throughout their husbands' lives.[2] Legal statutes prohibiting interracial sexual acts and interracial marriage emerged in Virginia in the late seventeenth century, and by the middle of the eighteenth century, six of the thirteen colonies had laws forbidding the marriage of Blacks to whites.[3] Such early slave laws upheld white patriarchy and racialized capitalism, privileging heteropatriarchal desire and sexuality. As enslaved women's offspring came to be legally defined as slaves throughout the colonies, white men could increase the number of enslaved children by raping and impregnating Black women. While some white enslaver fathers provided for their mixed-race children in their wills or manumitted them, as property, mixed raceness did not overcome the force of birthright. Free Black communities in cities such as Charleston, New Orleans, and Mobile were overwhelmingly mixed race in the nineteenth century, yet by ensuring slave status, these laws blunted the threat of a mixed-race population to the racially based premise of slavery.[4]

The mulatta's sexuality was a commodity—desired for the contradictions of chastity, based on her light skin, and hypersexuality, assumed because of her Black blood. Quadroon balls in New Orleans presented quadroons (one-quarter Black) as beautiful and sensual to white men so as to support sexual relationships for economic support. Accounts of these balls in travel narratives and antislavery literature fueled erotic fantasies of miscegenation for some whites and sparked outrage over racial mixing or the horrors of slavery and sexual victimization for others. The hemispheric reverberations of these quadroon ball social customs harkened back to Haiti, and from there, to New Orleans, and they reflected the hemispheric eroticization and commodification of the mulatta figure. Quadroon balls mirrored the same attitude toward mulattas' racialized sexuality as high prices for mulatta slaves on the auction block. The dominant culture's belief that mulatta women were sexually voracious fueled buyers' appetites.[5] The mulatta then emerged as a desired object of sexual availability, with a skin color that supposedly represented chastity and Black blood that carried hypersexuality. This perpetuation of eroticized images of light-skinned women of color has continued to embed itself in the popular imaginary.

The *mulata* figure in Brazil also has roots in the institution of slavery and sexual violence. Early twentieth-century scholars' comparisons between Brazil and the United States have often described Brazil's slavery as relatively more benign.[6] However, this is ahistorical, as conditions were often brutally harsh. As the largest importer of African slaves in the Atlantic trade, Brazil's slave prices were relatively low. Therefore, its slaves were far more expendable than U.S. slaves, who were harder to replace.[7]

The image of Brazil as racially more tolerant than the United States depended in part on the idea that racial mixing is more common in Brazil. Hypodescent rules, which assign racially mixed children the status of the subordinate group, obscure the actual frequency of interracial sexual contact in the United States, but Brazil's culture makes space for a racial continuum rather than dichotomy. The sexual availability of women of African descent has become integral to the national imaginary of a multiracial Brazilian family. In this perception, the *mulata* figure emerges as a symbol of Brazil's past and its unique national identity.

The unique demographics of the Brazilian colonial project influenced the development of the *mulata* figure. Unlike male colonists who brought white wives to the United States, Europeans who colonized Brazil generally came alone, and sexual relations with Black, Indigenous, and mixed-race women were common throughout Brazil's colonial period. The Portuguese Crown encouraged racial mixing between white male colonists and Indigenous women in order to claim greater control over the land. As in the United States, Brazil stigmatized interracial relations involving white women, treating them as the pure vector for constructing the family legacy resting on whiteness. Yet, as in the United States, discouragement of interracial marriage did not inhibit the sexual exploitation of enslaved women. Thus, the very premise of *mestiçagem*, the basis of Brazil's national identity, relies on colonial sexual exploitation.

The mythic role of a famous former enslaved woman who became one of Brazil's wealthiest slaveholders illuminates the links among gender, sexuality, and race. Born into slavery, Francisca "Chica" da Silva was the daughter of a Black slave woman and a white man. After João Fernandes de Oliveira, a diamond contractor from Portugal, purchased Chica in 1753, she became his concubine. He eventually freed her, and she became a wealthy enslaver herself. Numerous literary, theatrical, television, and film works have told her story, and many repeat the tropes of the sensual Brazilian *mulata* whose sexual relationship with her master is based on her seducing him. Some depict Chica as a manipulative, greedy woman, contrasting her to moral white women. Others use her as proof of racial democracy and women of color's ability to obtain upward mobility. The film *Xica da Silva* (1976) and telenovela *Xica da Silva* (1996–1997) represent her as a seductive *mulata* who used her Black sexuality to bewitch and manipulate her white lover. The proliferation of depictions of Chica suggests Brazil's ambivalence toward racial equality, investment in the idea of a racial democracy, and reliance on women's bodies to construct the narrative of the nation. This colonial myth of the seductive, social-climbing *mulata* naturalizes and exoticizes the hypersexuality of Black women, and it validates the national identity of mestiçagem and the possibility of ascension through racial blending.

Nonetheless, the presence of mixed-race people in the Americas provoked white anxiety and a variety of strategies of control. Racial classification proved a crucial instrument for upholding racial hierarchies. Historically, censuses contributed to institutionalized racial boundary making, assembling evidence to justify policies of white supremacy. In slavery's twilight years, the category of mulatto became a focus for racial scientists who sought to justify slavery through studying its members' characteristics. Lobbying legislators for the inclusion of the mulatto category in the national census of 1850, Josiah Nott, a noted racial scientist and slavery advocate, and other men argued that the census would prove that mulattoes were less fertile and had a shorter life span than their pure-race counterparts. In 1860, U.S. Census superintendent Joseph Kennedy predicted the gradual disappearance of the "colored" population due to racial mixing and physical and moral degeneracy.[8]

The United States considered Brazil a cautionary example. Louis Agassiz, a prominent scientist, traveled to Brazil in 1865 and 1866 to gather evidence of what he depicted as the degeneration of society that racial mixing had caused.[9] The northern United States abolished slavery before the southern states, leading to deep divides and a bloody civil war. Brazil, in contrast, only gradually abolished slavery, first passing the Law of the Free Womb, which in 1871 granted freedom to all children born to slaves, followed by full abolition of slavery in 1888. Regardless of the path to emancipation, the post-abolition containment of Blackness remained a paramount concern in both nations.

Mixed-Race Women and Sentimentalist Spectacles of Tragedy, Freedom, and Intimacy

Hemispherically, the figure of the tragic mulatta is a fundamental trope in anti-slavery novels. From Cuba to the United States to Brazil, she appears entangled in interracial liaisons destined to result in a tragic end for her.[10] In the tragic mulatta novels popular in both the United States and Brazil, a corrupt slave society victimizes a fair-skinned heroine who has the supposedly civilized traits of European women. She becomes the object of her white enslaver's desire and sexualized violence. Reflecting the influence of Romanticism and sentimental-ism, this tragic mulatta literature stressed the suffering of the mixed-race figure.

In the nineteenth century, white-authored works such as Lydia Maria Child's "The Quadroons" (1842) and Dion Boucicault's *The Octoroon* (1859), as well as *Clotel* (1853) by African American author William Wells Brown, used the mulatta as a sentimentalist literary trope to appeal to abolitionist sympathies. The tragic mulatta is usually light-skinned and beautiful, with aspirations of moral purity, but a small amount of Black blood is what dooms her. Due to her Black blood, she can never marry or merit the protection of white men and is at constant risk of sexual violence. Her tragic fate, often taking the form of a suicide after her white lover is unable to save her or else abandons her to marry a white woman, reaffirms the larger values of white heteropatriarchy. The ideals of respectable womanhood and sexual virtue were key to these antislavery tragic mulatta narratives. While the fetishization and objectification of the mulatta is consistent in these narratives, her Blackness is ultimately contained by her tragic fate.

The literary use of visibly white women of African descent to win abolition-ist sympathy also had an impact in Brazil. The worldwide popularity of Harriet Beecher Stowe's 1852 *Uncle Tom's Cabin* sparked the use of the mulatta trope in Brazilian abolitionist literature. *Uncle Tom's Cabin*'s mulatta, Eliza, escapes to Canada, and so the novel further contains Blackness in the United States by exiling and displacing it outside its national borders. The hemispheric dimen-sions of the mixed-race female figure are evident in Bernardo Guimarães's *A escrava Isaura* (1875, The slave Isaura), the most successful Brazilian novel of its day. *A escrava Isaura* popularized the Brazilian antislavery genre depicting cruel masters and virtuous slaves.[11] Isaura is the enslaved educated daughter of a Portuguese overseer and an enslaved *mulata* woman. After Isaura's biological mother dies, her white mistress prohibits Isaura from singing the songs her mother taught her, distancing her from her heritage and requiring her to focus on piano and classical music. With this forced forgetting of her mother as well as Afro-Brazilian culture and the author's emphasis on Isaura's white skin, the novel seeks to separate Isaura from Blackness.

Beautiful, modest, and virtuous, Isaura exemplifies the paradigm of ideal-ized white womanhood while juxtaposed against Rosa, her antagonist. As a hypersexual *mulata*, Rosa is an attractive, voluptuous temptress who threatens the Brazilian family and thus the Brazilian nation. Wishing to escape slavery, Rosa is envious of Isaura's ability to attract white male attention. Rosa's story ends in death—apt punishment for her attempts to seduce white men, while Álvaro, a rich white abolitionist, buys Isaura, frees her, and marries her. Her morality, exceptional beauty, and elegance are presented as her absolution from her Black peers, save for her enslaved status. Isaura's superiority, like mulatta heroines in the United States, is connected to her whiteness.

As with the U.S. versions of the tragic mulatta, the story of the Brazilian *mulata* maintains Black inferiority and uses her to appeal to white readers based on her semblance to whiteness. Yet unlike the U.S. tragic mulatta, Isaura's happy ending with her rescue and marriage affirms the power and virtue of white men. Nonetheless, her marriage, based on her desirability to white men, demonstrates the criticality of the mulatta within a sexual economy of slavery. While mixed-race characters are not fully embraced as full subjects in Brazilian literature, Isaura shows the potential of eventual belonging to the nation. She exists in a space in which she can position herself as worthy of belonging if she is fully disassociated from Blackness. Isaura's survival and marriage suggest a possible incorporation into the Brazilian national body if whiteness is privileged rather than the refusal in the United States to incorporate the mulatta. While Brazilian popular culture representations of mixed-Black characters managed the threat of Blackness with acquiescence to white superiority, U.S. popular culture has relied on the rejection and segregation of Blackness.

The Post-Abolition Mulatta/*Mulata* as a Threat to Racial Purity or a Path Toward Whitening

Following the abolition of slavery, the United States and Brazil took divergent approaches toward racial mixing and the role of the mixed-race female figure. Whereas the United States reinforced segregationist policies as a means of protecting white patriarchy as a national project, Brazil saw its large Black and Indigenous population as a threat to be diminished through miscegenation. White supremacy fueled both of these strategies of racial management.

The end of race-based bondage in the United States posed a very real threat to the racial hierarchy. As whiteness was premised on an opposition to Blackness, the Black freedom that followed slavery's end challenged a whiteness that in large part defined itself through its association with freedom. The response came quickly. By 1875, southern, northern, and newly formed western states such as California had ratified antimiscegenation laws. By the end of the nineteenth century, even though northern states had largely repealed such laws, southern states deepened them with the *Pace v. Alabama* Supreme Court decision in 1883 that upheld the prohibition of interracial marriage.[12] Such laws joined racial violence and the institutionalization of segregation as a means to protect white women from a perceived threat of Black male sexual predators.

Thus, women again became the conduits of a nation based on white purity and supremacy.

Against the backdrop of Reconstruction, fears of miscegenation, and political redistricting, the census became a crucial tool for differentiating Black mixture, fortifying racial categories, and ensuring white dominance. The 1890 census enumerator instructions indicated caution on distinguishing between Blacks, mulattoes, quadroons, and octoroons.[13]

Yet, the instructions gave no further information about how to measure and determine blood quantum fractions; census takers assigned categories by their own perceptions. Nonetheless, analysis of the results buttressed racial ideology and the increasing popularity of eugenics.

In order to uphold their social status, descendants of free people of color, the majority of whom were light skinned, sought to differentiate themselves from former enslaved people freed by the Civil War. Rather than free or slave, the separation between mulatto and Black expanded among communities of African descent in the United States. "The Wife of His Youth" (1898), a short story by African American writer Charles Chesnutt, depicted, among other social practices, the emergence of blue-vein societies—which barred people whose skin was too dark for veins to be visible on their arms. African Americans were increasingly divided between a light-skinned elite and the darker-skinned working classes. This colorism revealed a tension of association with and distancing from Blackness as these hierarchies and upward mobility depended on recognition of skin and class status within African American communities. Light skin became a form of social capital in upholding racial social structures within African American elite culture. White women, as the producers of white bloodlines, possessed the most social capital, and Black bourgeoisie took up racial uplift through emphasizing reproducing with light-skinned women.[14] Thus, from Reconstruction to the New Negro movement of the 1920s, the mulatta became a key symbol of African American racial uplift and mores of sexual respectability.

As African Americans migrated to northern cities between 1900 and 1930 and European immigration increased, whiteness absorbed immigrant groups previously considered racially distinct. Irish, Italians, and Jews became white along with reinforcement of the line between Black and white.[15] Depictions of mixed women's bodies in this period highlighted the threat of Black contamination of white bloodlines and the fragility of white privilege. The 1925 *Rhinelander v. Rhinelander* case was a public spectacle in this vein. Leonard Rhinelander, a white man from a wealthy family, sought to annul his marriage to Alice Rhinelander, a working-class mixed-Black woman he claimed had fraudulently hidden her Blackness.[16] The case invoked the idea of the mulatta as a danger because of her potential ability to pass into white society and thus produce children who unknowingly pass, and Alice's defense reaffirmed the essential nature of race as empirically discernible.

Brazil during this time period embarked on a trajectory from slavery to post-emancipation that leaned heavily on racial demarcation. Brazil declared its independence from Portugal in 1822, and after emancipation in 1888, the Brazilian *mulata* became a marker of potential degeneracy or mobility alongside eugenicist policies pursued in an attempt to better the Brazilian nation. Prior to abolition, Count Arthur de Gobineau, a leading proponent of biological determinism, published a short essay, "L'émigration au Brésil" (Emigration to Brazil), based on his observations and experiences as a French diplomat in Rio de Janeiro from 1869 to 1870. The essay condemns racial miscegenation in Brazil and predicts the eradication of Brazilian society due to the degenerative effects of miscegenation. Gobineau describes Brazilians as "a completely mulatto population, polluted in the blood and the spirit, and frighteningly ugly."[17] He argues that Brazil must isolate its most "damaging" racial elements and promote European immigration. With Brazil's growing nationalism in the wake of independence, Brazilian white elites feared that the nonwhite majority would block Brazil from entering into a perceived modernity alongside Europe and North America.

The Brazilian intelligentsia focused on challenging Gobineau's doomed assessment of national degeneracy by implementing a national project that embraced miscegenated Brazilian populations while simultaneously reinforcing racial hierarchies through concepts of racial difference.[18] With the hopes of intertwining whitening and modernization, the Brazilian government actively promoted and subsidized European immigration. In order to attract European immigrants, the Brazilian government used media campaigns and European expositions to project an image of a white wealthy Brazil. Approximately fifteen thousand immigrants responded every year from 1850 to 1930.[19] While African American leaders such as W. E. B. Du Bois expressed hopes for a racial utopia in Brazil, the Brazilian press discouraged African American migration, and the U.S. government worked with the Brazilian state to bar Black immigration from Brazil to the United States.[20] Regarded by the state as the unwanted remnants of a nation built on its forced labor, Afro-Brazilians remained relegated to the lowest paid jobs.[21]

Reconciling the idea of miscegenation as a solution for the emerging Brazilian nation with racist ideas of white superiority, Brazilian intellectuals argued that the influx of European immigration would overpower inferior Black blood.[22] For example, in 1911, João Batista de Lacerda, the director of the Museu

Nacional (National Museum) in Rio de Janeiro, predicted that due to whitening, Brazil would no longer have a Black population by 2012 and mixed-race groups would comprise only 3 percent of the population.[23] Similarly, Brazilian lawyer and historian Oliveira Vianna, who wrote the introduction for the 1920 census report, explicated his optimistic view of whitening and Brazil's racial future.[24]

Post-Emancipation Celebration and Fear of Mixed-Race Bodies in Popular Culture

Hemispheric narratives of white supremacy and Black exclusion defined post-abolition terrain for both Brazil and the United States. Like other Latin American and Caribbean countries' *blanqueamiento* (whitening), Brazil's whitening ideology, termed *branqueamento,* rested on the aspirations of whiteness as an ideal and the social transformations and practices enacted to achieve this ideal. Abolition put the privilege of whiteness in jeopardy, and post-abolition dominant popular culture responded by accentuating differences between Afro-descendants and whites. Cultural presentations of mixed-race women of African descent no longer portrayed them as nearly white in terms of beauty, grace, and morality. Instead, presentations focused on the threat they posed to the racial order in general and the nascent nation-building projects of whiteness specifically through their unbridled sexuality.

The connection between status and race became more tenuous in the United States in the post-emancipation period. Dominant culture portrayed the postbellum mulatta figure as morally vacant and sexually insatiable. The first cinematic appearance of the mulatta in D. W. Griffith's *The Birth of a Nation* (1915) maintained the linking of racial and sexual differences. The housekeeper, Lydia (played by white actor Mary Alden), is manipulative and sexually aggressive. She is hysterical, mentally unstable, and consumed both by sexual desire and a drive for power. The film idealizes white women, deploying Lydia as a marker of the perversion of Blackness, threatening white domesticity and white male morality. As photography and film created tension with the scientific racist view that race is visibly knowable, sexuality then became a key frame of racialization.[25] Sexually uninhibited, and thus unsuitable as a proper marriage partner, the mulatta was both the product of a sexual taboo and a sexual taboo herself.

The idea of a projected white nation also held currency in Brazil as the country struggled to reconcile the desire for white modernity with its newly emancipated Black population. After the abolition of slavery in Brazil, the legacies of slavery and a mixed-Afro-Brazilian population haunted the national racial future and threatened the preservation of racial hierarchies. As in the United States, the *mulata* emerged as a figure of racial and national degeneration. In Aluísio Azevedo's *O Cortiço* (1890; *A Brazilian Tenement*), a seminal text in the Brazilian literary canon, the *mulata* is the downfall of the prospective white nation. The iconic seductive and dangerous *mulata* character, Rita Baiana, is a corrupting influence on white immigrants. The narrative uses the *mulata's* sexuality as a way of shifting attention away from colonial legacies of racial and gender domination and directing blame on Black and mixed women themselves. In contrast to white women's chaste sexuality, Rita Baiana's sexuality is sinful and unrestrained. It victimizes white men such as Jerônimo, a hard-working white Portuguese man. His relationship with Rita Brazilianizes him and ultimately leads to his moral and physical degeneracy, the abandonment of his white wife, his descent into alcoholism, and the dissolution of his family. Rita and Jerônimo do not produce children, and thus the *mulata* is not the mother of a newly independent nation. Despite the unequal power relationships between white men and women of African descent, these depictions presented white men as innocent in their own sexual corruption.

In Brazil, ontologies of race emphasized visuality and racial mixing, clearly evident in visual art of the time. The gold medal painting in the 1895 Academia Imperial de Belas Artes (Imperial Academy of Fine Arts) salon, Modesto Brocos's *A Redenção de Cam* (*Ham's Redemption*) illustrates Brazil's whitening ideology. Depicting, from left to right, a Black grandmother, her *mulata* daughter, her white son-in-law, and her visibly white grandchild, the painting represents the dilution of Blackness. The Black grandmother raises her hands and eyes to praise God for whitening her family. The *mulata* holds the baby and the white immigrant gazes proudly at his child.

The painting conveys the disappearance of Blackness through sexual reproduction. The title references the biblical Ham, Noah's damned son who is considered the father of people of African descent. Proponents of New World slavery used the story of his wrongdoings to justify slavery. The title of the painting, then, posits that the elimination of the stain of Blackness is the path of redemption for Black people and the hope of a future white nation. The absence of men of color in this path toward redemption exemplifies the reliance on women of color for heteropatriarchal narratives of branqueamento and the exclusion of men of color from the vision of the nation. In the international vision of Brazil, Brazilian elites aimed to resolve the realities of Brazil's large mixed-race population and scientific theories that discredited mixed race. For example, João Batista de Lacerda, director of the Brazilian National Museum,

A Redenção de Cam (*Ham's Redemption*) illustrates Brazil's whitening project through racial mixing. Oil on canvas, 199×166 cm. Painted by Modesto Brocos, 1895. Source: Permanent Collection of Museu Nacional de Belas Artes, Rio de Janeiro.

reproduced Brocos's painting in his thesis and displayed it when he testified before the Universal Races Congress in London in 1911 to visually articulate his case on whitening.[26] Scientific thought and fine arts fashioned a national identity based on the visible disappearance of Blackness predicated upon the *mulata* body.

In the United States, the mulatta figure was used for different aims by white and Black producers. African American producers rewrote the script of colonial subordination and evoked a continuation, rather than an eradication, of Blackness. During the post-Reconstruction era, Frances Harper's *Iola Leroy* (1892) and Pauline Hopkins's *Contending Forces* (1899) used mulatta heroines to evince an honorable Black womanhood and a politics of respectability grounded in sexuality as a response to the exclusion of Black women from true womanhood.[27] In other postbellum novels by African Americans, among them Charles Chesnutt's *The House Behind the Cedars* (1900) and *The Marrow of Tradition* (1901), the mulatta characters reaffirm their Black identities and derive their morality from their affiliation with Blackness rather than whiteness. As had these novelists, Black director Oscar Micheaux presented African American imagery in which Blacks could thrive in a separate sphere. Offering an alternative to the racist imagery of films like *Birth of a Nation*. Micheaux's films, such as *The Homesteader* (1919), utilized passing narratives to celebrate Black pride and attachments to Black communities. In these narratives, the mulatta figure is the bearer of future racial bloodlines of Blackness.

Yet, Hollywood films, under largely white production, directing, and writing, exhibited anxieties about Black representation and racial mixing. The 1934 "Don'ts and Be Carefuls" guide published by the Motion Picture Producers and Distributors of America (MPPDA) and the official MPPDA Production Code suggest Hollywood's obsession with mixed-race bodies. These codes prohibited depictions of sexual relationships between whites and Blacks. Thus, Hollywood largely expunged interracial sexual relationships from the imagined vision of the nation and reinforced the established antimiscegenation laws.[28] Hollywood codes also implicitly instructed audiences on how to interpret and decipher race. With attention to the visibility of race and the threat of racial mixing, *Imitation of Life* (1934) caused apprehension within the Production Code Administration (PCA) due to the racial ambiguity of the light-skinned Black actor Fredi Washington, and her portrayal as Peola, a woman who crosses the color line. Leaving her Black college to pass as a white salesgirl, Peola's desire to assimilate and participate in a society that privileges whiteness consumes her actions and relationships. Whereas the tragic mulatta in nineteenth- and early twentieth-century narratives dies, here Peola loses her Black mother as punishment for passing for white. With Peola's return to a Black college, the narrative suggests that mulattas can find self-actualization by recognizing their own Blackness, yet ultimately this redeeming of Blackness is only to contain Blackness by maintaining segregation.

The yearning for freedom beyond the shadows of U.S. colonial legacies led to African American intertwined imaginings of Brazil and the mulatta. Harlem

Renaissance writers such as Nella Larsen, like their predecessors, used the mixed-race female character to criticize racism and refute notions of Black inferiority as the twentieth century wore on. Mixed race herself, Larsen depicted mulatta characters in *Quicksand* (1928) and *Passing* (1929) that challenged the ideal New Negro women and racial, sexual, and feminine norms espoused by the Black bourgeoisie. In *Passing*, Brazil becomes a site of escape without a color line. Other novels by African Americans about passing, such as Jessie Fauset's *Plum Bun* (1928), also used mulatta characters and Brazil to illuminate how U.S. racism led to the racial violence, fear, and cloaked histories embedded in the mulatta figure. Between emancipation and the start of World War II, African American leaders described Brazil as a nation without segregation and as possible Black refuge. The mixed-race symbol was essential to this discourse. For example, in 1914 W. E. B. Du Bois wrote in the *Crisis*, the National Association for the Advancement of Colored People's (NAACP's) magazine that "there are in Brazil 8,300,000 Negros and mulattoes; 3,700,000 Indian and mixed Indian-whites and 8,000,000 persons of European descent. All these elements are fusing into one light mulatto race."[29] Thus, Brazil is imagined simultaneously as a new frontier of racial mixing and of potential African American citizenship. As World War II began, the mulatta remained a figure of U.S. racial containment as well as a threat to the racial binary system.

The Mulatta/*Mulata* and Illusions of Inclusion in Brazil in the 1930s and 1940s

By the 1930s, Brazil's cultural and political expressions celebrated a mixed-race nation with the *mulata* as emblematic of mestiçagem. Unlike the United States, Brazil developed a national identity based on racial mixing. Whereas scholars such as Oliveira Vianna promoted policies of scientific racism in Brazil in the 1920s, Gilberto Freyre rose to prominence in the 1930s through his attempts to discredit prevalent ideas of scientific racism that doomed Brazil due to its racial mixing. Freyre put forward the idea that racial mixing created a hybrid vigor suitable for the tropics and that this new population would pave the way for a modernized, prosperous future. The Brazilian state embraced the idea of the union of three races—white, Black, and Indigenous—as a central discourse of mestiçagem. Freyre defined exceptional racial democracy because of racial mixing in direct contrast to the United States.

Freyre's work helped create a myth of racial democracy based on deeply gendered and sexualized relationships. His espousal of the benefits of mestiçagem, or racial mixing, carried forth into national lore the idea that all Brazilians could claim African, European, and Indigenous ancestry, and thus, racism in Brazil did not exist.[30] In *Casa Grande e Senzala* (1933; *The Masters and the Slaves*), which became very influential in the ensuing decades, Freyre described the sexual and cultural mixing and integration of African, Portuguese, and Indigenous elements as converging to form Brazilian national identity and a new hybrid tropical race.[31] Freyre framed miscegenation during slavery with a nostalgic affective stance and romanticized slavery as relatively benign. His work emphasizes domestic ties and intimacy between slave and free people in the form of children playing together, interracial sexual relationships, and Black servants affectionately observing white subjectivity. Freyre suggested that slavery brought different races together in harmony.[32]

The memory of slavery represented in *Casa Grande e senzala*, like that of the legends of Chica da Silva, relied on obscuring the unequal power dynamics of colonial Brazil and eroticizing the narrative of gendered and sexualized race relations. With pictorial and sensual detail, Freyre asserted that the relative shortage of white women and the "natural" attraction of Portuguese men for *mulatas* and Black women under the rural patriarchal family were essential to Brazilian colonization and nation-building. Freyre took the perspective of the male plantation owner, focusing on white male masters' union with Black and *mulata* enslaved women. His erotic narrative celebrated the *mulata* as the unifying symbol of brasilidade (Brazilianness) and as proof of Brazilian racial democracy.

Freyre's vision of slavery and mestiçagem depended on Black female slaves fulfilling white male desire both as a Black maternal figure and as a sexual object. As Saidiya Hartman notes, "the discourse of seduction obfuscates the primacy and extremity of violence in master slave relations . . . as the enslaved is legally unable to give consent or offer resistance, she is presumed to be always willing."[33] Black women, Freyre wrote, were the ones "who rocked us to sleep. Who suckled us. Who fed us. . . . The mulatto girl initiated us into physical love and, to the creaking of a canvas cot, gave us our first complete sensation of being a man."[34] This framework functioned in part because Freyre ignored colonial and sexual violence, framing interracial sexual relations as though they were based solely on love, and disregarding how the exalted sexuality of the *mulata* was used to justify sexual exploitation.[35] Freyre's vision of the past in which the *mulata* was evidence of a racially harmonious Brazil was characteristic of dominant ideas about race, gender, sexuality, and national identity.

Under Brazilian president Getúlio Vargas (1930–45 and 1951–54), the *mulata* became a symbol of national unity. Vargas relied on racialized concepts for the project of forging a modern nation. He posited mestiçagem as an alternative to the ideals of European superiority and purity. As an instrument of Brazilian national pride and identity, the valorization of mestiçagem contrasted with the Jim Crow segregation and racial binaries of the United States. Vargas sought to move away from the encouragement of European immigration as a solution to Brazil's race problem.[36] Rather than repress Afro-Brazilian cultural expression, Vargas validated these cultural forms, such as samba, as national symbols representative of a racially mixed Brazilian identity.[37]

Yet, Vargas's valorization of Afro-Brazilian culture masked a persistent racist patriarchal structure. His authoritarian government opposed any organizations or movements that challenged the nationalist project of mestiçagem, and thus, official state policy minimized racial differences and inequalities.[38] The state dismantled Afro-Brazilian organizations or political parties, such as the radical Frente Negra Brasileira (Black Brazilian Front), which had once backed Vargas.[39] For Vargas, the inclusion of Blackness had to be part of his own national policies and thus under his control. He viewed the assertion of a separate Black identity and of racial dissent as threats to the state. With the institutionalization of racial democracy, Vargas would not allow the questioning of racial inequalities, and he outlawed Black political organizing. Instead, the *mulata* became the pinnacle image of state-sanctioned racial democracy, consolidating the Brazilian narrative of mestiçagem while containing Blackness.

The refashioning of racialized femininity and sexuality in the United States relied on the domestic containment of Black sexuality and U.S. ideas of Latin America. During World War II, light-skinned African American film stars such as Lena Horne offered an illusion of racial tolerance for Black audiences, an acceptable beauty and entertainment for white audiences, even while her phenotype suggested histories of racial mixing. Horne represented the light-skinned respectable middle-class vision of racial integration, harkening back to the politics of Black respectability that began with Reconstruction.[40] Whether appearing in white-directed Hollywood musicals with all-Black casts, such as *Stormy Weather* (1943) and *Cabin in the Sky* (1943), or in other musicals with white cast members, no Hollywood production showed Horne in a relationship with white male characters. Musicals such as *Panama Hattie* (1942) and *Broadway Rhythm* (1944) Latinized Horne to avoid engaging with U.S. histories of racial mixing. The casting of the light-skinned U.S. actor Etta Moten as a Brazilian in *Flying Down to Rio* (1933) had a similar containment effect.[41] In keeping with U.S. ideas about Brazil as possessing racial categories that did not exist in the United States, Hollywood films reinforced notions of Brazil as a mixed nation while negating U.S. histories of racial mixing.

Following World War II, films such as *Pinky* (1949) utilized the mulatta character in the social-problem film genre that purported to tackle racial prejudice.[42]
The mulatta for whom the film is named has an offscreen interracial romance
with a white man, her fiancé, who, while aware of her heritage, requires her
to pass as white. After spending time in Mississippi helping her grandmother
care for her aging white employer, Pinky refuses to return to the North. "I'm
a Negro," she declares. "I can't pretend to be anything else. I don't want to be
anything else." The flaw preventing Pinky from full assimilation into white civil
society is her inherent Blackness and the threat of tainting white bloodlines.
As a reward, Pinky inherits money from her grandmother's employer, which
she uses to open a hospital for Black children.

Like earlier U.S. literature, from mulatta antebellum narratives to African
American literature post-Reconstruction, Pinky displays bourgeois respectability and values, which make her an exceptional Black woman. Her respectability
ultimately depends on knowing and adhering to her racialized social position.
The film presented a limited vision of democratic inclusion and citizenship
by reinforcing racial boundaries and evading the possibilities of mixed-race
identity and interracial intimacies. Indeed, the casting of white actor Jeanne
Crain as Pinky (as with the casting of white actor Ava Gardner as the mulatta
Julie in 1951's *Show Boat*) evidences the racial and sexual anxiety surrounding
actresses of known Black descent appearing alongside white actors in onscreen
romances. Nonetheless, the excision of Black actresses did not negate the preponderance of the imagined mulatta in U.S. cultural productions.

In contrast, Brazil espoused racial inclusion and eroticized interracial intimacies through the *mulata* figure. Starting in the 1930s, the *mulata* figure and samba
became intertwined signifiers of Brazilian national identity.[43] In popular music,
such as samba songs from the 1930s, and popular novels, the *mulata* represented
sexuality and sensuality. As Vargas's authoritarian government attempted to use
a populist agenda as a way of connecting to the masses, samba became a tool
for nationalization. National airwaves broadcast *samba-exaltação* (exaltation
samba) with state sponsorship. White musicians like Ary Barroso and Noel
Rosa began to enter the samba scene, a cultural expression that had previously
been most associated with Afro-Brazilians, and composed songs expressing
sexual desire for the *mulata*, such as Barroso's 1957 "É Luxo Só" (Pure luxury).
Other songs, such as Lamartine Babo's 1932 song "O Teu Cabelo Não Nega"
(Your hair gives you away; reprised in 1942, 1952, and 1981), demonstrated the
dual emotions of repulsion and desire. According to the lyrics, the *mulata* is
the epitome of Brazil, but her hair is a marker of her Blackness. Yet, because

her skin color doesn't rub off on him, the singer can love her. Implicitly, sexual intercourse will not contaminate his whiteness—an assurance that encodes his disgust for her Blackness.[44]

Afro-Brazilian musicians, such as Ataulfo Alves, often used the *mulata* figure as a way to enter into a masculinist interracial brotherhood with white men. For example, his 1930s song *"Mulata Assanhada"* (Restless *mulata*) romanticizes the sexual violence of slavery and places the singer in the position of white master dominating the *mulata* as his sexual possession.[45] United by their desire for the *mulata* and her sexual availability, Afro-Brazilian and white Brazilian men held common affinities for the *mulata* as a source of sexual pleasure. Thus, the *mulata* became a national symbol and a racialized sexual symbol simultaneously rooted in the discourses of mestiçagem.

Post–World War II Racial Orders: Desiring and Disciplining Blackness

While Brazil became a global model of racial harmony, the United States served as its antithesis in the international imagination. The mixed-race female figure then acted hemispherically as a testament to racial democracy in the former or as a symbol of racial discord in the latter. In the wake of the 1954 *Brown v. Board of Education* decision, segregationists sexualized school desegregation with the fearful prediction that mixed schools would lead to interracial sex and racial corruption. Capitalizing on the myth of Black men lusting after vulnerable white women, campaigns protesting desegregation used the idea of white purity and white female victimization as a rationale for violent opposition to Black civil rights.[46] Indeed, the international media images of the mangled body of fourteen-year-old Emmett Till in 1955 and the spectacle of federal troops accompanying nine African American children to school in Little Rock, Arkansas, in 1957 laid bare the continuing racial strife in the United States. Brazilian politicians called out the hypocrisy of racial discrimination and U.S. democracy as the ideal for the rest of the world.[47]

In contrast to the racism of the United States, Brazil emerged as a model of racial democracy. Following World War II and the Holocaust, UNESCO offered Brazil as a model for all former slaveholding nations. To counter the Soviet Union's mounting criticism of U.S. racism, the United States depicted Brazil as an exemplary capitalist country that had fixed racism.[48] In order to present itself as a beacon compared to the defeated racist Third Reich and Jim Crow United States, in 1951 Brazil distributed a pamphlet in English with a foreword from Gilberto Freyre exalting its benign race relations.[49] Yet, in the same year, Brazil was forced to reckon with media fallout after the barring of African American dancer Katherine Dunham from a high-priced Brazilian hotel. In the ensuing international public relations debacle, the Brazilian press spun the incident as a sign of the racist influences of U.S. capitalism in Brazil rather than of Brazil's own racism.[50] Legislators passed civil rights legislation, Lei Afonso Arinos, which prominent figures, such as Freyre, explained by asserting that foreign influence necessitated the law. Yet racial discrimination continued in Brazil despite the law's ban on the use of racial selection in hiring practices and discrimination in both public and private accommodations. Employment criteria such as *boa aparência* (good looks) used racially coded language that allowed discrimination.[51] Public discourses framed inequalities through class rather than race. The celebration of racial democracy and the persistent denial of racial discrepancies worked in tandem to perpetuate discrimination.

However, UNESCO and scholarly studies of Brazil in the 1950s and 1960s found pervasive racial inequalities that contradicted the notions of racial democracy. UNESCO's studies employed both Brazilian and foreign scholars, including Florestan Fernandes of the Universidade de São Paulo and future president Fernando Henrique Cardoso. They discredited the myth of racial democracy and emphasized persistent social structures that embedded racial inequalities. However, they largely advanced the notion that with greater industrialization and economic growth, racial inequalities would cease to exist.[52] According to UNESCO's influential report, the myth of racial democracy had both facilitated relative racial harmony in Brazil and masked deep racial inequalities and furthered racial hierarchies. Despite these scholarly findings, the Brazilian state continued to perpetuate the intertwined myths of racial democracy and mestiçagem, with the *mulata* as a symbol of both discourses throughout the late twentieth century.

Against the backdrop of civil rights advances and racialized backlash in the United States, the 1959 remake of *Imitation of Life* revived the tragic mulatta narrative. The ostensibly white Susan Kohner, who was actually Mexican and Jewish, portrayed the light-skinned daughter, Sarah Jane. Sarah Jane consistently rejects her Blackness and directs her anger at her mother, Annie, a dark-skinned domestic worker. Like the 1934 version, Sarah Jane disavows her mother in favor of passing for white. When her white boyfriend catches her trying to pass, he beats her and treats her abusively, denying her a white woman's privilege. The trauma of race relies on the body of the Black mother and, thereby, directly descends from colonial matrilineal slave status. Her father is absent, yet the presence of the Black mother and the mulatta daughter evokes the haunting of miscegenation, sexual coercion, and concubinage.

Unlike the 1934 version, the 1959 *Imitation of Life*'s mulatta plays into the tropes of the sexually excessive mulatta. With the *Brown v. Board of Education* decision and the fear of racial mixing due to school desegregation, Sarah Jane's mulatta is the manifestation of these anxieties. The film presented Sarah Jane's foil in the childlike and innocent Susie, the daughter of Annie's employer. Sarah Jane runs away from home to become a nightclub dancer, presenting herself as white. From her sultry voice to the jazz music associated with her character to her tight clothing, Sarah Jane's Blackness is revealed through upending white normative femininity. Indeed, Sarah Jane's strategy toward whiteness relies on the mulatta seduction narrative, yet ultimately it is this same spectacle of sexuality that marks her as Black.

Hegemonic whiteness is ultimately maintained. At the end of the film, Sarah Jane's mother has died of a broken heart. Sarah Jane returns home in time for the funeral, blaming herself for her mother's death. The punishment for the tragic mulatta is not her own death but the sacrificial death of her Black mother. Thus, in her quest to pass as white, Sarah Jane must disown her Blackness and her maternal ties. As in the 1934 *Imitation of Life*, the film manipulates audiences to critique the light-skinned daughter's rejection of her dark-skinned mother. The final image of the film shows three white people—Annie's employer's family—consoling Sarah Jane. Ultimately, the film reaffirmed racial hierarchies during the disassembling of legal segregation and contained the threat of Blackness.

In Brazil, Jorge Amado's novels exemplified how national discourses of mestiçagem and sexual objectification contained the threat of the *mulata*. Translated into various languages, *Gabriela, cravo e canela* (1958; *Gabriela, Clove and Cinnamon*) depicts the *mulata* Gabriela as hypersexual and exotic. As a group, his novels, several of which became bestsellers in the United States as well as Brazil, allegorize and further mythologize mestiçagem with white men and *mulata* women in a relationship of dominance of white over nonwhite. The sexual fantasy of hybridity and seduction reside within the *mulata* body.

Like Freyre's narratives, the novels of the 1950s and 1960s that featured *mulatas* naturalized colonial practices of racialized, gendered, and sexualized domination. Amado's emphasis on sensuality and overt sexuality made Gabriela a continuation of Azevedo's Rita Baiana in *O Cortiço*. Both *mulatas* are exotic and primitive figures with a lack of control over their raw sexual impulses, but, unlike Rita Baiana, Gabriela is an asset rather than a liability to the nation. Economically and socially subservient to her white lover, Gabriela conforms to racialized and gendered norms. Amado reinforced hemispheric patterns of modernist writers' attempts to recover the nation through the exaltation of mixed-race female figures and the reinforcement of sexual objectification. Thus, the recuperation and celebration of Blackness also relied on the containment of this Blackness through the naturalization, commodification, and exotification of this figure. The eroticization of the *mulata* body through a male gaze paralyzes her Blackness in a heteropatriarchal vision of mestiçagem.

Struggles for Empowerment: Producing and Contesting Iconic Mixedness and Blackness

By the late 1960s, the mulatta no longer played such a prominent role in U.S. cultural expression. Following the Los Angeles Watts riots in 1965 and the assassination of Martin Luther King Jr. in 1968, the civil rights project of integration appeared to splinter. Despite significant civil rights gains, such as the 1964 Civil Rights Act and the 1965 Voting Rights Act, large-scale problems such as housing segregation and underemployment remained. The emergence of the Black Panther Party signaled that public attention was turning from moral persuasion and integration to confrontation and self-determination and Black power. The slogan "Black is Beautiful" and the aesthetic adoption of Afro hairstyles set up an oppositional alternative to white beauty standards. While Black nationalist movements often emphasized a recouping of Black masculinity, Black female activists reimagined Black womanhood through frames of revolution, militancy, and global solidarity.[53] Emerging from 1970s social movements, the Combahee River Collective, a group of radical Black feminists, insisted on addressing the intersections of racial, class, sexual, and gender oppressions. The text, the Combahee River Collective Statement, critiqued the limitations within both white middle-class feminism and male-dominated Black nationalist movements and how multiple systems of domination generate and cloak Black women's lived conditions. Articulating a transnational vision of liberation by centering Black women's knowledge and experiences, the Combahee River Collective provided a legacy for future Black feminist praxis.[54]

Amid these civil rights gains and growing disillusionment with civil rights integration, *Loving v. Virginia* struck down the last of the Jim Crow laws—antimiscegenation laws—in 1967. Challenging the hierarchy of white supremacy, the U.S. Supreme Court case overturned Virginia's 1924 Racial Integrity Act, which prohibited interracial marriage between a white person and a nonwhite person. Chief Justice Earl Warren's decision argued that "the fact that Virginia prohibits only interracial marriages involving white persons demonstrates that the racial classifications must stand on their own justification, as measures designed to maintain White Supremacy. We have consistently denied the constitutionality of measures which restrict the rights of citizens on account of race." The court had legitimated heterosexual multiracial families, and an expanding number of interracial marriages tested the boundaries of racial categories and national identity. The *Loving* case is significant for its resistance to the institutionalization of white supremacy yet has largely been co-opted as a colorblind narrative that ultimately re-centers whiteness. By the 1990s and 2000s, as the following chapters will demonstrate, the mulatta thus reemerged as a key symbol of U.S. racial hope, anxieties, and ultimately as a necessary containment of Blackness.

The *mulata* had a more enduring position as a symbol of brasilidade. After a military coup in 1964, the ideology of racial democracy became even more integral to national consolidation. The military dictatorship, with the support of Gilberto Freyre, determined that any challenge to racial democracy should be considered subversive, anti-Brazilian, and communist. The dictatorship exiled Florestan Fernandes and Fernando Cardoso and prohibited studies on racial discrimination.[55] By 1970, the military government decided to go further, omitting racial or color categories on the census to prevent scholarly research into educational, income, professional, and health disparities among different races. The state wished to avoid activism along the lines of the U.S. civil rights movement, extinguishing the potential ruptures in racial hegemony through repression, violence, and censorship.[56]

Growing political Black consciousness in Brazil emerged with the formation of the Movimento Negro Unificado (MNU; Unified Black Movement) in 1978. As the first national Afro-Brazilian organization to form since the 1937 ban of the Frente Negra, the MNU demanded recognition of the pervasiveness of racism in Brazil and called for social, economic, and political reforms to remedy it.[57] In the late 1970s, with the gradual opening of democracy, pressure from social scientists and Black activists succeeded in restoring the race question to the 1980 census. Similar to dominant strands of U.S. Black nationalism, the male-dominated Afro-Brazilian movement often marginalized Afro-Brazilian women's voices and concerns.[58] Like the U.S. women's movement, which focused largely on the concerns of white middle-class women, Brazilian feminist movements also largely ignored Afro-Brazilian women's social locations and experiences. Expressing intersectional identities and sociopolitical locations, and marginalization, Afro-Brazilian women, like U.S. Black women, critiqued the multiple forms of marginalization within these movements while highlighting the specificities of Afro-Brazilian women's experiences.[59]

By the late 1980s, organizations such as Criola and Geledés emerged to address Afro-Brazilian women's issues and to combat intertwined gender, racial, class, and sexual oppression.[60] Such growing Black consciousness and activism would lay the foundation for Brazilian affirmative action advocacy in the 1990s and 2000s. Yet, the adoption of the myth of racial democracy by the state and major periods of authoritarian state rule, 1937–45 and 1964–85, had hindered Afro-Brazilians' capacity to challenge the state and to organize movements for recognition and equality. The *mulata*, as a narrative of national unity, remained entrenched as a means of disavowing racial inequities.

The mixed-race figure as an icon of sexual pleasure operated hemispherically despite shifting political and social dynamics. The U.S. civil rights movement and the emergence of the Black Power movement brought along a questioning of racial representations and a critique of light-skinned characters. Blaxploitation films of the 1970s were prime examples of media that arose to fill the newly opened space for representation. While most films focused on Black men, Pam Grier, an actor of Black and Indigenous descent, starred in films such as *Coffy* (1973) and *Foxy Brown* (1974). As heroines seeking justice and revenge against white patriarchal systems, Grier's characters are neither the tragic helpless mulatta nor imprisoned in sexual servitude. While scripted with Black rather than racially mixed heroines, these films reflected anxieties of interracial mixing. Grier's highly sexualized roles and fetishized body contained her Blackness in a way that recalled presentations of the mulatta. The films presented interracial sex between Black men and white women as consensual, but sex between Black women and white men as assault.

The mulatta figure haunted these films, a reminder of unequal power relations and sexual violence. In the Hollywood-produced *Sparkle* (1976) with an all-Black cast, the tragic sexual mulatta theme persisted by featuring mixed-race actor Lonette McKee as the beautiful and promiscuous Sister, who defies familial sexual mores, descends into drugs, and eventually dies. The ideological function of mass popular culture in the 1970s continued to work within a management of Black women's sexuality.

The containment of Blackness also resonated through both the invisibility of Black actresses and the sexualization of the *mulata* in Brazil. As in the United States in the 1940s and 1950s, actresses racialized as white in a Brazilian context often played roles scripted as *mulata* roles in the 1970s and 1980s, such as Betty Faria as Rita Baiana in *O Cortiço* (1978) and Lucélia Santos in *Escrava Isaura* (1976–1977).[61] Walter Avancini, director of *Escrava Isaura*, claimed that there were no suitable actresses of African descent for the roles and that only white women could draw the audience he desired.[62] Thus, even as the figure of the *mulata* remained evidence of racial democracy, the media elite argued that desirable audiences would not accept nonwhite characters. Until the 1990s, most telenovelas only featured Black actors in slave-period productions or in roles such as maids and prostitutes.[63] Not until 2009 did the first primetime television show feature a Black actress in a protagonist role, Taís Araújo in *Viver a Vida*.

Adaptations of Jorge Amado novels, such as the 1975 telenovela *Gabriela*, the 1983 film *Gabriela, cravo e canela*, and the 2012 television miniseries *Gabriela*, presented the *mulata* character as sexually available. As Gabriela in the 1975 telenovela and 1983 film, Sônia Braga became both a national and international icon of brasilidade. With her curly hair and tanned skin, she presents a hetero-patriarchal ideal of Brazilian racial flexibility in that she manifests hybridity without material consequences. The focus on Braga's sensuality heightens notions of mestiçagem and in her stardom while eliding Black familial origins and distancing traumas of racial mixing and racial inequalities from brasilidade. Gilberto Freyre commented in 1987 that Braga's beauty represented the triumph of Brazil's meta-race.[64]

While the vast majority of cinematic and televisual representation focused on white women, presenting the *mulata* as the epitome of brasilidade gained prominence in samba show spectacles. From the 1970s to the 1990s, white Rio businessman Oswaldo Sargentelli, a self-described *mulatólogo* (*mulata* expert), presented samba spectacles of scantily clad dancing women to the Brazilian elite and tourists alike.[65] With the branding of brasilidade as a sexual paradise of *mulatas*, the archetype of the sensual, sexually available *mulata* who dances with abandon represents a thematic fixture memorialized in popular Brazilian cultural politics and the international imagination of Brazil. In 1993, TV Globo's Carnival-related programming featured the Mulata Globeleza, a body-painted nude dancing muse of Carnival. Each year, the Mulata Globeleza displays the eroticism, dancing skills, and sexual availability represented by the trifecta of the *mulata*, samba, and Carnival. This iconography of the *mulata* as a consumable sensual pleasure who seduces audiences harkens back to the colonial imaginary, into Getúlio Vargas's Estado Novo, and into the contemporary notion of *mulata* sexual availability.

From the slavery era to the 1970s, the gendered and sexualized politics of the mulatta/*mulata* figure were grounded in a dominant frame of exploitation and the devaluation of nonwhite difference. Inscribed in these colonial legacies, the mixed-Black female body legitimized a racial, gender, and sexual system of oppression. These racial regimes stemming from colonial cultures regulate the mulatta/*mulata* and how racialized sexual intimacies are imagined as a mean to maintain racial hierarchies. Media representations of mixed-race women in the 2000s cannot be divorced from historical racial legacies. Dominant culture has constructed and utilized these depictions of mixed race to advance white patriarchal privilege. Both the United States and Brazil value some racialized bodies more than others. The mulatta/*mulata* demonstrates the continued salience of white hierarchies and anti-Blackness as she embodies and troubles both the U.S. and Brazilian racial projects. Demographic changes in the United States present a challenge to binary views of race as well as white supremacy as the actual national body politic shifts. Brazil's history of racial mixing without eliminating racism presents an alternate narrative of race and national identity that nonetheless relies on white supremacy.

Framing Blackness and Mixedness

The Politics of Racial Identity in the Celebrity Texts of Jennifer Beals, Halle Berry, and Camila Pitanga

In June 2012, *Complex* magazine commemorated the forty-fifth anniversary of the *Loving v. Virginia* decision by publishing "The 50 Hottest Biracial Women." The magazine detailed how, "considering the rainbow of races we now have in celebrity culture, it's hard to conceive that it took an act of the Supreme Court for beautiful women like Alicia Keys and Rashida Jones to legally exist.... So, here, enjoy these mocha-colored, honey-tinted, caramel-complected babes."[1] Referencing the *Loving v. Virginia* decision, the magazine reduces civil rights and mixed women to commodified racial desirability. Biracial women like Jennifer Beals and Halle Berry graced the list. This type of fetishizing of mixed women's bodies could be seen in Brazilian magazines as well, as when *VIP* magazine featured Brazilian actor Camila Pitanga in an article titled "Pitanga, cravo e canela."[2] A clear reference to Jorge Amado's 1958 novel *Gabriela, Cravo e Canela* (*Gabriela, Clove and Cinnamon*), Pitanga was used to evoke the iconic eroticized exotic mixed-race figure that has played a key role in the construction of Brazilian identity.

In both the United States and Brazil, actresses of mixed-Black descent appeared as the commodification of a consumable sexual and racial desire. Through the exchange of mixed-Black bodies as commodities, the mixed-Black celebrity enters into a political and social vision of race. In the personas of Jennifer Beals and Halle Berry in the United States and Camila Pitanga in Brazil, these celebrities have a variety of racial and sexual meanings inscribed onto their bodies according to national racial projects. Hemispherically, intertwined histories of white supremacy and capitalism converge to direct these celebrities as celebratory embodiments of racial progress and exotic desire. This chapter takes up an intersectional analysis of power to formulate how logics of capitalism, patriarchy, and neoliberal inclusion act with and against subjectivity and agency. The star texts of these mixed-Black celebrities provide acceptable chronicles of difference that disavow historical and material racialized conditions while refashioning tropes of multiracial Blackness to affirm neoliberal racial projects. With the neoliberal commodification of identities, mixed celebrities acquire cultural and symbolic capital even as these same celebrities have exercised their agency through a critique of racial hierarchies. While these actors mobilize and cultivate individual racial subjectivities, they nonetheless straddle limits of subversive agency within hegemonic racial landscapes. This chapter examines how mainstream and Black press representations of mixed celebrities regulate racial identity and sustain models of nationhood.

Celebrities facilitate the mediation of mixed-race identities and prompt racial and sexual anxieties.[3] Their public personas trouble hegemonic racialized national landscapes, yet these subversions are ultimately contained through commodification and the repositioning of mixed Black femininity into dominant narratives. In a U.S. context, Jennifer Beals privileged multiracial identity and Halle Berry emphasized Black identity while acknowledging a mixed racial heritage. These two actors provide contrasting embodied imaginaries of racial essentialism and multiracial utopias in the public sphere. Yet, like the United States, the existence of mixed-race identities in Brazil has not necessarily led to greater social justice. Brazilian actor Camila Pitanga identifies as Black as a personal and political stance. A star's self-identification, how viewers categorize her, how media tells her story, the narratives she participates in, and the political statements she makes often operate independently of each other. Unraveling racial constructions of celebrities demonstrates how racial meaning is inscribed onto visually fetishized bodies rather than expressive of these bodies. Taking these star texts together, I draw a larger portrait of how race operates through and on mixed-Black celebrities in the United States and Brazil.

Celebrity Public Personas

Stars are highly symbolic models, and female celebrities embody ideals of beauty, desirability, and femininity. Mixed-Black actors like Beals, Berry, and Pitanga present forms of racial commodification and symbolic racial transformation beyond the national racial landscape. As studios generally assume that audiences are white in the United States and Brazil, they market stars in a way meant to deactivate threatening racial elements and maintain white hegemony. While the commodification of nonwhite celebrity images often reinforces the superior position of whiteness through the containment, neutralization, or deactivation of race, how these actors negotiate their racial identities can demonstrate resistance to structures of racial visibility and heteronormative notions of ancestry that determine belonging.[4] Beals, Berry, and Pitanga participate in and shape discourses regarding race. However, they cannot completely control their own images, given the media framing and the historical legacies of mixed figures.

Time and national borders separate these three actors. This chapter moves from the U.S. 1980s climate of Black-white binaries to the 1990s era of hopeful racial tolerance characterized through wistful overcoming of racial divisions to the 2000s, when multiraciality was packaged as a promising postracial order. Meanwhile, in Brazil, I begin with the 1980s and 1990s, which brought about political reforms aimed at combatting racial inequalities, and advance to the 2000s in which questions of defining Blackness and blurring racial identities become key components in debates regarding the legitimacy of such reforms. Beals's star text is enmeshed within narratives of passing, Berry's celebrity challenges and fits into the tragic mulatta trope, and Pitanga's stardom contends with the sensual mulatta as a Brazilian emblem.

Through diverse strategies of mixedness and Blackness, these actors assume their positionalities within broader struggles of resistance. Their own attempts to represent themselves function as a form of what José Muñoz calls disidentification—the strategy of survival that minority subjects utilize to "perform the self" in a manner that neither conforms to dominant ideologies that pathologize minority subjects nor completely discards them. This performance "tactically and simultaneously works on, with, and against" ideology. Subjects form their identities in negotiation with the "cultural logics of heteronormativity, white supremacy, and misogyny" so as to counter them from within this model to "envision and activate new social relations."[5] Subverting a Black-white binary, Beals frames her mixedness first as a liminal space and eventually fashions a biracial identity. Berry and Pitanga assert the value of Black women and Pitanga in particular uses her celebrity persona to advocate for the well-being of the Black majority in Brazil. Yet, ultimately, the actors are contained and reincorporated into the national body politic in which Blackness has been excised at the same time that colonial legacies and structural inequalities have been forgotten.

Celebrities, as sites of meaning, shape and reflect broader political discourses. The focus on these celebrities' racial identities parallels the rise and decline of affirmative action, changes to the U.S. census, and shifts in national racial narratives. Beals's star text anticipates the 1990s debates over racial classification while Berry's celebrity arises within this context. In the 1990s, multiracial organizations participated in a reshaping of racial identity. The Association of Multiethnic Americans (AMEA), primarily composed of minorities, proposed a new "multiracial" group as a way to join the ranks of protected racial groups in order to make an argument for equal rights. In contrast, Project RACE, a multiracial advocacy group that existed primarily under the auspices of white mothers, saw the census as a way to promote individual identity.[6] Civil rights leaders such as Jesse Jackson termed the multiracial movement a "diversion, designed to undermine affirmative action," while others feared that the multiracial category threatened the enforcement of antidiscrimination laws and the zoning of legislative districts.[7] Jackson further proposed that the movement was a "plot to create a 'colored' buffer race in America."[8] Asserting the multiracial category as a form of passing or opportunism, many Black leaders, including the former executive director of the United Negro College Fund, Arthur A. Fletcher, testified against the category in front of a House subcommittee. Other Black leaders, among them Ralph Abernathy III, John Conyers, and Carol Mosely Braun, disagreed with this position at multiple hearings and through their public support of shifting racial classification, indicating that Blacks could claim Blackness while maintaining a multiracial identity.[9]

Meanwhile, conservatives used the multiracial movement's seeking of the multiracial category as a way to promote nationalism and obscure racial inequalities. Aligned with Project RACE, Newt Gingrich, Speaker of the U.S. House of Representatives, supported the bill for a multiracial category. His testimony at the 1997 hearings included this statement:

> Millions of Americans like Tiger Woods . . . have moved beyond the Census Bureau's divisive and inaccurate labels. We live in a Technicolor world where the government continues to view us as only Black and white. Ideally, I believe we should have one box on federal forms that simply reads "American." . . . We should . . . stop forcing Americans into inaccurate categories aimed at building divisive subgroups and allow them the option of selecting the category "multiracial," which I believe will be an important first step toward transcending racial division and reflecting the melting pot which is America.[10]

Newt Gingrich's testimony previewed a postracial social order that would render racial identity itself obsolete. Like other conservatives in the 1990s and

2000s, Gingrich strategically utilized multiracial figures to employ a color-blind rhetoric to justify dismantling civil rights programs. The deployment of multiraciality blurred racial distinctions and posited racial classification as a state intrusion on individual rights. Paralleling 1930s Brazilian nation-building projects that emphasized Brazilian identity over racial identity, U.S. conservatives advocated using "American" as the only identity signifier. Like Brazilian national rhetoric, the basis of this U.S. racial harmony rested on mixing and the denial of racial inequalities and ultimately, the negation of Blackness.

Eventually, the U.S. Office of Management and Budget (OMB) reached a compromise: a multiple check box option on the census, dubbed the "mark one or more option" (MOOM). This system of reallocation protected race-based legislation while allowing for multiple racial identifications.[11] The 2000 U.S. census acknowledged racial mixing for the first time by permitting respondents to claim multiple races. For Black people in particular, this provided a significant shift from the historical legal invocation of the one-drop rule of hypodescent.

By the 2010s, conservatives once again utilized the multiracial population as a strategy for dismissing racial structures despite racial inequalities. In the 2013 oral arguments for *Fisher v. Texas*, Chief Justice John Roberts repeatedly questioned why a one-quarter or one-eighth Hispanic would qualify under affirmative action, while Justice Antonin Scalia followed by interrogating whether universities determine diversity by who looks Asian, Black, or Hispanic or by proportions of their ancestry.[12] By 2016, in the dissent from *Fisher v. Texas*, Justice Samuel Alito criticized the university's failure both to define racial groups and to explicate what it means to be African American. Citing statistics regarding increasing interracial marriage rates among Asian Americans and Latinos, Justice Alito determined that, due to the "more integrated country that we are rapidly becoming" and the growth of the multiracial population, the university's classification system is largely invalidated and is an "invitation for applicants to game the system."[13] While reducing racial ancestry in fractions derived from grandparents and great-grandparents, Justice Alito utilized the multiracial population in his argument against affirmative action. Thus, like the 1990s distorting of the multiracial movement for the dismantling of racial policies and programs, the continued use of the multiracial population seeks to invalidate pursuits of racial diversity. Furthermore, this conservative use establishes that multiracial experiences are irrelevant and inauthentic.

During the same years that the United States moved toward less race-conscious policies while multiracial collectives, identities, and politics reemerged on the national scene, Brazil began to shift toward explicitly race-conscious public policies that challenged the myths of mestiçagem and racial democracy. Camila

Pitanga's celebrity emerged in the midst of racial reforms, and her rise to stardom is part of the larger social and cultural consequences of these shifts. In the 1980s and 1990s, the end of the Brazilian dictatorship and military rule catalyzed activity in Afro-Brazilian movement and transnational Black alliances. With the Brazilian government's legacy of positioning itself as a model of harmonious race relations and its global reputation at stake, the 2001 Durban World Conference Against Racism offered an opportunity for a vocal delegation of Afro-Brazilian activists to disprove the myth of racial democracy and demand implementation of race-conscious policies. Brazilian media coverage of the conference spurred intense dialogue about race. In effect, Durban was the state's chance to satisfy domestic and international concerns by demonstrating its commitment to confronting the problem of racism on the home front and asserting itself as a leader in global efforts to combat racism. Following Durban, official policy measures, most notably affirmative action, began implementation.[14]

Like the debates over racial categories on the 2000 U.S. census, racial designations open up parameters of racial identities and the institutionalization of race. In 2001, the Rio de Janeiro state legislature became the first state to establish racial quota admissions at public universities with the Universidade do Estado do Rio de Janeiro (UERJ) and the Universidade Estadual do Norte Fluminense (UENF) ensuring that 40 percent of the students they admitted were negro or pardo.[15] Many other states followed suit. A plethora of court challenges to the quota system followed, with white applicants suing for discrimination. Recognizing that the Supremo Tribunal Federal (Federal Supreme Court of Brazil) would likely invalidate the quotas, by 2003 the state legislature revised the conditions such that pardos were eliminated, and only 20 percent of admissions went to self-declared negros. By subsuming pardo under negro, this addressed the concerns of some who favored affirmative action but felt concerned about who might benefit, because they believed that white students were less likely to apply as negro than pardo.[16] The elevation of self-declaration as the determinant in a legal context—requiring individuals to legitimate their own racial identification—represented the embrace of a policy that broke with the essentialism of race based on color or biology.

In 2004, the Universidade de Brasília (UnB) created a very different construction of racial formation, classification, and identity to qualify applicants for quota-based admission. It established a committee consisting of an anthropologist and a sociologist affiliated with the school, a student representative, and three Black movement activists.[17] The committee had the mandate to accept or reject each applicant's claim to negro status based on its review of applicant photographs of self-declared negros.[18]

While systems that require outside review of individuals' claims to a protected category engage with the Black movement's concerns about the gaming of a system based on self-identification alone, they also have the capacity to disadvantage racially ambiguous individuals. In a highly publicized case from 2007, Brazilian media reported that two identical twin brothers, sons of a Black father and a white mother, both applied for admission at UnB under the racial quota system, but the committee initially identified one as negro and the other as white.[19] While the twin deemed white won a reversal through appeal, the unreliability and inconsistency of a racial classification system based on third-party perceptions and phenotype was clear.[20] Although this quota evaluation system is now defunct, these cases highlight the media utilization of racially ambiguous bodies to emphasize color-blind discourses that undermine affirmative action. Like controversies over the 2000 U.S. census, the affirmative action policies in Brazil revealed the slipperiness of racial terminology and racial identity in a multiracial society.

The quota systems ignited public debate in newspaper, magazines, and books in the 2000s and challenged Brazil's self-concept as a country of unity and tolerance. Supporters of quotas and other affirmative action measures described them as a means to advance higher education and upward mobility for Afro-Brazilians as a historically disadvantaged group, while their opponents regarded affirmative action as a U.S. import that would also bring in U.S. racial formations and racism. Using the discourse of mestiçagem, opponents further argued that Brazil's racial fluidity rendered race-based policies obsolete and that altering this racial flexibility based on mestiçagem would fundamentally alter Brazilian national identity for the worse. Public discourse largely focused on racial quotas for those with African ancestry. In manifestos such as *Carta Pública ao Congresso Nacional: Todos têm direitos iguais na República Democrática* (Public letter to National Congress: all have equal rights in a democratic republic) and *Centro e treze cidadãos anti-racistas contra as leis raciais* (113 Antiracist Citizens against the Racial Laws), academic critics took to the media, academic journals, and eventually were at the forefront of a Supreme Court challenge to affirmative action. In claiming that the implementation of affirmative action in Brazil would constitute racism, the legal brief referenced Jim Crow segregation in the United States and suggested that U.S. legacies of institutionalized racism differed from the exceptionalism of Brazil's absence of legal segregation. The hostile media reaction to racial quotas and the greater resistance to quotas for Blacks than for other groups underscored the class-centered framing of inequalities in Brazil and a continuing discomfort with recognizing race, specifically Blackness, as a significant barrier to social equity.[21]

In 2012, the Federal Supreme Court declared the Universidade de Brasília's affirmative action policy constitutionally valid.[22] Affirmative action was then institutionalized across all public federal universities. All federal public universities were to reserve admission spots for public high school graduates, low-income students, Afro-descendants, and Indigenous students proportional to their relative populations within each state. These cases of supposed racial fraud are ongoing in Brazil and demonstrate a potential institutionalization of race that determines who is Black and who is not.[23] Like the 2016 dissent of *Fisher v. Texas* in the United States, the charge of racial authenticity supports racial essentialism and thereby empowers opponents of affirmative action to employ multiraciality as proof of the obsolescence of race-based policies and to mark such policies as illegitimate. At the same time, the ambiguous body that passes for Black questions the entire racial system of branqueamento and linked ideas of mestiçagem and racial democracy. Pitanga's celebrity is entangled in debates regarding the definition of Blackness and Brazilian identity.

Jennifer Beals from the 1980s to the 2000s: Shadows of Passing Intertwined with the New Biracial

The media framing of Jennifer Beals has consistently focused on the tensions inherent in her racial ambiguity, amid shifts in Beals's articulation of her identity from the 1980s to the 2000s. Passing, as racial performance, as strategy, and as misidentification, is a major motif in Beals's star text. From media framing to the roles that she plays, passing reveals shifting power dynamics and valuations of whiteness, Blackness, and mixed race. Ultimately, Beals has declined to identify as solely Black or white. Her reluctance to utilize her celebrity and assert a Black identity has led to some media framing of her identity as a rejection of Blackness.

Beals's phenotypical features have allowed her to play racially ambiguous characters and a variety of different ethnicities, including roles audiences might read as white. In interviews, she has described herself as the daughter of an African American father and a white mother, and has called herself biracial instead of Black. Before the 1983 release of *Flashdance*, Paramount Pictures expressed concerns about Beals's racial background and whether she would appeal to audiences. In her study of the production of *Flashdance*, Rachel Abramowitz reports that men found Beals physically attractive and women found her more appealing than "suburban-looking" actresses the studio also tested for the role.[24]

In other roles, Beals has explicitly played a mulatta archetype. For example, in the television movie *A House Divided* (2000), she plays the daughter of a plantation owner who believed her mother white; in the course of the movie she discovers her mother was enslaved. In the cable television miniseries, *The Feast of All Saints* (2001), Beals plays a quadroon brothel proprietress who arranges quadroon balls. In the 1995 film noir, *Devil in a Blue Dress*, her character's penchant for soul food and jazz clubs undermines her ability to pass for white.[25] The fact that Beals has often acted in stories set before the civil rights movement suggests film and television in the 1980s and early 1990s largely preferred to contain mixed Blackness in the past. The historical memory of passing lingered on in these cultural productions. Furthermore, Beals's performances of passing destabilizes the visuality of race while also serving to racially authenticate herself into mixed Blackness.

Through subtle references to notions of Black mixedness, Beals's characters exemplify the idea of the mixed body relying on forms of sensation other than the visual. While other white actresses also tested for Alex Owens in *Flashdance*, the character was meant to have an apparently innate ability to pick up break dancing—including improvisational skills. This may be one way that perceptions of Beals's racial origins played a role in her casting. The representation of Owens's body as sexually available through her dancing in erotic nightclubs and the camera's intense gaze on her body invoke mulatta tropes of corporeality and sensuality.[26] Beals's character also relies on her white boss-turned-lover to achieve success. After watching her perform in a strip club, her boss becomes overcome with lust, which leads him to help land her an audition at a dance conservatory. This storyline plays into narratives and histories of mulatta concubinage and of socioeconomic ascendancy hearkening back to the New Orleans quadroon balls. In *The L Word* (2004–9), Beals exerted some control over the part of Bette, who was scripted as biracial at her request. Nonetheless, the character enacts mulatta tropes—she cannot control her sexual impulses or remain faithful to her partner. Mulatta narratives creep into the text and hence use Beals's mixedness as part of the text itself.

Before the burgeoning multiracial movement and the marketing of multiraciality as "cool," which coincided with the broadcast of *The L Word* in the early 2000s, media framing of Jennifer Beals often slid from a focus on her mixed heritage to surprise at her African American heritage, or else derision for her lack of open affiliation with Blackness. Both the mainstream press and the Black press have noted her Black heritage, and she has openly acknowledged her racial heritage in interviews. She won an NAACP Image Award for *Flashdance* and was nominated for her roles in *Devil in a Blue Dress* and *The L Word*. Nonetheless, the idea of passing has haunted her image. For example, a 1995 *Vibe* magazine article was titled "Regarding Jennifer: Mystery and Mistaken Identity Follow Beals Everywhere. The Star of the Upcoming Thriller *Devil in a Blue Dress* Sets the Record Straight."[27] The title and the article itself enhanced an aura of mystery around Beals that is directly tied to her biracial identity. Even though many mainstream media sources such as the *Los Angeles Times*, *US Weekly*, and *People* magazine specifically noted her mixed racial heritage and the June 6, 1983, edition of *Jet* magazine featured her on the cover, Beals continued to be connected to the specter of passing and subject to suspicion about her racial allegiances.[28]

The mainstream press focus on Beals's ambiguity allowed for a containment of her Black element, along with their threat to white hegemony, while also activating discourses of exotic sexual desirability attributed to non-white women. Following *Flashdance*, publications such as *People*, the *Chicago Tribune*, and the *Los Angeles Times* focused on Beals's complexion, always emphasizing her "olive" or "caramel" skin when discussing her mixed racial heritage.[29] By fetishizing her skin color, they marked Beals as a familiar and accessible yet exotic beauty. Beals has at times played into this fetishization. For example, in a feature in the *Los Angeles Times*, Beals explained that for a long time she felt like a "mongrel" but eventually found an alternative description: "Someone told me that there's a breed called the Black Irish that was born when the Moors invaded Southern Ireland a long time ago. It's a lot more exotic than saying I'm a mutt."[30] Beals's mother is Irish American, but her father is likely descended from enslaved African Americans. When Beals focused on her Irish heritage by identifying as Black Irish, she relied on ambiguous whiteness rather than an ambiguous Blackness, thus removing herself from a history of Black slavery, all while implying that despite its prevalence, being mixed race is actually unusual in the United States.

In the same feature, the *Los Angeles Times* described Beals's college admissions essay, which told a fairy tale about a heroine living among the princes and princesses of Chicago's Gold Coast, only to discover that she doesn't really belong. The article contrasted Beals-as-outsider with the white upper-class Chicagoans who attended her elite private school. Implying that her Black heritage and upbringing could have hampered her rise to success, journalists have often presented her biracial heritage and childhood on Chicago's South Side as part of her struggle.[31] Similar to later media discourse that would emphasize the absent Black father of another notable biracial figure, Barack Obama, the mainstream media also downplayed Beals's Black heritage by continuously pointing out that her father died when she was a child.[32] Mainstream media outlets have emphasized the centrality of her white mother in her upbringing, her attendance at predominantly white schools, and her family's move from the Black South Side to a whiter neighborhood in a way that implies she escaped the socioeconomic barriers and stigmas associated with Blackness. Yet these same news sources credited her early working-class experiences with enabling her to play a working-class welder and aspiring dancer in *Flashdance*.[33]

Far from presenting Beals as tragic, the mainstream media accentuated tropes of exceptionality, talent, and attractiveness—all qualities assumed to be a consequence of her racial mixture. A 1985 *Chicago Tribune* film review noted that "a portion of Beals's confidence must have come out of her personal upbringing and background. She is the product of a racially mixed marriage. Beals has also emphasized her individual exceptionality: "I've always felt sort of special and on my own in some way. . . . Sting told me [regarding her mixed parentage] that I was probably farther along on the evolutionary scale. I don't know if that's true, but I do know that I don't feel like I'm a member of just one group or another. I feel very much like an individual."[34] Rather than the evolutionary anthropology of the nineteenth century that emphasized racial mixing as pathological and degenerative, Sting's reference to Beals reinforced race as biology but situated Beals as the evolutionary terminus, and thus the epitome, of progressive development. The cultural logics of individual autonomy and choice operate in tension with Sting's suggestion of biologically given potential. Beals's star persona and her 1980s focus on individual rather than group belonging was a premonition of the 1990s and early 2000s multiracial movement's discourses of social recognition and rights by reason of individual autonomy.[35]

In the same year that the mainstream press struggled to reckon with Beals's ambiguity, the Black press defended Beals for playing multiple ethnicities or racially ambiguous characters. In a 1985 letter to the *Los Angeles Sentinel*, a reader asked why romantic plots always place Beals with white actors. In response, the writer for the *Sentinel*'s "Celebrity Lookout" column wrote that "Jennifer Beals is a great actress and she is an American. Isn't it great that an actress in America can play any part she is lucky to win and qualify for? You are as bad as many white Americans who deny opportunities to Black people, not because of their talent but because of the color of their skin. You are a bigot."[36] By highlighting Beals's national identity, the magazine suggested her success exemplified a racial progress and equality that was uniquely American. By naming the reader a bigot for noticing and naming race, the writer also supports a color-blind exceptionalism. Another *Jet* magazine article made similar assertions when it praised her inclusion in *The Bride*. The article stated that the director called Beals "ideal" for the part, citing her Black father and Irish mother as making her "the perfect Eva, a character who embraces the ideals of freedom, independence, and intelligence."[37] A mixed racial heritage became an implicit affirmation of inclusion.

The limited representations of women of African descent in mainstream media places a burden of representation on actresses in a terrain in which white celebrities can be seen as individuals rather than representatives of nondominant groups.[38] Celebrities of African descent are thus expected to vocally and visibly represent Blackness. Instead of a biracial subject, Beals was largely converted into an object of debate over Black politics in the 1980s and 1990s. By the 1990s, the Black press castigated Beals, alleging she had denied her Blackness offscreen. Articles in *Ebony* and *Jet* such as "Who's Black and Who's Not: New Ethnicity Raises Provocative Questions About Racial Identity" and "Are the Children of Mixed Marriage Black or White?" listed her among celebrities who were unsure of their racial identities and who failed to acknowledge their Blackness.

The fact that audiences sometimes read her as white heightened the stakes of asserting a Black identity. *Ebony* received numerous letters objecting to the use of skin color as a barometer for racial identification. For example, Ramona E. Douglass, vice president of the Biracial Family Network of Chicago, specifically noted that identification as biracial does not mean being ashamed of one's African American heritage, but rather is an acknowledgment of one's full heritage.[39] Yet elsewhere, the Black press accused Beals of depriving the Black community of a Black celebrity, a Black success story, and a Black role model. This points to the social, economic, and political stakes involved in assigning race categories.

With their criticism of Beals, Black magazines hint at the gender dynamics involved in the treatment of mixed-race women, especially women whose physical features allow them to potentially be read as white. Figures like Mariah Carey have been subjected to similar criticism.[40] *Ebony*'s article contrasted women like Beals with actors such as Jasmine Guy, who are mixed race but identify as Black. Thus, women of mixed-race African descent already on the borders of Blackness are even more tightly bound to racial communities as both the reproducers and caretakers of these communities. Mixed-race women are deemed biologically bound to race within the continuing cultural legacies of the one-drop rule. Given the centrality of heteropatriarchy, women of African descent are often charged with Black uplift. Thus, without a visible engagement, such women are presented as betrayers to Black communities in ways that are reminiscent of the Brazilian "mulatto escape hatch." Carrying the physical marker of racial and sexual transgressions, women representing these racial boundaries must be reclaimed back into Blackness. Within this contextual memory of mulatta narratives, refusing to be claimed is also refusing to serve as a feminine, sexualized object of desire.

The burden of proof lies with Beals as she remains outside of U.S. recognizable and intelligible visible markers of Blackness. To be nonnormative in the United States is to be nonwhite, which requires that one either continually out oneself or not pass. Certainly, Beals and other multiracial celebrities would have been considered Black in previous generations according to the one-drop rule. These controversies also demonstrate struggles over what it means to be Black, how Blackness should be measured, and what makes one authentically Black. In the 1980s and 1990s, the mainstream press framed issues of racial authenticity and racial fraud with individuals who sought to be recognized as African American for public gain and often in the context of affirmative action cases.[41] Thus, Beals's star persona is immersed within these debates about racial authenticity and identification alongside the destabilization of racial constructs and the relevance of race-based policies.

In the 1980s and early 1990s, the trope of the tragic mulatta and the disavowal of the passing mulatta denied the possibility of mixed-race subjectivity, despite the dismantling of legal segregation. In Caroline Streeter's words, mixed-race individuals of the post–civil rights generation have "not experienced the historical imperative to identify as Black."[42] Without this historical imperative, Beals's position as a racially liminal figure became even more significant as a means to secure an investment in Black community, politics, and identity. Beals's case indicates that ancestry alone cannot assign Blackness. Rather, appearance and racial identification also come into play.

Beals drew criticism from Black-targeted magazines when she commented that "I thought I would never get in [to Yale]. I thought they only took geniuses. But, I was lucky because I'm a minority. I'm not Black and I'm not White, so I could mark 'other' on my application, and I guess it's hard for them to fill that quota."[43] In the context of conservative assaults on affirmative action, Beals's statement provokes concerns about opportunistic identity claims. The designation of affirmative action as "lucky" marks Beals a race traitor as surely as her statement that she's "not Black." At issue here is the accusation that Beals and others who do not identify as Black undermine Black solidarity. The issues of *Jet* and *Ebony* that called Beals out for these statements anticipated the controversy that would arise in the 1990s over the multiracial category on the 2000 census. Similar to the concerns of Black leaders and the Black press to U.S. census changes, the criticism of Beals alludes to allegations of passing or racial opportunism.

By the 2000s, many multiracial celebrities and public figures self-identified as biracial and were depicted as biracial or multiracial in mainstream popular media. The use of the language of mixed race, biracial, and multiracial grew within public discourse. Beals's public representations reflected these changes. Many articles about her appearance on *The L Word* explicitly describe Beals as "biracial." However, as Catherine Squires notes, "most mainstream media coverage of multiracial identity reinforces what some scholars have identified as a 'conservative consensus' on race in the United States . . . that rejects the notion that race has any meaningful influence over life outcomes or group inequalities."[44] Beals's biracial persona was largely disconnected from issues of racial equality, but rather focused on the increasing visibility of biraciality.

Beals herself has pointed out that there are very few acting roles for mixed-race characters.[45] By asking writers to script the character she plays as biracial—as she did for the 2011 television series *The Chicago Code* and for *The L Word*—Beals acknowledges the importance of providing multiracial images to viewers that presents a more inclusive vision of the United States and an onscreen expansion of Black experiences. Beals may also see it as advantageous for her career to present herself as multiracial, given the increased recognition of such identities in the United States. Indeed, Beals has helped change the media landscape with an increase in biracial characters and interracial families. For example, ABC Family's *The Fosters* (2013) features a lesbian couple with a mixed-Black mother and a white mother who have biological, adoptive, and foster children. A 2013 Cheerios ad depicts an interracial family, with a Black father, white mother, and mixed-Black daughter. The 2018 Hollywood film adaptation of *A Wrinkle in Time* reimagines the protagonist as a mixed-Black girl with a Black mother and a white father. Within a consumerist society, multiraciality is now a brand but also offers the opportunity to show multifaceted mixed characters and families.

However, Beals emphasized that being biracial made her an outsider in relation to her part in the *L Word*. In a 2011 interview with Tavis Smiley, she reflected: "Well, with 'The L Word,' when I first met with Ilene Chaiken about the role, I asked her to consider making the character biracial because I thought it would be an interesting way to talk about race and quite frankly, when I was a child, there was nobody on television who looked like me. I had Spock. That was kind of it. I was hoping to give somebody some other kind of representation, maybe with different ears."[46] By suggesting she "looked" more like Spock from the television series *Star Trek*—because his character is mixed alien and human—than like Lieutenant Uhura, Beals implied that even Black communities excluded her.

While Beals highlighted biracial identity and mixed-race experiences, this focus on difference also functioned to "other" biracial people in relationship to both Blacks and whites through an emphasis on being special and unique. However, an increase in mixed-race images, voices, and character representations in popular culture can weaken this focus on exclusion and exceptionality. In a 2004 speech, Beals stated:

> I got a little older, and I was more aware of television and magazines, I searched for images of girls that looked like me. As a biracial girl growing up in Chicago there wasn't a lot there, positive or otherwise. . . . Somehow my story just wasn't there. I was too young to start reading Faulkner; I hadn't seen *Imitation of Life* and so I wasn't aware that I was supposed to be the insane, oversexed tragic Mulatto gal. Certainly my otherness was sometimes so palpable it was a wonder that anyone could see me. I was that invisible. And certainly, when society fails to write your story there is an unspoken message that the story is not worth telling.[47]

These statements suggest Beals wanted to see positive images of multiraciality onscreen; she expressed a desire for multiracial individuals and communities to be recognized.

Regarding her role on *The L Word*, Beals states that she "wanted to explore what it means to be biracial in a larger cultural context and what it means within the gay community."[48] Beals's public claim that she is not solely Black, but biracial, demonstrated a reconfiguration of positions regarding racial identity in a post–civil rights context. The way she shaped the role of Bette as explicitly biracial and the way she used biraciality as a key part of the narrative demonstrate an attempt to mark a racialized positionality to critique white privilege and the complicity of racial invisibility. Beals's assertion of multiraciality evoked the process of disidentification. Beals did not identify as Black or white in a Black-white binary system, but she also did not identify as raceless in the denial of race. Rather, Beals attempted to change the way we talk about race. Yet, by merely reconfiguring racial identifications and biraciality instead of attacking racism itself, she vocalized how her body often stands in tension with racial taxonomies rather than a dismantling of racial hierarchies. Beals's biracial celebrity persona and her attempt to increase the number of biracial characters opened an opportunity to reshape cultural imaginaries of the nation. With a greater number of mixed-race public voices and characters onscreen, media can engage a wider spectrum of experiences and questions about identity. In such a situation it is imperative not just to have mixed-race role models, but to understand how mixed-race voices and cultural representations of mixed-race can work toward abolishing oppression.

In the 1980s and 1990s, Beals's public persona demonstrated that biraciality can be co-opted toward a raceless politics in which race has meaning but no social, economic, or political weight. However, by the 2000s, Beals's biraciality was grounded not in a default near-white or disassociation from Blackness, but as a way to interrogate the complexities of racial identity. While Beals and many multiracial advocacy organizations attempt to use biracial identities as a means of recognition, such identities must also actively challenge anti-Black racism in order to transform apolitical multiculturalism into an antiracist multiculturalism. In the 2000s, while Beals has championed LGBT, women's, and environmental activism, she has not actively utilized her celebrity in service of racial struggle. Yet, Beals's ability to make her own choices to prioritize certain causes requires an understanding of celebrities as complex social actors that feel empowered to take on certain activist stances at particular moments.

Rather than assume issues of racial authenticity based on visual appearance or the explicit claiming of racial identities, Beals's case demonstrates how attachments to racial categories are placed on racially ambiguous individuals. Indeed, her role in *The Last Tycoon* (2017) demonstrates how historical racial categories and divisions reflect on contemporary understandings of race. Playing Margo, a character inspired by the 1930s actor Merle Oberon, who passed for white and hid her Asian background, Beals adapts the multiple meanings of passing as a mediation of racial ambiguity and racial identification. As Margo passes for white with her Black mother as her maid, Beals's ambiguous racial features and performativity challenge scopic regimes of racialization. Yet, this specter of passing and the mystery around Beals harkens back to not just actresses such as Merle Oberon, but also in the very aura of the mixed-race female figure.

Beals's casting and the way in which she talks about her roles points to the instability of narratives and performances of race. When comparing the character of Margo to Merle Oberon, Beals references Margo as "having the reins" and "unlike 'Imitation of Life' where the girl is embarrassed about her mother. It's very different. I wanted to take this notion of shame away and have a plan."[49] Referring to *Imitation of Life*, Beals correlates the image of the desirable but tragic mixed-race woman against the understanding of Margot as possessing strategic agency. Rather than passing as a betrayal of ancestry, history, family, and identity, passing here as articulated by Beals becomes way to transgress social order and an illustration of the saliency of race instead of a raceless vision. In a *Vanity Fair* interview, the article states that, "for her part, Beals—who's always been open about being biracial—says she doesn't think anyone would go to the lengths Margo and Oberon did to hide their heritage these days, when information is so accessible."[50]

With the rise of social media and the Internet, passing has become more difficult. In the early 2000s, websites such as the now defunct mixedfolks.com "outed" celebrities of mixed descent.[51] Yet, the article later recounts how Beals was horrified to learn from Carl Franklin, the director of *Devil in a Blue Dress* (1995), that he had met with several actresses who admitted to passing.[52] The article again reinforces that Beals has never passed and reasserts a biracial identity. Historically, passing as a social practice assumes the strategic denial of one's racial identity for social mobility and escape from racial violence. Beals's racial identity has often been misread, and her inadvertent passing should not be collapsed with a conscious strategic passing. The allegation of passing relies on the notion of an authentic biologically rooted racial self and racial fraud. Passing then relies on surveillance, regulating, and containing racialized bodies. Beals's star text, from the press framing of her racial identity to her performance roles as mixed women passing for white, marks tensions between misrecognition of race, racial authenticity, and the notion of racial imposter in the post–civil rights era. The focus on racial masquerade absolves structural white privilege while further surveilling Black bodies. For Beals's star text, the specter of passing divulges the ambiguity of race and refutes notions of racially legible authenticity. In contrast to the strategies of racial ambiguity employed in the 1980s and 1990s evidenced in Beals's star text, by 2017, biraciality has become a racialized self-expression. In the post-Obama, Trump era, Beals and her biraciality no longer portend a postracial future.

Halle Berry: The Tragic Mulatta between White Progress and One Drop of Blackness

When Halle Berry won the Oscar for Best Actress in 2002, mass media trumpeted the historic moment: she was the first Black actress to win that particular award. Her speech demonstrated that she was highly aware of her positioning as a Black figure rather than as a mixed-race figure. She articulated her place among other pathbreaking Black actresses: "The moment is so much bigger than me. This moment is for Dorothy Dandridge, Lena Horne, Diahann Carroll. It's for the women that stand beside me—Jada Pinkett, Angela Bassett—and it's for every nameless, faceless woman of color that now has a chance because this door tonight has been opened."[53]

Berry places herself in a pantheon of talented Black actors who faced limited opportunities for recognition and advancement due to racial barriers. By naming Pinkett and Bassett, she aligned herself with contemporary Black actresses who are the heirs of Dandridge, Horne, and Carroll. She asserted a continued struggle against racial oppression and strategically aligned herself with Black communities while paying homage to earlier actresses. Many celebrities have used their speeches to advocate for political and social causes, and Berry followed that long tradition. The Black press took a similar approach, celebrating Berry as a trailblazer. For example, the cover of the November 2005 issue of *Ebony* showed her with two other Black actors who had recently won Oscars, with the heading, "Denzel, Halle, and Jamie: Celebrate 60 Historic Years of Civil Rights, Movies, Sports, Politics, Music, Religion, TV, Fashion, Black History, the Arts, and More!" The magazine presented the trio as historic and placed Berry among a pantheon of Black U.S. heroes.

Berry's speech revealed much about her role as a light-skinned, mixed-Black actress. She mentioned neither Whoopi Goldberg nor Hattie McDaniel, both of whom won Oscars for Best Supporting Actress, but she used the term "women of color." Her omission of the first two Black women to win Oscars may reflect Berry's identification with actresses such as Pinkett, Bassett, Horne, and Dandridge, women who have been recognized as beautiful, while Goldberg and McDaniel, as a result of phenotype and body size, do not conform to dominant beauty norms. Dandridge and Horne, like Berry, were promoted as exotic yet accessible to white audiences due to their light skin color and other phenotypical features. Yet even as she took her place among these women, and solely referenced actresses of African descent, she also used the term "women of color," inviting non-Black women to identify with her victory, and highlighting a broader invisibility of women of color in Hollywood.

During Berry's speech, the camera repeatedly cut to Berry's white mother, Judith Ann Hawkins, who was seated in the audience next to Berry's Black husband, Eric Benét. The juxtaposition in this image illuminates constructions of Blackness and mixedness and points to the construction of mixed-race as inclusive within a Black identity. Therefore, Berry's choice to identify as Black does not necessarily correlate with a disidentification with her white mother. While many multiracial activists have argued that choosing a monoracial category such as Black makes multiracial children choose one parent or disidentify with the other parent, Berry's appearance at the Oscars with her mother demonstrates her ability to inhabit a space of Black mixedness. Berry's positioning of herself among other Black actresses points to an intersectional and strategic approach to racial identity that reinforces the intertwining of racialized interpellation, national historical context, and self-identity. Her strategic alignment with Black actresses and the understanding of the historical significance of her Oscar awards show how the moment reinforced the political understanding of Berry as Black.

Berry's reference to Dorothy Dandridge in her speech also suggests that she saw her Oscar win as a fulfillment of Dandridge's legacy. Berry played Dandridge in the 1999 HBO film, *Introducing Dorothy Dandridge*; as Caroline Streeter has argued, the public discourse around Berry and the marketing of Berry and the film positioned the actor as Dandridge's heir.[54] Like Berry, Dandridge's stardom is understood in relation to discourses on racial mixing. The intertwinement of the two figures illustrates how the media framing of Berry both resists and slots into the tragic mulatta trope.

Dandridge's star power and her marginalization from mainstream Hollywood stem from the imbrications of gender, sexuality, race, and class in a postwar context. Dandridge became a star with recognized crossover appeal in *Carmen Jones*, an all-Black musical. She plays an overtly sexual, fallen woman who dies for her sins. Donald Bogle argues that Dandridge embodied the tragic mulatta in the 1950s, and her role as Carmen paralleled her own death from a drug overdose at age forty-two and the violence of her racialized hypersexuality in Hollywood.[55] The collapsing of Dandridge with her cinematic role as Carmen blurs the lines between character and celebrity similarly to the eliding of tensions between the haunting of racialized sexual exploitation and desires for racial mixing without the weight of the past. Following *Carmen Jones*, in films such as *Island in the Sun* (1957), and *Tamango* (1957), Dandridge mostly played mulatta seductress roles. Through marketing and narrative strategies, Hollywood constructed Dandridge as a beauty, yet dangerously erotic and exotic. Describing this image in opposition to the sexualization of Elizabeth Taylor, Marilyn Monroe, and Ava Gardner, Dandridge is quoted as stating, "My sex symbolism was as a wanton, a prostitute, not as a woman seeking love and a husband, like other women."[56] Although in 1955 Dandridge became the first African American woman that the Academy of Motion Picture Arts and Sciences nominated for Best Actress, she never achieved the rich and varied career that a white starlet could.

The fascination with light-skinned women as mulatta figures has continued in Berry's star text. The stardoms of both Dandridge and Berry stem from their mulatta beauty, which is equated with sophistication and class yet also with loose sexuality.[57] Berry, the 1986 Miss Ohio and a spokeswoman for Revlon Cosmetics beginning in the 1990s, is also famed for her beauty. As Sika Dagbovie-Mullins notes, the fixation on Berry's beauty resembles how early U.S. literature depicted mixed-race women as possessing an exceptional beauty in a way that allured and unsettled readers familiar with social taboos concerning racial mixing.[58] While Berry's mixed-race heritage, light skin, and European features have granted her privileges, celebrity access, and crossover appeal, Berry cannot pass for white. Unlike Beals, Berry does not have the option nor the specter of the mulatta-passing narrative nor can she play characters Hollywood deems "raceless." As Dandridge did, Berry negotiates shifting standards of beauty, femininity, and sexuality within the Hollywood industry.

Like Beals, Berry has also played the passing mulatta figure. In *Queen* (1993), Berry played Alex Haley's paternal grandmother, a daughter of a Black slave and a white enslaver. As cultural critic Lisa Jones points out, the series "drag[s] out mulatto clichés from every B movie and paperback."[59] The casting of Berry, unlike Beals's, provides a resonance that Blackness must still be visually evident. Thus, the actor's perceived heritage authenticates her portrayal. The miniseries reinforces nineteenth- and early twentieth-century notions of mulatta exquisiteness and the hereditary taint of mental instability. The trope of mulatta exceptional beauty and insanity in *Queen* continues to linger in Berry's star persona.

Berry played roles in the 1990s that treated her as unambiguously Black: the young urban Black professional and desirable girlfriend in Black-targeted films such as *Strictly Business* (1991), *Boomerang* (1992), and *B.A.P.S.* (1997); and major Black characters in social problem films such as *Losing Isaiah* (1995) and *Bulworth* (1998). Yet, as Berry's manager, Vincent Cirrincione, recalls, "when Halle was up for 'Strictly Business' in 1991, they didn't want her at first. They said she wasn't Black enough, that she should get a tan."[60] Berry describes the press's interest in her biracial heritage as disproportionate: "I never once announced that I am interracial. I was never the one to bring it up. I've always said, 'I'm Black, I'm African American.' But reporters constantly ask what childhood was like for an interracial person. And believe me, being interracial wasn't as big an issue as these articles might lead you to believe. Sure, there were problems, but there were other things in my childhood that caused me more pain than being interracial."[61]

According to Berry, her own racial identity is often at odds with how the media constructs her persona. Indeed, a 2003 *New York Times* article on multiraciality and the census singled her out, discussing "role models, like Halle Berry and Tiger Woods, who celebrate their multiracial background."[62] Yet, Berry herself has never appeared to embrace a biracial or multiracial identity. A 2001 *Jet* article cited Berry and Woods as "among a growing number of Americans who acknowledge their Black roots and multicultural heritage as well." The issue focused on "the emergence of a multiracial nation" and "the redefinition of Blackness" but did not state that multiraciality and Blackness are incompatible.[63] Indeed, *Jet*, *Ebony*, and *Essence*, as magazines aimed at a Black audience, have been crucial for defining and refining parameters of Blackness and instilling a sense of Black identity and community. By the 2000s, the Black press treated multiracial stars such as Berry as part of the panorama of Blackness and unlike the mid-1980s and 1990s did not present multiracial celebrities as confused, in denial of Blackness, or tragically between races.

Introducing Dorothy Dandridge reinscribed Berry as a mulatta. As Caroline Streeter argues, the imagined relationship between Halle Berry and Dorothy Dandridge carves out a popular narrative trajectory of the mulatta from tragedy to triumph, yet nonetheless both actors function as sexual mediators between white and Black femininities.[64] The marketing for *Introducing Dorothy Dandridge* showed Berry in a glamorous low-cut dress above images of the Hollywood sign and a mansion with the text, "Right Woman, Right Place, Wrong Time." It suggests that Berry, as a Black woman whose career takes place in an age of multiculturalism rather than an age of segregation, is in the right place and the right time.

Two articles in *Ebony* represent Berry as a reembodiment of Dandridge. The first, in August 1997, "Who Should Play the Tragic Star?," quotes Berry: "For me, the paradox that makes Dorothy such a fascinating character is that she was a pioneer who possessed incredible inner strength to achieve ... but ultimately the industry did not know what to do with her. I see many parallels in my life today. It is tough to get good roles, and personal tragedies can often overshadow professional triumphs." The title of the second, "Halle Berry: On How She Found Dorothy Dandridge's Spirit and Healed Her Own," in March 1999, makes the reincarnation almost literal.[65] The association of Dandridge as tragic mulatta with a doomed fate haunts Berry's film image and her public persona. These articles simultaneously reify and deny the idea of Berry as the tragic mulatta.

Dominant mainstream media represented Berry as tragic because of her multiple divorces, experience of domestic abuse, and attempted suicide. Unlike Beals, who was largely positioned as racially exceptional, as an outsider, or as assimilated into whiteness, Berry carried the tragic trope framed by gender and sexual vulnerability. As Dagbovie-Mullins observes, the media needlessly highlighted her racial background when describing her adversities, and thus the media framing recalls early U.S. literature depictions of mixed-race women marked by beauty and misfortune. Such an understanding is typified by articles like the 2001 *New York Times* article, "The Beautiful and Damned," and the 2002 *New York Times* article, "Halle Berry, Bruised and Beautiful, Is on a Mission," and a biography titled *Halle Berry: A Stormy Life*. In a 2010 interview with CNN, Berry talked about witnessing the domestic abuse of her mother and how this experience accounted for her low self-esteem.[66] Furthermore, she has recurrently acknowledged that intimate partner violence made her deaf in her left ear and linked her mother's history of domestic abuse with her own: "I chose partners that mimicked my father."[67] If the 1994 *Redbook* article "Beauty and the Brave" described her then-husband, Major League Baseball player David Justice, as restoring the trust in men destroyed by her father's abandonment and a series of abusive relationships, later articles in magazines such as *People* would describe her as fearful about her safety with Justice.[68] The media also portrayed Berry as a victim when her husband Eric Benét was unfaithful to her.[69] A 1999 *Washington Post* article, "Halle Berry, in Character: For the Actress, Dorothy Dandridge Is a Star Worth Shooting For," cemented the understood connection between Berry's pain and Dandridge's. Drawing parallels between the two stars, the reporter implies that Berry is Dandridge reincarnated. The article compares the two women's difficulties in finding suitable roles, as well as equating Berry's suicidal attempts after her divorce from Justice with Dandridge's death. These images of vulnerability connect Berry to Dandridge and to the tragic mulatta iconography.

The emphasis on Berry's vulnerability recalls nineteenth-century models of the idealized tragic mulatta. Very few articles mention Berry's acting skills; instead they focus on her personal life and tribulations. The 1999 *Washington Post* article concludes by expressing hope that Berry will ultimately find more opportunities than Dandridge did: "everybody is waiting to see whether this actress will reprise her character role as a tragic beauty, or take her turn at star."[70] The media posed that, while tragic misfortunes plague Berry as they did Dandridge, and other tragic mulatta figures, Berry may enjoy a better fate.

Suspended between the status of mulatta heroine and victim, Berry is depicted as a vulnerable exotic vessel of the hopes and failures of neoliberal multiculturalism. A 2002 *New York Times* article reported that "Ms. Berry will talk about the racism she has experienced only if asked. Though, she may have been a victim at times in life, she does not act like one." Thus, both in terms of racism and gender violence, she must demonstrate her subjection, her moral rectitude, and she must demonstrate her powerlessness in the face of abuse, her moral righteousness, and her self-reliance. When contemplating casting Berry in *Monster's Ball*, director, Marc Forster recalled that "I also saw incredible sadness in her eyes from her past. I thought I'd be able to tap into that."[71] The Black press, such as *Ebony*, also framed Berry's life as a saga of obstacles marked by her race and gender: "Halle's life contains enough anguish for any actress to draw on as motivation—her abandonment as a child by her father . . . her confusion over her racial identity . . . years of mentally and physically abusive relationships with men she let use her because she was so desperate to be loved."[72] Berry's media framing as a fragile, sympathetic woman coexisted with her exotification and sexualization.

Much of Berry's sexual desirability relies on a sense of white male entitlement to the bodies of women of color, specifically to the mulatta body. Adrien Brody exemplified this when Berry announced his Best Actor win at the 2003

Academy Awards, taking hold of her and kissing her, to her evident surprise. Brody later explained to a reporter, "if you ever have an excuse to do something like that, that was it."[73] Narratives of mulatta sexuality simultaneously made Berry's consent presumed and framed her as so sexually irresistible that Brody could not be held responsible for his actions. *USA Today* described Brody's assertion of privilege and use of the mulatta body as signaling his own desirability, proclaiming, "with an impromptu kiss, a sex symbol was born." The article romanticizes the inherent violation as a seduction: "If all the underdog nominee from *The Pianist* had done while accepting his best-actor statuette was to put the smackdown on presenter Halle Berry—and a swooningly smooth scoop-and-dip it was, too—many female TV watchers would still be fanning themselves over the impulsive act."[74] The incident demonstrates the interconnection between white male sexuality and mulatta sexuality, figuring Brody's demonstration of power as making him both masculine and desirable and is largely reflective of the media industry and access to women's bodies.

Berry's turbulent relationship with white Canadian model Gabriel Aubry, which produced a daughter, inspired discussions of racial conflict. After Berry and Aubry's breakup, various gossip media sources introduced the racial and gender dynamics of their custody battle with headlines such as "Halle Berry's Baby Daddy Hurled 'N' Word at Her."[75] The controversy over whether Aubry did use a racial slur during the breakup, as Berry alleged, and the countervailing idea that Berry is crazy, feeds into stereotypes of the unstable tragic mulatta. It also negates the vision of a postracial society generated by interracial relationships and mixed-race children.

The racial makeup and identity of Berry and Aubry's daughter, Nahla, has also generated much media discussion. In the March 2011 issue of *Ebony*, Berry stated: "I had to decide for myself and that's what [Nahla's] going to have to decide—how she identifies in the world. And I think, largely that will be based on how the world identifies her. That's how I identify myself. But I feel like she's Black. I'm Black and I'm her mother, and I believe in the one-drop theory."[76] The statement evoked a tension between race as biological and race as a political, cultural, and social identity. As the multiracial movement pushed back against the state imposition of a monoracial identity, the 2000 census, growing awareness of multiracial populations, and the increasing popularity of multiracial celebrities has decreased adherence to the one-drop rule in U.S. society. Berry's comments conjures images of Jim Crow laws and a U.S. history of racial segregation based on the one-drop rule.

While Beals has articulated a historically negated biracial identity, Berry acknowledges racial mixture within Blackness and bluntly rejects the idea of

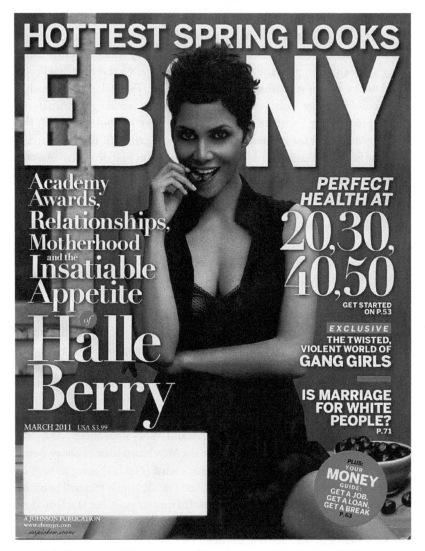

Halle Berry on *Ebony*'s March 2011 cover. Courtesy of Johnson Publishing Company.

a postracial United States. She implies that racial differences still matter and racial identity is a combination of how one self-identifies and how one is defined by others. Furthermore, Berry's choices regarding how to identify herself racially and how to frame her racialized beauty also informs her deliberation on Black politics for herself and her daughter. Berry refutes the optimism of a post *Loving v. Virginia* era and the individualism and free choice attributed to multiracial advocacy such as the "Bill of Rights for Racially Mixed People" that refuses to check one racial designation.

Furthermore, Berry's 2011 statement anticipates the U.S. Supreme Court questioning of mixed-race candidates for university affirmative action programs. Berry's "one-drop theory" statement does not claim that multiracial Blackness is new and distinctive, but rather it encompasses a long history of Blackness in the United States. While Berry's and Justice Alito, Justice Roberts, and Justice Scalia's statements reify race, Berry's position points to an understanding of structural racism and the lived experiences of people of African descent. Meanwhile, the justices' questioning signals race as meaningless unless discretely biologically constructed, and thereby their questioning fails to challenge white privilege.

Berry's invocation of the one-drop rule reflects an awareness rather than a disavowal of race. Berry also notes that she sees Nahla as Black, even though she acknowledges that Nahla may not see herself that way. She refutes racial identity as genetic and ancestral, while saying she follows the one-drop theory. In other interviews, she relates how her white mother prepared her for how the United States would racially view her: "My mother helped me identify myself the way the world would identify me. Bloodlines didn't matter as much as how I would be perceived."[77] Rather than assuming blood is the primary conveyor of race, Berry destabilizes the links between Black and white while affirming a Black identity. While she notes that she sees Nahla as Black due to her maternal status, Berry's white mother could not pass on her racial identity to her. Race and gender operate so that Blackness can be passed down, but whiteness cannot. Nahla was older when Berry told a reporter for the *Huffington Post*:

> I want [Nahla] to embrace all of who she is. Her father is French-Canadian. I have a white mother. I've always identified myself as Black. That's a choice that felt right for me. It wasn't like I decided. I was always Black. Nobody knew I had a white mother unless I said it. So, I hope she will grow and decide for herself how she wants to define herself in the world. I think the world will also tell her how she is going to define herself, by how they will define her. She will have to be ready to accept that, too. But whatever it is, I want her to feel good about who she is, where she comes from, embrace her little curly hair and everything about her.[78]

Celebrity motherhood is a significant facet in the construction of racialized femininities. As a maternal figure and as an icon of beauty, Berry relies on tensions between a racial familiarity coded as white and racial Otherness. The politics of hair regarding Berry's daughter reinforce these divides. Hair texture became a touchstone in a mediated representation of custody negotiations between the actor and Gabriel Aubry. Berry told the court: "I continue to worry about the potential psychological and physical damage to Nahla that can be caused by the use of chemical hair treatments and the psychological message that it conveys to Nahla, and to implore the court to put a stop to Gabriel's attempts to alter our daughter's appearance and most probably cause her to wonder why her natural appearance is not good enough."[79] Berry attempts to respect her daughter's non-European features, linking natural hair appearance with pride and empowerment and chemical altering with a devaluation of Blackness.

As girls and women are most often the target of beauty products designed to alter Black phenotypical traits such as hair-straightening products and skin-bleaching creams, whitening is gendered. Berry alleged that Aubry had chemically altered, lightened, and straightened Nahla's hair in an effort to make her look less African American. Hair can be changed through styling in a way that skin color or nose shape cannot. Thus, Nahla's hair as a symbol of her Blackness is also subject to the continuing legacies of colonialism and whitening.

The media framing of childrearing and hair is clearly about racialized beauty and control over Black female bodies. Headlines such as *Vogue*'s "Team Natural: Why Halle Berry's Lawsuit over Her Daughter's Hair Matters" suggest the stakes. Whereas *Vogue* and the Black target consumer magazine, *Vibe*, positioned Berry as a maternal protector, mainstream gossip news described Berry as irrational, hysterical, and as using race to prolong the custody battle, in articles under headlines such as "Gabriel Aubrey: Halle and Nahla's Hair Can Both Relax."[80]

The judge's decision mandated that neither parent could alter Nahla's hair and that Nahla's hair should be allowed to grow naturally. The conflict highlights racial differences rather than a color-blind rhetoric that negates a tight connection between the everyday personal and the political. Berry challenged straight hair as a normative standard and thereby resisted the dominant Eurocentric ideology of beauty. This court battle participates in a long history of politicizing Black hairstyles and especially those of Black women. Nahla's hair in its natural state is a site of visual physical resistance to whitening, given the denigration of Black hair textures in the Americas.

Through her battle to prevent Aubry from straightening their daughter's hair, Berry resists a collapsing of white identification with Black women's bodies. Berry expresses racial identity formation as a response to racism while also claiming her daughter's right to determine her own identity. Expressing agency through how she chooses to represent herself and the hopes that she has for her daughter's identity, Berry refutes notions of postracial transcendence. Her conflicts with Aubry challenge color blindness as default whiteness.

Berry's success and her claim of space for Black women in beauty industries and in Hollywood has reverberated in Brazil as well. *Raça*, which bills itself as "a revista dos negros brasileiros" (the magazine of Black Brazilians), featured Berry on the cover in 2006. Inside, an interview quotes her: "Every day, I wake up with my brown skin and it does not matter how much money I have, how many films I have done, how many prizes I have. Every day, I have consciousness that I am a Black woman in a country that still has a certain discrimination."[81]

As a diasporic figure, Berry reaffirms Black identity and challenges anti-Blackness through an appeal to awareness rather than color blindness.

Both Berry and Beals are intertwined with tragic mulatta and the passing mulatta tropes even as their own racial self-labeling in the media often repudiate national racial narratives. Examining Brazilian and U.S. celebrities together demonstrates that Blackness and mixedness are unfixed concepts that often work with each other, and, most importantly, how Black and mixed-race identities hold different meanings depending on national, political, social, and cultural contexts. Juxtaposing readings of the celebrity personas of U.S. actors Jennifer Beals and Halle Berry alongside Brazilian actor Camila Pitanga points to the political valence of self-consciously asserting a racial identity that negates national racial norms, yet it also illustrates the fetishization of light-skinned racial ambiguity as a form of sexual allure in the Americas.

Camila Pitanga as Black, not *Mulata*, not Morena

Celebrations of mestiçagem and the idealization of the *mulata* as the object of desire have long circulated in Brazil. In this context, Camila Pitanga's self-identification as negra (Black) refutes the hegemonic Brazilian national identity that privileges mixed identity. During the 2000s, the Brazilian state began making policy choices that sought greater social equality. With affirmative action policies targeting Afro-Brazilians, the diminishment of poverty, and the growth of Black middle classes under Lula da Silva's and Dilma Rousseff's presidencies, the potential of racial inclusion in the public sphere included the opening-up of televisual spaces occupied by Afro-Brazilian celebrities.

Since that era, the growth of the Afro-Brazilian middle class has by no means eliminated racial inequities in Brazil. Black youths comprise 77 percent of all youth homicide victims in Brazil, and only 8 percent of these cases are even tried.[82] While official reporting on racialized police violence is notoriously irregular and inaccurate, Black youths are grossly disproportionately the targets of murder by police. The pervasiveness of racialized police brutality and state-sanctioned violence that have galvanized #BlackLivesMatter in the United States exists in Brazil as well. The persona of Pitanga, like that of Beals and Berry, both reinforces and disrupts the racial politics of the supposedly postracial United States and Brazilian racial democracy.

Pitanga's star text emerged within this context of Black political activism and a questioning of racial democracy. From the start of her career, Pitanga has taken on a Black positionality as a way to self-define herself in the Brazilian landscape that encourages a disidentification with Black identity. In 1996, she appeared alongside her darker-skinned father, the renowned actor Antônio Pitanga, with the headline, "Camila Pitanga: Tenho orgulho de ser negra" (I am proud to be Black), in the second issue of *Raça*, the first nationally circulated magazine directed at Afro-Brazilians.[83] The headline affirms Black identity and the visual image of a light-skinned daughter with her famous dark-skinned father refutes the Brazilian form of whitening, branqueamento. Opting to be understood as negra rather than as morena or as white, Pitanga claims Blackness instead of the dominant default of *morenidade* (brownness) that emphasizes ambiguity and racial mixture while minimizing racial difference and blackness. By affirming herself as negra, Pitanga refuses racial democracy and the ideology of whitening.

With light skin as a privileged form of beauty, social capital, and opportunity, Pitanga challenges the visual representation of what it means to be Black in the public sphere. *Raça* quotes Pitanga:

> In all aspects, I always want to be as optimistic as possible, but prejudice exists. Here in Brazil, it is camouflaged. It is stamped out in our advertising. Just analyze the commercials. I am the only Black woman that does publicity for all products. I have done perfume commercials, cars, everything.... And still I have to be with colleagues, business people, and a whole lot of people saying to me, "You are so light, why do you say that you are Black?" They are awful and even Blacks will give this type of advice. This is nonsense, living proof of prejudice. I am Black with the utmost pride.[84]

In addition to showcasing Pitanga's connection to her father, this article presents her as the sister of the darker-skinned actor Rocco Pitanga and as the stepdaughter of Benedita da Silva, a well-known Afro-Brazilian senator. Largely absent from her childhood, Pitanga's mother, Vera Manhães, is a former model and actor of mixed African descent. Considered for the title role of the iconic *mulata* in *Gabriela*, Manhães was snubbed for lighter-skinned actor Sônia Braga, who underwent tanning treatments to play the part.[85] Pitanga has described the prejudice she experienced as a model, pointing out that the privileging of light skin indicates the presence of inequities that belie the notion of Brazil as a racial democracy. By acknowledging her light-skin privilege and advocating for visibility for people of African descent, Pitanga stakes a claim to an inclusive Blackness and an equitable Brazil.

In Brazil, celebrity stardom is mediated through the TV Globo telenovela industry. While TV Globo regularly exports its telenovelas, the U.S. mainstream television industries do not air these programs except as subtitled or dubbed series on Spanish-language television. Thus, while Hollywood films still dominate the Brazilian market, very few Brazilian stars have successfully entered the U.S. market, with the exception of actors Carmen Miranda, Sônia Braga, and Alice Braga. Even these actors would be considered white in the Brazilian context and have also been heavily critiqued by Brazilian audiences for catering to U.S. productions rather than maintaining their national roots. However, Pitanga's celebrity, tied with TV Globo as the principal exporter of telenovelas, provides recognition for her activism within Latin America.

Considering the fact that success abroad in U.S. markets is often contingent on a resemblance to whiteness and the performance of exoticism, an examination of Pitanga must also content with a history of asymmetrical political and cultural exchange. Camila Pitanga, along with Afro-Brazilian actor Taís Araújo, has had crossover success from Brazilian television to Brazilian film. Yet, as celebrities also reach their audiences through their embodiment of race, gender, and sexuality, these actors again have phenotypical traits that nonetheless act as sociocultural currency to both uphold and challenge ideals of racial democracy.

The paucity of characters and actors of African descent in Brazilian film and television in general, as well as the fact that most roles for actors of color are maids or other stereotyped roles, reflects Eurocentric dominance in the culture.[86] However, the number of characters and actors of African descent on television has increased in recent years. In 2009, TV Globo's *Viver a Vida* featured Taís Araújo playing the first Black female protagonist in a primetime telenovela. Araújo's role as a high-fashion model reflected a historic moment in Brazilian mass media related to the intensification of Afro-Brazilian activism and the emergence of race in public discussions. As universities adopted affirmative action policies in the early 2000s, public figures such as Araújo became integrally positioned as visible symbols of progress toward racial inclusion. Yet, in the Brazilian media world, which favors whiteness, Pitanga is still an exception in that she has modeled in advertising campaigns and starred regularly in telenovelas.

However, the majority of Pitanga's roles play into tropes of women of African descent. Pitanga's light skin color and appearance have allowed her to enter telenovelas, though only within restricted roles and terms. Pitanga's casting in telenovelas unmasks the limits of the myth of racial democracy. This illusion of progress is a crucial comparison for the United States in light of the use of mixed-race people to promote a postracial agenda in the mid-2000s.

Brazilian media culture idealizes whiteness while a national identity based on a celebratory mestiçagem solely valorizes and objectifies the sexuality of mixed women of African descent. The term "morena" can be used in various linguistic contexts to refer to almost any combination of darker physical features, as a polite way to refer to a woman with dark hair, regardless of her skin color. The very ambiguity of this term allows for a contextual relationship in which racial signifiers are constantly shifting. Many magazines, articles, and publicity materials use the term "morena" to describe Pitanga. Since Blackness has low status in Brazilian social hierarchies, many women of African descent hesitate to admit their own Blackness. Many Brazilians consider calling someone "negra" or "preta" to be rude. Pitanga has said that she has been told that she is morena because she is too pretty to be negra.[87] The transnational manifestations of Eurocentric beauty norms rely on the commodification of light-skinned mixed Blackness while devaluing Blackness as ugly and appraising whiteness as an aspirational ideal. Anti-Blackness is embedded within these capitalist and affective forms of beauty. The term "morena" highlights Pitanga's ambiguous racial looks. In the popular imagination, the morena body is permeable and flexible, yet not accessible to very dark-skinned Black women. At the same time, it is rare for an article about a white actress to mention her race at all. Pitanga points out this inconsistency when she says that the incorporation of Black characters represents less than true progress—true progress will come when magazines do not even mention her race.[88]

The ideology of branqueamento dominates how Brazilians perceive beauty. As Pitanga notes, "I do not care, for example, about the comments that I heard after appearing on the cover of *Raça*. Some fans wrote and said to me that they did not understand the fact that I was interviewed by a publication targeted for Blacks. I repeat: I am Black."[89] Given her light skin, when Pitanga espouses a negra identity she is making a conscious choice to repudiate the practices and discourses of branqueamento in favor of standing in solidarity with people of African descent in the diaspora. By appearing on the cover of *Raça*, Pitanga claims a space to inscribe herself within the Black public sphere.

In spite of her self-identification and her famous Afro-Brazilian actor father, when *Folha de São Paulo*, a major national newspaper, surveyed people

Camila Pitanga on the cover of *RG Vogue Brazil*, December 2005.
Courtesy of the Condé Nast Publications, Inc.

regarding the racial makeup of various celebrities and politicians, only 27 percent considered Pitanga *negra*. A greater number, 36 percent, termed her *parda* (a census category meaning brown or mixed).[90] She has played her father's daughter in two telenovelas, *A Próxima Vítima* (1995) and *Cama de Gato* (2009–2010). Given the visibility of her family in the public eye, Pitanga's familial relationships would seem to sufficiently legitimate her Black identity. However, in Brazil, visual appearance carries more weight in racial identification than in the United States. While she has the option to identify as *mulata*, morena, or parda, Pitanga negates assimilating racializing norms and instead works within the parameters of Blackness.

Pitanga's self-identification as negra is an oppositional response to the dominant national identity based on mestiçagem. Understanding actresses such as Camila Pitanga as racially mixed fits into a physical realization of mesticagem as demonstrated by descriptions in magazines such as a 2005 *RG Vogue Brazil* cover proclaiming her as "A síntese do Brasil" (The synthesis of Brazil). Like the *mulata* archetype, Pitanga is presented as a natural resource signified as an exploitable object for capitalist accumulation. By portraying Pitanga as the embodiment of sensuality and desirability, *Vogue* reinforces how Brazil manifests itself as a site of racially harmonious mixture. The cover of the March 2006 issue of *Claudia*, a women's magazine, features Pitanga with the caption "talento com sabor de Brasil" (talent with the flavor of Brazil). While the magazine typically features white models and actresses, Pitanga, along with the Afro-Brazilian actor Taís Araújo, remain exceptions to hegemonic white beauty and consumerism. Such media present bodies that do not fit into the norms of whiteness or into the dominant parameters of Blackness are presented as exotically consumable, yet also authentic, figurations of Brazilian national identity. Similarly, *VIP*, a men's magazine, featured Pitanga on its July 2000 cover, with the title "Pitanga selvagem, dá vontade de catar, morder, e . . ." (Pitanga, wild, she makes you want to pick up, bite . . .).[91] Presenting her as part of the tropical pleasures of Brazil, the magazine describes Pitanga's allure as based on her authentic exoticism. Both the dominant feminine and male gazes position Pitanga as a site of pleasurable, wild difference and consumption in these magazines primarily targeted to white readerships. The eroticism and beauty attributed to Pitanga is part of the iconography of the *mulata* figure.

As mixed-race female figures are offered as the epitome of racial democracy and thereby function to limit discussions of racism, Pitanga's identification as Black is especially salient. Consider that she identifies as negra at a time when there has been a push to group Brazilians of African descent as negro rather than maintaining multiple gradated color categories. The Afro-Brazilian movement in Brazil has increasingly pressured the state to include the term negro in legislation.[92] Although negro has never been an official census category, race-conscious Afro-Brazilian organizations such as the Frente Negra Brasileira in the 1930s, the Teatro Experimental do Negro in the 1940s, and the Movimento Negro Unificado Contra a Discriminação Racial (MUCDR) in the

1970s and 1980s have used it as well as publications such as *Raça*.[93] The term potentially rearticulates Afro-Brazilian identity as the Brazilian state has long used a tertiary system of branco (white), pardo (brown), and preto (Black). The negro category subsumes preto and pardo classifications. The proposal of the negro category self-consciously rearticulates race making for specific political purposes and reopens racial identification as a matter of public discussion.

By aligning herself with the Black movement and arguing for more parts for Afro-Brazilian actors, Camila Pitanga defies stereotypical assumptions about the morena, who aspires to enter into whiteness by rejecting associations with Blackness. Unlike Beals and Berry, Pitanga speaks out explicitly in favor of Black political movements. While both Berry and Pitanga insert themselves into a legacy of Black actors, Pitanga uses her celebrity to change power structures within society. She does so in a time when Brazilians see claiming a Black identity as symbolizing Black resistance to racism. In Pitanga's case, it also negates the erotic symbol of the *mulata* in a white patriarchal framework. The emergence of the Black movement challenges the myth of racial democracy, and by identifying with it, Pitanga works against the dominance of mestiçagem. Yet, the construction of Pitanga as a sensuous *mulata* tethered with her identification as Black reveal conflicts over histories of racial mixing and corresponding racial categories versus appeals to racial solidarity. By emphasizing the undervaluing of Black women and the sexualization of the *mulata*, Pitanga relocates Blackness to the center through highlighting the diversity of Blackness itself.

While both Halle Berry and Camila Pitanga identify as Black in their respective national landscapes, Berry invokes the historical one-drop rule when attempting to influence how people in the United States see her. Pitanga, in contrast, works against historical paradigms of mestiçagem and how many Brazilians see her. In her interview with *Raça*, Pitanga stated: "I consider myself active in the pro-Black movement. I repudiate any form of prejudice, discrimination, and aggression, not just against Blacks, but also against women, children, slave labor, etc. I believe that to exercise this social function is a choice of citizenship, independently of the profession that someone occupies. I understand that my profession increases this focused attention and it is a good form of power to have this visibility that I have to defend causes that I believe in."[94]

Race, for Pitanga then, is not a function of color or biology but of political commitment. Like Jennifer Beals, Pitanga resists the way in which the nation she lives in has ascribed racial identities. However, Beals and Pitanga have different political stakes in that Pitanga's identification as negra is part of her crusade for racial equality. The differing racial politics of their generations and nations facilitated the structure of these choices. A neoliberal framework highlighting individual agency and mobility as an approach to social change obscures the privileged status of light-skinned mixed Blacks in comparison to darker-skinned Blacks. While Beals and the media covering her emphasized her outsider status, Pitanga's avows an identity that places her within an Afro-Brazilian collective. The media depiction of Beals frames her alterity rather than her place within a multiracial and/or Black community. In contrast, Pitanga inserts herself as an insider rather than an outsider—even when responding to comments that she does not look Black. She enacts what Muñoz would term "disidentificatory practices" that rely on a strategy of resistance and survival. She claims the very position that the dominant culture denigrates.[95] For Pitanga, the tension of disidentification depends on a questioning of the national racial ideology of mesticagem. By disidentifying as morena, Pitanga also resists a gendered and sexualized notion of beauty and desirability resting outside of Blackness. Unlike Berry and Beals, who distance themselves from a dark-skinned devalued Black womanhood, Pitanga connects her role as a public Black figure to other struggles against forms of oppression. She performs and asserts her identity in opposition to the expected norm of morenidade, which has been considered more desirable and beautiful than *negritude* (Blackness). In this sense, Pitanga's identity is neither a Black nationalist response nor a reenactment of racial binaries, but rather an example of how to use Black identity as part of a larger pursuit of social justice. Her identification as negra accounts for variance and diversity. However, the politics of individual racial identity does not take place in isolation. The naming, meaning, and physical markers of the racial term she embraces are part of significant national debates—for example, over affirmative action and racial quotas—with real material effects.

Just as the highly publicized 2007 case of the differential admissions treatment of identical twin brothers catalyzed debates over racial policy and definitions of Blackness, Pitanga, as a celebrity, also structures how race is talked about, understood, and enacted. A 2007 case arguing for inclusion under racial quotas referenced Pitanga: A mixed-race Brazilian student with a Black father and a white mother was denied admission to the UFPR under the racial quota system. Arguing for a reversal, the student's counsel said that she was Camila Pitanga's color and therefore, should be allowed to enter under racial quotas.[96] The counsel described the student, Ana Gabriela Clemente da Silva, as the daughter of a Black father, who defines himself as "moreno escuro," with the same color as Naomi Campbell. While acknowledging that Ana did not possess her father's racial traits, as she has a "rostro afilado" (sharp face) associated with whiteness, the attorney pointed out her "parda" coloring to designate a brown skin tone linked with racial mixture.[97] The counsel argued that discrepancies

between ancestry, phenotype, self-identification, and the commission's inter-
pretation of a student's race made for an arbitrary system. Clemente da Silva
won the case. Her success in using Pitanga's public statements points to how
popular culture can shape political and social meanings, with consequences
for policy. The case also demonstrates a gap between self-identity and social
interpellation and privileges the visualization of race, with profound material effects on public policies and collective identities. If da Silva's claims were
found invalid, the implication would be that Pitanga is passing for Black within
a passing binary of authenticity or fraud.

By invoking Pitanga, her lawyer countered the notion that Clemente da
Silva had sought to pass for Black and enacted a racial opportunism, qualifying
for racial quotas the commission had judged her too light-skinned to merit,
based on the idea that she did not suffer the discrimination the quotas seek to
remedy. It is important to stress that the notion of the "mulatto escape hatch"
in that brown and mixed-race people are able to flee poverty and occupy an
intermediary position in comparison to pretos has been disproven.[98] Rather,
the incomes, higher educational opportunities, and social mobility prospects
of pardos and pretos are roughly similar, and both groups face significant prejudice rooted in anti-Blackness.[99] Furthermore, the university admissions view
prescribes rigid definitions of Blackness and precludes racial coalitions that
go beyond skin color. Much of the opposition to racial quotas in Brazil suggests that potential applicants will commit racial fraud and therefore there are
parallels with U.S. affirmative action cases in the early 1990s in *Malone v. Civil
Service Commission* and the 2016 dissent of the *Fisher v. Texas* case.

Under these terms, Black identification represents a radical resistance to racism and oppression. This Black political identity, however, differentiates from
those such as the 2015 case of Rachel Dolezal, a white woman who purposefully presented and performed herself as Black as an act of deception. In both
the United States and Brazil, the blurriness of racial categories has provoked
anxieties about fraudulent and opportunistic racial identity claims. In the U.S.
context of the one-drop rule and multiracial movement strands emphasizing
racial identity as a choice, passing is nonetheless framed as shifting the perception of one's authentic racial self. Black identification in Brazil dismantles white
hegemony and recognizes racial ambiguity not as an act of passing for what one
is not, but rather to embrace Blackness. However, this denial of racial identity
in Brazil does not preclude a possible future in which the visual fetishization
of race trumps racial identity as a way to fight racism. In 2009, when an inter-
viewer in *Raça* commented that many people still do not consider Pitanga to
be Black, Pitanga responded that "I have heard that many times, and I think

that this is another demonstration of the amount of racial prejudice that can be hidden even if there is not consciousness of this."[100] The slippage between the terms "morena" and "negra" used to describe Pitanga destabilizes phenotypic visuality as the primary witness for understanding race in Brazil by undercutting the reliability of the viewer. These discrepancies in how Blackness is defined in Brazil and the United States call for new lenses in the construction, meaning, and utility of Blackness.

As a crucial figure within Brazilian celebrity culture and contemporary media practices, Pitanga's star text allows for new understandings of Blackness in Brazil. Combined with heightened media coverage of racial inequalities and controversies surrounding racial quotas, Pitanga's fame comes at a time when she is able to take up both discursive and television space in the Brazilian public sphere. The 2009 telenovela *Cama de Gato* features Camila Pitanga in the role of a maid. However, significantly, Pitanga's character is the protagonist. Two years later, she played a mixed-race female executive in another telenovela, *Insensato Coração*. Her character is romantically involved with an upwardly mobile Black architect (played by Lázaro Ramos). The 2015 telenovela *Babilônia* casts Pitanga as a poor beach kiosk worker who aspires to attend university. The program's ensemble notably has numerous Afro-Brazilian characters, and Afro-Brazilian actors play Pitanga's parents. These narratives suggest that the representation of Afro-Brazilians may be shifting past the tropes of subservient Afro-Brazilian characters, who largely stand in the background of white characters' stories and/or have no desires, aspirations, or familial networks of their own.

However, the heteronormative mandate of branqueamento is still prevalent—in all of these telenovelas, Camila Pitanga's characters end up marrying wealthier white men. These changes in television programming also reflect the growing Afro-Brazilian middle class and the commercial power of the nonwhite population in Brazil. Between 2003 and 2011, approximately 40 million people, known as classe C, entered the middle class in Brazil. More than half, 53 percent, of classe C are negros and pardos.[101] The rise of affirmative action in universities and public service jobs has shifted the culture. Pitanga has become a bankable celebrity and commodity. She was the most visible celebrity in television commercials in 2012 in a media industry that relies heavily on advertising revenue from telenovela programming.[102] Like Berry, Pitanga's start as a model grounded her star text in beauty, and both Berry and Pitanga appeal to an audience that includes people of color without significantly altering Eurocentric beauty standards. Yet, as Pitanga's rise in fame coincides with increasing Afro-Brazilian mobilization, her racial identification is at least in part strategic and intended to encourage racial critique in dominant spaces.

Recognizing her privileged access to the public, Pitanga has taken on a marginalized identity to intervene directly in the dominant racial ideology of branqueamento. Unlike Beals and Berry, Pitanga's political identification with Blackness is grounded in political action. As the national ambassador of UN Women Brazil, Camila Pitanga is the first Latin American celebrity to serve as a spokesperson for UN Women. Referencing the personal and the political connections in her own life, Pitanga participates in enacting transnational frameworks of social change. Her movements and activism cross borders, positioning her as a racialized and Black diasporic subject. Utilizing her celebrity platform, Pitanga has also participated in the Amnesty International campaign Jovem Negro Vivo, (Young Black Lives), openly advocating for racial justice. Pitanga capitalizes on her celebrity platform to communicate the Black movement's message and to publicly display an ideological commitment to Black valorization. In a 2015 *Marie Claire* interview, Pitanga cites the case of a missing Black man that became a touchstone debate about racialized police violence and abuse: "I find this issue really important as a Black woman and as a mother. We need to stop with this anesthesia, to stop pretending that this is natural and that there are only exceptional cases such as that of Amarildo."[103] As a visible and vocal celebrity, Pitanga articulates her intersectional positionality as a Black woman. Furthermore, she evokes Black mothering as a form of mobilizing activism and as a form of resistance to anti-Black state violence. As opposed to Berry, Pitanga places Black motherhood as not solely individual, but as asserting communal and institutional change. Later, in a 2016 UN campaign video promoting gender equality, Pitanga affirms that she is negra, not morena or *mulata*.[104] While Pitanga has built her influence through the commodification of mixed-race femininity, she deploys her celebrity as a voice of intersectional Black feminisms. Through interrupting the intertwined national narratives of racial democracy and mestiçagem, Pitanga helps shift the conversation around anti-Blackness and racial identity.

Mixed Blackness and Celebrity Culture

Berry, Beals, and Pitanga negotiate the differentiated politics of inclusion of women of African descent and tensions over the management of Blackness in the Americas. The struggle to redefine the parameters of racial identities involves not only policy changes and legislation but also cultural shifts in how the respective publics in each country view Black and mixed identities. In Beals's case, the conventions of the passing mulatta intersected with her representation in the 1980s and early 1990s, amid a post–civil rights era in which the

Black-white binary was still dominant. The 1980s and 1990s context of multicultural inclusion onscreen also coincided with concerns over affirmative action and the census. By the 2000s, the burgeoning multiracial movement, the growing consciousness of mixed-race identities, and the sharp increase in multiracial stars, provided a context in which Beals was able to assert a biracial identity. Berry, in contrast, claimed a Black identity but acknowledged her mixed-race heritage. Her celebrity image drew on the iconography of tragic mulattas such as that of Dorothy Dandridge but also presented her as surpassing this image in an age of neoliberal multiculturalism despite racial inequalities.

Yet, the continuing fascination with racially mixed actresses and the allure of Berry's mulatta sexuality facilitated Berry's stardom and ultimately reinscribed the mulatta for the 2000s. For example, Beyoncé's commodified Blackness also draws on the intersections of racialized sexuality and consumption. Beyoncé's star text draws on a reverie celebrating her Louisiana Creole heritage and the aesthetics of her light skin and blond-highlighted hair juxtaposed with the fashioning of her "bootylicious" sexual allure. The legends of mulatta sensuality from slavery are reworked into global capitalist cultural exchanges. By the later 2000s, celebrities who came of age post-*Loving* have also grappled with the hauntings of the mulatta and racial authenticity policing. Thus, the mulatta symbol is a signal not of a path toward the obsoleteness of race, but rather of the fetishization of race. By 2016, the rematerialization of race in the mulatta figure as a structuring force rather than a race-neutral figure emerges in the wake of postracial discourse.

On the Netflix series *Dear White People* (2017), Joelle (played by Ashley Featherson), a Black female student, references her fellow student, Sam's (played by Logan Browning) identity: "You're not Rashida Jones biracial, you're Tracee Ellis Ross biracial—people think of you as Black."[105] This statement draws attention to the role that celebrities play in crafting racial identity as well as the role of the viewer in the interpellation of these identities. Rashida Jones and Tracee Ellis Ross are celebrities who connect notions of mixedness and Blackness, their very legibility stemming from the star texts of Jennifer Beals and Halle Berry. The fixation on gazing the mixed-Black body for skin color and phenotype undergirds the sociohistorical context from the Obama era forward.

Rashida Jones, like Camila Pitanga, has a well-known Black father in the culture industries. As the daughter of music producer Quincy Jones, she carries the U.S. familial ancestral ties to Blackness to the public sphere. Like Beals, her racial ambiguity, which is often read by viewers as white, also permeates her celebrity text. In the television series *Parks and Recreation* (2009–15) and the comedy film *I Love You, Man* (2009), she largely plays "raceless" roles that exclude her family and, hence, her racial background. While she outwardly recognizes a Black identity, her roles circumscribe viewers, unaware of her famous father, to read her as racially white.[106] Furthermore, like Beals and Pitanga, she is most often paired with white love interests. Unlike Beals, Jones's fame arises during heightened neoliberal postracial discourses that emphasize individual choice and the ability to cast off racial identity. Jones's racial flexibility and appearance in comedy genres allows her to bypass the hypersexual imagery associated with Black women, yet it still marks her as attractive due to simultaneous coherence and differentiation with white aesthetics. Jones's roles are safe and acceptable markers of racial representation that can appeal to multiple viewing audiences without disrupting the racial status quo.

Like Beals, the specter of passing has also followed Jones into the twenty-first century, yet her famous parents also undercut these currents. In a 2005 *Glamour* article, Rashida's sister notes that Rashida passed for white. In response, Rashida retorts, "Passed?! I had no control over how I looked. This is my natural hair, these are my natural eyes! I've never tried to be anything that I'm not." Jones negates the idea of any intentional choice to pass or be white, while leaving unacknowledged the entitlement that her phenotypical features give. While Rashida's sister has the same father and mother, the siblings have distinct racial experiences based on their differentiated phenotypes. In order to pass, the passing woman must also deny Black familial relationships. Countering these claims of passing, Jones affirms her biological family ties and disturbs the essentialism of Blackness to darker skin. The accusation of passing implies an act of denial and the notion of an authentic Blackness hinging on visibility. The one-drop rule, despite claims of racial fluidity, continues its hold on U.S. racial consciousness. Jones herself in interviews challenges clear racial definitions and criteria.

Similar to Pitanga, Jones expresses pain at the insinuation that she is not Black and at the racism that stems from her light-skin privileges. In the same interview, she responds, "And I get: 'But you look so white! You are not Black!' I want to say: 'Do you know how hurtful that is to somebody who identifies so strongly with half of who she is?'" This unintentional passing is not a denial of Blackness, but rather demonstrates the primacy of whiteness and the signaling of visual markers of race in the U.S. imagining of multiculturalism. She continues to point out the limits of visuality in the U.S. imagination: "When I audition for white roles, I'm told I'm too exotic. When I go up for Black roles, I'm told I'm too light." Thus, "exotic" becomes a reference to nonwhite bodies and signals racial difference while the dominant racial reading of Black does not encompass Jones's phenotypical features. Thus, the supposed postracial United States is constrained by racial structures of whiteness with a simultaneous demand for racial authenticity.

The constant misrecognition of Jones facilitates the assertion of both a Black and biracial identity. Hence, the policing of authenticity along with the restructuring of racial orderings puts forth race as both an in-between state and as a marker of identity. In a 2008 interview, Jones remarked: "I'm lucky because I have so many clashing cultural, racial things going on: Black, Jewish, Irish, Portuguese, Cherokee. I can float and be part of any community I want. The thing is, I do identify with being Black, and if people don't identify me that way, that's their issue. I'm happy to challenge people's understanding of what it looks like to be biracial, because guess what? In the next 50 years, people will start looking more and more like me." Jones mobilizes her body in relation to a futuristic racial order in which mixedness and ambiguity are dominant assumptions. The reference to fifty years in the future is significant in that the year 2050 is when the U.S. Census Bureau predicts that non-Hispanic whites will become the minority population in terms of demographic numbers. The public imagination of this prediction often revolves around a specific visual image of light-skinned women with racially ambiguous features. Hence, Jones herself also adopts and romanticizes this futuristic mode of seeing race. By 2013, mixed identity has developed further as a possible site of identity rather than as a threat or as an anomaly. In an interview discussing casting, Jones noted that "I wasn't Black enough. I wasn't white enough. I was just kind of in the middle. But, in the past ten years, there have been a lot more biracial actors and actresses."[107]

Yet Jones is continuously subsumed into a broader category of whiteness that reaffirms the normalization of whiteness. On a red-carpet interview in 2015, reporter Danielle Demski remarked to Jones that "you look like you've just come off of an island or something! You're very tan. Very tropical." Jones's response that she was ethnic was met with laughter from the reporters. As tans are associated with leisure and beach resorts, Demiski associates Jones with the embodiment of celebrity capitalism and within the parameters of whiteness. By designating Jones as possessing a white identity, Demiski posits her tan in contrast to the brownness of people of color in the United States. Jones was forced to justify her racial body within the realms of idealized commodified beauty that relies on exotic fantasies of the tropics. By responding that she is ethnic rather than Black, Jones places herself outside of established U.S. racial categories and hints at differential appearances and identification.

The reading of bodies as possessing an ambiguous near-white appearance rather than an ambiguous nonwhite appearance stands with rather than against notions of racial purity. Such readings emphasize the naturalization and fetishization of mixed bodies rather than the ways in which the viewer has historically sought to view bodies. Hence, the cultural meanings that viewers ascribe to bodies rather than the bodies themselves construct race. In contrast, Rashida Jones has appeared on *Black-ish* as the sister of Rainbow (played by Tracee Ellis Ross). Tracee Ellis Ross, like Jones and Pitanga, has a famous parent, Diana Ross. Yet Tracee Ellis Ross is consistently viewed as Black. Hence, phenotype is consistently associated with authenticity. In interviews, Ross has asserted that "I've never not known I was Black." Yet, like Jones, she also claims both a Black and a mixed identity. In an interview with Trevor Noah, another mixed-Black figure, she stated that "I am mixed and I have never actually played a mixed person. And though 'Bow's experience of being mixed is different than mine, I am still very pleased to put that experience on the map and on television. . . . Black is not a monolithic experience and that looks different for all of us. . . . There is no one way to be mixed."[108] Together, Jones and Ross defy notions of monolithic Blackness and mixedness.

Both in Brazil and in the United States, much of the racial identification of celebrities revolves around phenotype and the perceived performance of Blackness and mixedness. These celebrities push back against the notion of a monolithic Blackness. Camila Pitanga's public affirmation of herself as negra does not necessarily correlate with her representation and interpellation in the public sphere and in films and telenovelas. Yet, her identity as negra also coincides with the emergence of new understandings of Blackness in Brazil and the material stakes involved in claiming a Black identity. For light-skinned Afro-Brazilians, who do not identify as preto as part of their experience, the rise of Black consciousness and the term negro offers up new possibilities of political participation. In the public sphere, Pitanga's use of negra reimagines a politicized Black identity. Along with discourses spurred by race-based legislation and policies, Pitanga's star text revises dominant notions of Blackness and national narratives of mestiçagem. Hence, these actors function as a threat to the racialized national imaginary—Beals and Berry in the binary racial divisions of the United States and Pitanga in the celebratory rhetoric of mesticagem.

Yet, the media that surround them often tame and reinscribe actresses of African and European descent back into racial, gender, and sexual orderings through mixed-race tropes with a long history in film, telenovelas, and U.S. television. Their star texts emphasize that race is a product of social relations rather than a truth that resides on the body. The following chapters examine some of the roles that Pitanga, Berry, and Beals have played in relation to a negotiation of racial and national identities. The narratives at work in these cultural productions contain and nullify Blackness through a focus on the regulation or sexual deviance of the characters. Yet, many of these same cultural productions do allow a potential small space for seeking mixed-Black female agency.

The Morena and the *Mulata* in Brazilian Telenovelas

Containing Blackness in a Racial Democracy

The slim, statuesque maid, her hair pulled tightly back into a high bun and her crisp dress buttoned to the top of her collarbone, cooks and cleans in the kitchen with humility and grace. With her light brown skin, she is not fair-skinned like the majority of the women onscreen in the telenovela, *Belíssima,* but, the audience wonders, will her beauty and goodness be enough to attract the attention of a wealthy man in this Cinderella story? As it turns out, they are. White, wealthy men are captivated by her looks, celebrate her purity, virginity, and goodness, and rescue her from a life of toil and labor. Mônica's straightened hair, light skin, and virginity allow her to climb social class and to be presented and perceived as elegant and a "dama"—a lady. From living in the back quarters of her employer's luxury apartment to dancing the waltz as an exuberant bride to being an expecting mother, Mônica's bewilderingly rapid transformation is facilitated by intertwined narratives of whitening, class mobility, and reproductive labor.

In contrast to the virginal Mônica, *Paraíso Tropical's* Bebel is strikingly sensual with her curly hair of locks and tight-fitting bright embellished clothing that accentuates the curves of her brown body. With her hips swiveling from side to side, her stride takes on rhythmic movements accompanying the samba soundtrack. While Mônica's loveliness and inherent goodness capture the attention of white suitors, Bebel is a sex worker who aspires to become a dama. But will Bebel achieve the happy ending with a white wealthy suitor? Instead, her excessive brown body oozes carnality rather than marriage. Although from a low social class like Mônica, Bebel does not possess inherent grace nor potential for sophistication that would enable her social ascension to the prized status of upper-class wife and mother. Instead, her brown body, exhibiting her sexual accessibility and exotic allure imbued by Blackness, draws in viewers to consume the *mulata*. Through the commodification of difference, Bebel, as a *mulata* sex worker, converts racial predicaments into racial sexual pleasures. Camila Pitanga played both of these figures, which together display the complexities mixed-Black women bear due to the weight of history.

Nineteenth- and twentieth-century cultural productions of mixed-race women of African and European descent in Brazil, as in the United States, demonstrate Eurocentric heteropatriarcal perspectives and the linkages of this system of dominance to mestiçagem (racial mixing), branqueamento (whitening), and Blackness. Into the twenty-first century, contemporary systems of power have reworked the objectification and commodification of women of African descent. These legacies of colonialism and nation building have endured in telenovelas, although contemporary adaptations mask them and modern conditions have changed them. By observing these legacies and the reinscription of the mixed-race female body alongside limited displays of social agency or resistance to branqueamento, this chapter explains national and racial identities as a process of negotiation.

In the early 2000s, the advent of race-based policies such as affirmative action fueled ideological debates around racial equality and mestiçagem as centerpieces of Brazilian identity. As these hegemonic ideologies of racial democracy and mestiçagem began to fray in public discourse, telenovelas increased media visibility of mixed-Black women while reconfiguring them to largely deploy these same ideologies. Telenovelas frame racially ambiguous women of African descent within national narratives, and thereby fit them into logics of racial management and Black containment.

Telenovelas and Mass Culture

The telenovela is a key site of race making and a powerful conduit for the Brazilian national imaginary. Telenovelas developed soon after the advent of television in Brazil in 1950 and expanded after the Kubitschek government (1956–61) aimed to use television as part of a movement toward modernity. Television functioned as a way for the government to provide information to a geographically dispersed population with low literacy rates. Seeking to project a unified national identity, the military government imposed strict limits on foreign programming and censored criticism.[1] TV Globo emerged as a private venture in 1965, with financial and technical support from U.S. media company Time Inc. and Brazilian government investments and political favoring that facilitated the company's rise as the dominant media force.[2] The network used its programming to project an image of Brazil as progressing toward modernity, consumerism, and upward mobility. TV Globo maintains audience leadership with a national average share over 53 percent and the majority of television advertising revenue bolstered by its signature product—the telenovela.[3] TV Globo, as the primary television network, is a protagonist in a "national tele-dramaturgy."[4]

Brazilian telenovelas use melodrama and sentiment in service of a project of modernity and nation building. As Adriana Estill argues, telenovelas have become the twentieth and twenty-first centuries' "foundational fictions" and have replaced the Latin American novel of the nineteenth century as major agents of nation building.[5] Through a sentimentalist "erotics of politics," nineteenth-century romantic narratives conjoined different or conflicting segments of the nation via heterosexual marriage.[6] Like nineteenth-century novels, telenovelas rely on heteronormative and patriarchal models of national identity through romantic plots. However, whereas nineteenth-century novels featured lovers of different races, most Brazilian telenovelas typically focus on whites, with Afro-Brazilian characters playing supporting roles. The exceptions of big hits, such as *Xica da Silva* (1996–1997) and *Da Cor do Pecado* (2004), demonstrated continuity of the themes of racial mixing of Black women and white men as a form of upward mobility.

As television is parceled as one of the tools and institutions of the white ruling class, telenovelas reflect whiteness as the pinnacle of femininity. However, by the mid-2000s, the use of mixed-race female figures in telenovelas, accompanied by large-scale engagement with racial issues during the administration of Lula da Silva, presented a potential opening within the racial national imaginary. The telenovelas coincided with the economic and political advancement of Afro-Brazilians and low-income groups, yet containing Blackness continued to be the dominant dynamic displayed. Hemispheric strategies of containing Blackness reimagine racial utopias as bereft of a politicized Black identity. Mixed-Black women are only legible based on proximities to white ideals and fantasies of Black exoticism—both of which uphold gendered and sexualized racial hierarchies. The telenovela mixed-Black figure generates a sustained abjection and consumption of Blackness.

While the romance narrative is an important structure in the Brazilian telenovela, the melodramatic nature of the genre is key to viewing audiences' affective relationship with it. Specifically, telenovela narratives often focus on characters who encounter major obstacles as they seek to maintain or improve their social status. By emphasizing the challenges faced by individual characters or family units, the telenovela invites viewers to identify with the characters, and hence with the imagined national community. Telenovelas mediate meanings that people identify with as part of a greater set of values within the nation and as such, telenovelas articulate the cultural imagination.[7] Thus, telenovelas are integrated as part of everyday lives and influence and articulate identity formations.

With new episodes six days a week over an average duration of nine months, telenovelas function as a kind of open serial, which Samantha Nogueira Joyce terms an "open text."[8] The writers are still writing the script for later episodes as the season begins to air, and they change the script based on public sentiment and audience reaction, with an eye toward building viewership rates. This feedback process is integral to the production of telenovelas, making the telenovela more of a national form than a novel or film. The most popular telenovelas air during the coveted primetime slots. Telenovelas are integral to the public sphere in Brazil, as they offer a means in which people can engage in a dialogue about the nation and its future.[9] Through the participation of writers, directors, producers, actors, audiences, and external institutions, telenovelas become a site of negotiation of social issues and meanings attached to gender, sexuality, class, and race.

The viewing public thus has a strong influence on the content of telenovelas, but TV Globo's monopolistic legacy and relationship to the government persists. Currently, one of the largest networks in the world and the most dominant channel in Brazil, TV Globo has been fundamental in the development of the telenovela genre into a contemporary medium distinguishable from other Latin American telenovelas for their high production value, commercial success, and realistic style that utilizes colloquial language and references social and political events.[10] Telenovelas have thus become a mirror of national identity, fulfilling the state's desire to project a modern identity with its rapidly growing economy, urbanization, and the rise of the middle class to affluence.[11] Since the late 1970s, TV Globo has exported its telenovelas to more than 130 countries, and its programming reaches more than 100 million viewers per day.[12] Thus, as a domestic and international product, the TV Globo telenovela also participates in transnational race making.

Like the Hollywood studios in the 1930s and 1940s, TV Globo both produces and broadcasts telenovelas. Brazilian television stations also employ a star system that binds actors to networks with permanent contracts, a system that facilitates an intensification of identification with actors in which Globo will heavily invest. Globo only invests in a few leading actors at a time. Given the marginalization of Afro-Brazilian actors onscreen, Camila Pitanga is one of the few female actors with sufficient prominence to capture the attention of audiences in Brazil.

Although Afro-Brazilians were onscreen in the 1960s and 1970s, they were largely relegated to playing maids, bodyguards, and butlers to the elite. With the decline of the military dictatorship and censorship in the mid 1980s, telenovelas began to address social and political issues, such as strikes and political corruption, more openly.[13] During the early 1990s, middle-class Afro-Brazilians began to appear, but these characters, like many of their U.S. counterparts in the 1970s and 1980s, consistently lacked Black familial or social networks.[14] As Joel Zito Araújo argues, Afro-Brazilians have largely been imperceptible onscreen due to their social invisibility and marginalization in the narrative.[15] The very few Afro-Brazilian media professionals employed within mainstream networks have little power to insert content or storylines.[16] Racism largely remained off-screen, even as Afro-Brazilian political and social mobilization rose in Brazil. Until the early 2000s, the official Brazilian state ideology was that Brazil was a racial democracy without racial tensions, and thus, until quite recently, discussing racial inequality has been largely taboo in the public sphere.

Telenovelas from the late 1990s and early 2000s suggest a complex negotiation of racial inclusion and citizenship. Beginning during Cardoso's presidency, the Brazilian government finally admitted that racial inequality existed and, as a redress, began to implement public policies, such as quotas, legislation (e.g., Estatuto da Igualdade Racial, Racial Equality Statute), and the creation of the Special Ministry for the Promotion of Racial Equality (SEPPIR). While the national law that enforced quotas in all federal universities passed in 2012, the debate surrounding racial quotas began around 2001 when the State University of Rio de Janeiro (UERJ) and the Universídade de Brasilia (UnB) first started experimenting with quota implementation. From fashion designers' complaints that the mandating of Black models inhibits creativity and the blatant ignoring of the 10 percent Black model quota for São Paulo Fashion Week to the large number of academic scholars and journalists that have vehemently opposed university racial quotas, debates over the role of race in national identity and national politics abound and demonstrate the disjuncture between various public arenas and the state.[17] This shift in discussions of race in the public sphere, deepened the incorporation of social issues and more Afro-Brazilian actors into principal roles. Thus, these telenovelas, *Belíssima* and *Paraíso Tropical*, and Camila Pitanga herself, are immersed in the periodization of racial debates in the early to mid 2000s.

The iconic figure of the mixed-race woman in Brazil stands within these complex negotiations of national identity and constructions of race, gender, and sexuality. In telenovelas, the mixed-race figure recalls earlier literary tropes (see chapter 1), as hypersexual seductresses such as Rita Baiana in *O Cortiço*, and the virtuous marriageable beautiful Isaura from *A escrava Isaura*. Yet, these tropes are reinvented for a new era in the early 2000s, when critiques of oppressive racial and class systems entered the Brazilian public sphere. Media stigmatization of Afro-Brazilians as inferior has combined with the relative absence of Afro-Brazilian actors in principal roles to marginalize Afro-Brazilians in the public sphere. Therefore, visibility in telenovelas is an important facet of struggles over power. As telenovelas hold a significant presence in the everyday lives of Brazilian audiences, these telenovelas also have important potential in the promotion of public discussions, the articulation of citizen identities, and the contributing of a common cultural citizenship among Brazilians.[18]

From the late 1990s onward, there has been an increasing presence of Afro-Brazilian actors onscreen and heightened sociopolitical conversations about race and national identity, as shown in public policy debates surrounding affirmative action and racism. Telenovelas function as a crucial space for including Afro-Brazilians into the public sphere. Given the telenovela's potential for a public forum regarding the articulation of citizenship and political emancipation, in what follows, I argue that the mixed-race female figure in Brazilian telenovelas figures in discussions of national identity and cultural citizenship in the early 2000s. The mixed-race figure thus contributes to a form of racial subjection in which the discourses of mestiçagem deny racism. Yet these telenovelas demonstrate how the mixed-race figure is contested so that her symbolism allows for possibilities of inclusion and exclusion, even as it relies on the management of mixed-race Black female sexuality so as to promote the future whitening of the nation and the neutralization of Blackness.

The Morena and the *Mulata*: Mothers of the Whitened Nation or Erotic Objects of Desire

From colonial times to contemporary settings, women of African descent in Brazil have systematically been consigned to a social structure that requires them to serve white elites, either sexually or economically.[19] Racialization is not always contingent on actual phenotype, but it is contingent on notions of sexuality and labor. Within a hemispheric racialized genealogy, Brazil, like the United States, connects morality with proper civil subjects, whereas mixed-race women who do not conform to these norms are regulated within this social order.

The function of the morena and *mulata* in the sexual political economy is key to racialization. *Mulatas* are frequently characterized by hypersexuality, promiscuousness, desirability, and the ability to dance samba. The term "morena" can signify an olive-skinned brunette to a dark-skinned woman and is considered a polite way to refer to someone with darker features. Unlike the term *"mulata,"* the term "morena" is not always associated with African descent and therefore is not always highly sexualized. The morena often distances herself from Black ancestors and instead emphasizes European descent or, at times, Indigeneity. This distancing of Blackness allows her to be respectable.[20] Preta (Black), although an official census category, is often associated with domestic labor and often carries a derogatory meaning. In contrast, "negra" is often associated with race consciousness.

The national imaginary of women's roles intertwines gender, sexuality, and class in Brazil's racial hierarchy. The popular Brazilian saying, "Black women for work, *mulata* women for sex, white women for marriage," encapsulates understandings of women of various races expressed by the many terms associated with different phenotypes and their associations. Brazilian culture continues to perpetuate the legacies of African slavery and European colonization that prescribed racial, gender, and sexual norms. On this spectrum, white women represent ideals of beauty and chastity, the *mulata* woman represents sensuality and sexual desire, and Black women represent manual labor. Racially ambiguous female characters can occupy several roles within telenovelas and their inclusion or exclusion from the nation and cultural citizenship is often based on the presentation of the character's gender and sexuality in relation to heteronormativity and respectability.

Telenovelas demonstrate that race cannot always be read off the body. The moralizing, pathologizing, and/or eroticization of subjects influence the meaning of their phenotype. Visual representations are not the sole source of racialization; rather, sexuality is key to the racialization of women in Brazil. Proximity to respectable heteronormativity is key to racialization and to the inclusion or exclusion of citizenship. The notion of citizenship as social and cultural practices that give a sense of belonging limits racialized, gendered, sexual, and classed subjects who are relegated to the realm of the invisible in Brazil. Race is unstable and shifts depending on the manifestations and variabilities of other mutable categories such as sexuality and class. Dominant modes of sexuality then dictate that respectable moral women, represented through the morena figure, participate in the nation through branqueamento and thereby help facilitate national myths of Brazil gradually becoming a less Black nation. The sphere of morality lies with the morena figure. In contrast, when sexuality is deemed to be hypersexual or excessive, the *mulata* figure is used to help justify her own exploitation as this hypersexuality is naturalized as a need to be sated.

Telenovelas show how women's bodies are controlled for the sake of the family and the nation. Sexual activity and marriage, therefore, also become racial projects. The sexuality and reproductive labor of women in Brazil are tied to the fate of the nation and are therefore politicized. The ideal woman represents values of female chastity and motherhood. However, Black sexuality, as represented by the *mulata* figure, precludes her from serving as a prototypical mother. She can give birth, but, due to her innate primitive sexuality, she cannot be maternal, nor even a productive citizen. The morena figure, in contrast, can be redeemed from Black ancestry and phenotypes through the eventual capacity to be whitened and serve as a mother of Brazil.

Through this control over women's bodies, the nation pursues whitening by containing Blackness. While some bodies of African descent, such as the morena figure, can be disciplined, the *mulata* figure must be contained. Brazil's national imaginary creates a duality of the morena as pure and moral or the morena as hypersexual and deviant. Like the hypersexual mulatta figure in the United States, the *mulata* figure in Brazil represents racial, sexual, and gender excesses. The *mulata* is not marriageable, but is available for sexual pleasure and exploitation.

Given that telenovelas both reflect and mediate the Brazilian imaginary, it is not surprising that they naturalize the sexual exploitation and economic marginalization of characters of African descent. Just as sexuality can Blacken or whiten in Brazil, money can whiten while poverty can darken.[21] When metanarratives in telenovelas present an opportunity for economic and social ascent for women of African descent, rather than grappling with the lack of opportunities faced in a racially stratified country, the telenovelas emphasize whitening through liaisons with white Brazilian men, who have supreme social status, and downplay the existence of structural racism. The location of Afro-Brazilian women in social and political economies is key to the intersection of race, gender, and class.

This narrative of young beautiful mixed-race women falling for white male romantic partners is part of other hemispheric mestizaje narratives in which whitening is a key part of the nation's future. Therefore, these Brazilian telenovelas, like other Latin American telenovelas, are rooted in these foundational fictions and carry with it a whitening ideology. Just as in Gilberto Freyre's narratives of mestiçagem and national identity in *Casa-Grande e Senzala*, mixed and Black women are sexual objects who desire white men, and hence white men fall under their sexual spell. Meanwhile, Black men are largely absent.[22] Mixed-race female figures in Brazilian telenovelas are a continuation of these national narrative myths.

In the Brazilian national imaginary, interracial romance is the sole path for Black women's mobility. In *Paraíso Tropical*, the character Bebel, a sex worker, is sexually exploited. In *Belíssima*, Mônica works as a domestic servant within white homes and institutions, and moves socially in terms of upward mobility only through sexual relationships with white men. The telenovelas individualize inequalities and thus deny the underlying social structures that place these women in positions as sex workers or domestics. For the morena figure, the narrative follows a racial self-transformation through branqueamento and marriage to white men. For the *mulata* figure, the narrative emphasizes their eroticized and racialized physical attractiveness and also shows the possibility of economic gain through liaisons with white men. Race in Brazil has largely been regarded as through phenotype, rather than through ancestry in the United States.

An analysis of Camila Pitanga's roles in *Belíssima* as Mônica and in *Paraíso Tropical* as Bebel demonstrates that race is interpreted through class position and sexual behavior. Mônica is read as morena because she is sexually pure and upwardly mobile in a way that Bebel is not, while Bebel is continuously racialized through her sexuality and lack of class. Yet these narratives are in the position of communicating hope of upward mobility to the vast majority of low-income women in Brazil. Therefore, telenovelas function as a technology of citizenship that creates a vision of proper citizenship according to racial, gender, and sexual norms.

Belíssima: Melhorarando a raça (Improving the Race)

Belíssima revolves around a love triangle. Camila Pitanga portrays Mônica, a domestic servant in the home of Mary Montilla. She is the guardian of her deceased friend's son, whose wealthy father, Alberto Sabatini, wants nothing to do with him. When Alberto Sabatini, meets Mônica, however, he decides to make contact with his son for the first time so he can pursue Mônica. Cemil, a middle-class head of factory workers in the Belíssima lingerie factory, where Alberto is on the board, pursues her as well. Mônica agrees to marry Cemil but jilts him at the altar because of a lie Alberto has told her about him. She eventually agrees to marry Alberto, but after catching him cheating on her repeatedly, she marries Cemil.

Mônica achieves upward mobility through alliances with wealthier men. In Brazil and many other Latin American countries, the narrative of the mocinha boazinha (a moral and obedient young woman), who obtains good fortune, happiness, and love despite various hindrances, is commonplace.[23] Often the mocinha might come from a modest or poor household. Her natural beauty and virtue attract the attention of a wealthier man, who presents her with a better life. Thus, the primacy of heterosexual romance creates a highly gendered narrative of feminine beauty and purity that generates social ascension. Often, the mocinha might suffer temporarily, yet she is rewarded for her morality and virtue with a happy ending. These narratives reinforce normative views of femininity, compensating morality and punishing women who use their sexuality for manipulation or display loose sexual morals. Foremost, these telenovela narratives reward adherence to norms of white womanhood.

As the telenovela's title implies, the story is replete with explorations of how race, gender, and class define standards of beauty. From the opening credits of *Belíssima*, the perception of beauty is already given a race and class bias: a young thin woman with straight blond hair dances to Caetano Veloso's song, "Você é Linda," with the lyrics "Linda, mais que demais, você é linda sim" (You are beautiful, more than the rest, you are beautiful yes) during the opening credits, then after every commercial and at the close of every episode. The phrase "more than the rest" seems to emphasize the association of blondness— a demographic rarity in Brazil—with beauty. Similarly, all of the models for the Belíssima lingerie company campaigns are white women with light eyes. Clearly, the ideal of beauty resides in whiteness.

While affirming the link between beauty and whiteness, the narrative also makes social mobility dependent on beauty. The telenovela reflects popular fashion magazines, which primarily feature white Brazilian women or women with light skin and light eyes. Unlike most telenovela Cinderellas, however, Mônica is not white but morena. Conformation to Eurocentric standards of beauty is necessary to be able to be recognized as beautiful and transcend social classes. While there are many working-class women in Brazilian telenovelas, many of these women are virtually absent in the plot and are usually Black domestic servants. It is quite rare that a Black maid is able to ascend socially because she is already not recognized as beautiful. In contrast, a white woman with a menial job is more frequently able to have this Cinderella role because she has the potential to be beautiful.

Mônica represents virtuous virginal beauty. While Camila Pitanga is darker skinned than most female telenovela actors, she is lighter than actors like Taís Araújo, who played a character called simply Preta (Black) in 2004's *Da Cor do Pecado*. Pitanga is light enough to avoid significant controversy, but her darker skin and features also make her identifiable and believable as a domestic servant. Mônica typically wears her hair straightened and pulled back into a bun. Although on her days off she sometimes wears it in loose waves, it never appears in the tight curls associated with Blackness. With Camila Pitanga's representation, Mônica has less Africanized features not only from her skin color but also from her straight nose and straight hair, which allow for inclusion into dominant Brazilian and hemispheric ideas of beauty.

Mônica then stands in as the pleasing morena that official popular claims of brasilidade assert as representing typical beauty. While her skin color is darker than any of the other characters, with her phenotypical characteristics resembling that of the show's white female characters, Mônica does not present a radical departure from conventional standards of beauty in Brazilian media. On the contrary, it reinforces dominant notions of desirable phenotypical characteristics. Furthermore, white actors play her father and brother, which directly conveys her potential social mobility. When Alberto expresses surprise that she is so morena with a white brother, Mônica simply explains that her biological mother was negra. The telenovela *Cama de Gato* (2009–2010) makes the connection more explicitly with Rose, another character played by Pitanga. The character's father, portrayed by Afro-Brazilian actor Antônio Pitanga, is an untrustworthy *malandro* (hustler). Although Antônio Pitanga is actually Camila Pitanga's father, the character she plays discovers that her actual biological father is white, which enables her to break away from him and from her lazy deceitful Black ex-husband and pursue social mobility through her eventual marriage to her white employer, the wealthy executive Gustavo. Rose later becomes pregnant by Gustavo and, thereby, also helps whiten the nation. Both Rose and Mônica are uplifted through their associations with whiteness.

In *Belíssima*, Mônica and her brother, André, have different mothers. The different biological mothers help explain the different physical characteristics between them. All that is known about Mônica's mother is that she was Black; she never appears. The absence of relatives of African descent despite Mônica's skin color allows for the audience to see Mônica as already nearly white. Mônica's racial ambiguity near whiteness enables an identification of mestiçagem and branqueamento in the telenovela. Thus, Mônica's presence in the telenovela does not challenge notions of whiteness.

Although the mixed-race female body is celebrated, the semiotics of appearance favors whiteness, which becomes a form of social capital.[24] Brazilian ideals of whitening, based on European and U.S. scientific racism and eugenics, shaped public policies related to immigration, reproductive health, housing, and education from the late nineteenth century onward.[25] Lilia Moritz Schwarcz observes that early twentieth-century Brazilian intellectuals outlined a racialized national agenda in which they argued for the hopeful national project of potentially perfectible Brazilian populations while simultaneously reinforcing Darwinist racial hierarchies.[26] White women as reproductive vessels were key to this Brazilian national project. Accessing this history, *Belíssima* suggests that white beauty is a national project.

While Gilberto Freyre's visions of morenidade as the epitome of Brazilian physical beauty still holds weight in Brazilian society, the ideologies of branqueamento are also present. This paucity of women of color in Brazilian media differs substantially from the national image of mixture that Brazil espouses. While the cultural imaginary of Carnival and samba feature women of color, these women are absent in mainstream media. Even as women of color have recently begun to appear in magazines and other media texts in greater numbers in the twenty-first century, the privileging of European features is also evident. Therefore, mestiçagem works to beautify other nonwhite bodies. Mônica, as a morena with European features, is not the epitome of physical beauty for the elite. However, she is white enough to be considered physically desirable to white men, and therefore she represents a whitening aesthetic through mestiçagem.

The effect on the viewer cannot be overstated. The Cinderella narrative of the mocinha allows viewers, especially working-class women, even if they are not themselves white, to imagine their own Cinderella tale in which they transcend their social position. These narratives normalize romance as a vehicle for social mobility, reinforce the family as the primary unit of social relations, and place consumerism, through upward mobility, as central to national belonging and citizenship.

From Domestic Worker to Madame: Consumerism, Class, and Mobility

Telenovelas and the popular imagery of the morena emphasize upward mobility. In *Belíssima*, this mobility is achieved through consumption and through marriage to white men. Thus, in a neoliberal framework, agency is equated with love and consumerism. Rather than provisions from the state that afford opportunities, citizenship is bestowed through the capacity to whiten through marriage. As Joel Zito Araújo notes, most Afro-Brazilians are cast in minor roles such as domestic servants. Thus, the character development of Mônica offers a departure from these racializing norms and invisibility in the public sphere. Thus, while TV Globo telenovelas, along with other media forms, have naturalized the relegation of Black women as servants, the emphasis on Mônica's mobility does not rely on shifts in social structures or an increase in educational and occupational opportunities. Absent in the telenovela is the potential for upward mobility through policies or labor organizing. It was not until 2013, after the airing of this telenovela, that a constitutional amendment passed that included domestic workers under workers rights and labor protection legislation. Historically, after the abolition of slavery and with limited labor opportunities, Afro-Brazilian women remained trapped in domestic work.[27] Furthermore, the happily servile sexually desirable domestic worker is a trope stemming from colonial legacies and illustrated in Gilberto Freyre's paternalistic romanticization of master-slave relations in the household and his characterization of Afro-Brazilian women as sexually available willing participants in mestiçagem. Instead of unmasking the myths of racial democracy, in *Belíssima*, domestic bliss and consumer prosperity are gendered and racialized as rewards for branqueamento.

By the time of the airing of *Belíssima*, women comprised over 93 percent of domestic workers, over 59 percent of whom were preta (Black) and parda (brown). Furthermore, the lack of labor rights solidified the marginalization of domestic workers and the extension of racial and gender dynamics stemming from slavery. Within the industrial area of greater São Paulo and in other Brazilian urban areas, the maid is an indicator of middle-class status, albeit a middle class that depends on cheap domestic labor. Middle- and upper-class white femininities are in part defined by the control of Black female labor.

The legacies of colonial slavery seep into Brazilian ideas of modernization so that relationships of inequality are normalized both in intimate spaces of the home and in the public sphere. Brazil has located much of its modernization in consumerism. Therefore, a glamorous white universe is the primary onscreen representation. Indeed, like previous telenovelas, in *Belíssima*, the primary personifications of luxury, elegance, and modernity are still white upper-class women. Brazilian telenovelas convey the desirability of capitalist culture, and hence the need for consumerism, through advertisements, product placement, and programming. They structure consumer desire, launching fashion trends and instructing on the use of new products. Through the interpellation of consumer products and telenovelas, consumption produces what Thaïs Machado-Borges calls "a feeling of belonging, a feeling of collective participation in national rituals and national passions."[28] Telenovelas then transmit ideas of modernity, new forms of expression, language, style, and significantly, new habits of consumerism.[29]

The imaginary of a white upper-class modernity onscreen is tied in with the assumption that target audiences desire to see this world projected. The end of the military dictatorship in Brazil in the 1980s led to greater emphasis on the market and the influence of opinion and audience research of Instituto Brasileiro de Opinião Pública e Estatísticas (IBOPE; Brazilian Institute of Public Opinion and Statistics) in crafting television shows. Through IBOPE, marketing teams, advertisers, and television producers construct images of the audience. Television has become a vehicle for publicity and advertising consumer products, and networks like TV Globo seek to appeal to an audience considered the likeliest to consume.[30] As such, historically, Afro-Brazilians have not been counted as part of this ideal audience.

The telenovela market develops its audience as consumers before they are formed as citizens. As Néstor García Canclini observes, consumers are not merely passive targets of capitalist messages, since their consumption of goods, especially cultural goods, becomes a means of citizen participation in society. He argues that in Latin America consumption has become a central practice of citizenship and class relationships.[31] However, given the consistent disparagement of Blackness and racial inequalities, Afro-Brazilians have been denied full citizenship. Although consumerism offers an avenue toward participation in the national and transnational capitalist cultures, this practice of citizenship is limited in a racially and class-stratified society.

With Brazil exhibiting one of the highest wealth inequalities in the Americas, the 2002 election of President Lula da Silva, a working-class uneducated former union leader detested by Brazilian elites, brought about a new promise of social class ascension. By the airing of *Belíssima*, President Lula's government had already begun implementing social policies such as 2003's Bolsa Familia, which provided cash transfers to families for ensuring that their children attend school and are vaccinated. The combination of Brazil's growing economy and President Lula's policies helped millions of Brazilians rise out of extreme poverty and helped millions more become part of a new middle class. Hence, the potential telenovela audience and product consumer shifted demographically. Nonetheless, with the dominance of the politically conservative TV Globo network, more Afro-Brazilian actors and characters appeared onscreen without the network adequately addressing structural inequalities. Although the presence of Afro-Brazilian onscreen appears as a radical disruption of racial hierarchies, the telenovela narratives obscure systemic racism and institutional barriers that shape Afro-Brazilian experiences. Telenovelas are a way for audience members to mobilize identities as consumers, citizens, and as members of certain gender and class categories. Hence, the inclusion of people of African descent onscreen is integral to a sense of belonging. Yet, onscreen visibility alone does not necessarily radically restructure racial, gender, and sexual norms.

Likewise, the lower class cannot obtain the symbols of consumption that maintain the classist narratives of the telenovelas. While most telenovelas represent the upper class who have the largest amount of disposable income, the lower and middle classes compose the majority of viewers. Nonetheless, the allusion that members of the upper class use a certain product gives the consumer product a certain amount of prestige, luxury, sophistication, and desirability.[32] By making *Belíssima* the name of a lingerie company in the telenovela, the show makes beauty itself consumable. The equation of beauty with whiteness thus excludes people of color from Brazilian society. Therefore, beauty is something to work on, aspire to, and consume. The linking of beauty to whiteness makes the consumption of beauty and the investment in cosmetic and aesthetic practices part of the whitening process.

A popular Brazilian saying holds that money whitens—a sentiment evident in the telenovela. The show's narrative whitens Mônica by allying her with Alberto and Cemil. Mary, Mônica's employer, influences Mônica's decision and emphasizes that her wedding to a wealthy man would facilitate her social mobility. Mary says Mônica is a *burra* (donkey) who only likes Cemil because she has never experienced the weight of precious jewels on her fingers or the warmth of a fur coat. Therefore, Mary posits love as calculated in terms of materials goods and consumption. Mônica's friend Dagmar says that she will learn to love Alberto in the same way she loves Cemil when she gets used to his wealth, which will make her a "madame" (woman of high social class and refinement), equating wealth with respectability. When Mônica deems many of the items Mary proposes for her wedding to Alberto too luxurious, Mary tells her to stop thinking like a small-minded or poor person, now that she will become a Sabatini. The intimate values of romance are coded in terms of a discourse of female mobility through consumption. Her wedding then becomes a demonstration of taste, social mobility, and success that demonstrates ways of behaving and spending for these new Brazilian middle classes, yet the behaviors are very much in line with narratives of domesticity and branqueamento. Mônica's transformation into a madame also relies on the assumption that she will no longer work as a maid and, conversely, might have a maid of her own. Therefore, part of Mônica's class and racial whitening is related to her capacity to choose not to do physical labor.

The cloaking of racial inequalities in telenovelas stems from the similar rationales used by Gilberto Freyre's *Casa Grande e Senzala* that situated interracial intimacies in slaveholding homes to show congenial racial relations. Many telenovelas attempt to evoke a friendly relationship between a *patroa* (female household employer) and her maid, similar to that of Mary to Mônica. The emphasis on friendship obscures the fact that Mônica's physical labor enables Mary to shop, socialize, and pursue business ventures. Nonetheless, Mary asks Mônica to find another maid to replace her even as she leaves to marry Alberto. This comment serves the function of reminding Mônica that she is still just a maid. Furthermore, only the invisibility of Black domestic labor can make the idealization of white upper-class womanhood possible.[33] As illustrated in the telenovela, the extensive use of cheap domestic labor in Brazil buttresses the link between whiteness and power and naturalizes Black women's subservient position. Mônica's marriage to Alberto not only changes her labor status but places her within a narrative of branqueamento and upward mobility.

The Virtuous Mocinha:
The Labor of Sexuality and Whitening

The whitening of Mônica occurs not just through aesthetic stylistic choices, but also by assigning Mônica some of the tropes of white womanhood. As a virgin, Mônica represents the Madonna. Yet, Mônica is also a mother due to her surrogate status following her friend's death. As the guardian of Toninho, who is white, she is the mother of a white son and a virgin, two ideals of white womanhood. Like the U.S. tropes of true womanhood, piety and sexual purity became dominant norms of femininity. Yet, in Brazil, like other Latin American nations, the exaltation of the Virgin Mary such as la Virgen de la Caridad del Cobre, the patron saint of Cuba, and la Virgen de Guadalupe, the patron saint of Mexico, the mixed-race woman becomes a symbol of national racial syncretism. Here Mônica occupies the aspirational tropes of this racial syncretism that allows for her place as a national symbol, yet nonetheless her role as a morena is to whiten and thereby eventually purify the nation of its Blackness.

Mônica can be pure, virginal, and virtuous, in part because she is disassociated with Blackness. Alberto is interested in Mônica as soon as he meets her, but learning she is a virgin makes him obsessive. Therefore, Mônica's purity drives Alberto's interest in the hopes that he can conquer her. While he is Toninho's biological father, he has no emotional link to his son until he becomes involved with Mônica. In this way, Mônica, Alberto, and Toninho become a family through affective rather than biological means, with Mônica as the primary link. The whiteness of future progeny, as represented by Toninho, remains intact. Mônica can be a maternal figure and therefore represent the cultural and emotional miscegenation without biological racial mixing. Furthermore, Mônica acts a surrogate mother for the Brazilian nation. Through her labor as a mother for Toninho, Mônica fulfills the task of reproduction for the Brazilian nation without having physically reproduced herself.

Mônica's virginity connects her to the Virgin de Nossa Senhora Aparecida, the patroness of Brazil. Doubts as to Nossa Senhora Aparecida's racial origins and appearance have reflected the racial anxieties of Brazilian national identity. She has been, alternatively, a figure of idealized white purity, Brazilian racial mixture, or Afro-Brazilian, all of which point to different visions of the nation. Similarly, the controversies over Nossa Senhora Aparecida also relate to questions as to who can represent Brazil onscreen and in what capacity. Archbishop Raymundo Damasceno declares that Nossa Senhora is not Black and maintains, "Nossa Senhora Aparecida é um fator de integração racial, reunindo devotos de todas as cores e condições sociais" (Nossa Senhora Aparecida is a factor of racial integration, gathering devotees of all colors and social conditions). On the other hand, Emanoel Araújo, the director of the Museu Afro Brasil, contests, "diferentemente do brasileiro, que quer ser branco, a santa foi ficando negra. Para um país mestiço como o nosso, a Padroeira nacional tinha mesmo que ser negra" (differently than the Brazilian, who wants to be white, the saint remained Black. For a mixed country like ours, the national patroness had similarly to be Black).[34] Nossa Senhora has a significant national function as a spiritual symbol of the struggle against slavery and the redemption of the nation through racial democracy. Fluid identities and significations on the one hand and racial anxieties in Brazil manifest in this figure; and Mônica, as a virginal morena figure, represents this dual notion of motherhood and chastity. In this story of a mother of a white son, the nation is also allowed to further whiten rather than retain racial hybridity for the future. The telenovela idealizes this virgin mother image.

At the same time, the narrative constructs Alberto's fetishization of Mônica's virginity and his manipulative seduction as white masculine conquest and domination. After Alberto has taken Mônica's virginity, he cheats on her repeatedly and when she leaves him admits that he misses her because she ironed his clothes and made him snacks—thus signifying that she continued to perform the domestic duties of a maid as his wife, suggesting potentially that as a nonwhite woman she cannot fully penetrate the upper class, as white elite men such as Alberto must have white children. Ideals of domesticity and femininity are intertwined in her role in Alberto's life. Mônica's life centers on taking care of others and their homes, from Mary, her former employer, to Toninho, to her elderly father, to, of course, Alberto. Selfless nurturing defines Mônica's feminine virtue in the telenovela. Even her distress over Alberto's extramarital relationships puts her in the role of passive receiver of pain and suffering. However, she does not leave Alberto for Toninho's sake, even though it causes her pain.

As Mônica grows increasingly dissatisfied with her situation with Alberto, Mônica leaves Alberto for Cemil. At first Cemil does not think that he would still have a chance with Mônica because, as Cemil notes to his father, Mônica is now sophisticated and well-dressed and is now considered a madame, whereas when he met her, she was a maid and he was still just a middle-class head of factory workers. By the closing episodes, Cemil is promoted to Alberto's position as factory director and Alberto is also promoted within the company. The *final feliz* (happy ending) of the telenovela is not with the very wealthy Alberto but with the faithful Cemil. Nonetheless, her suitor is white and does not belong to lower economic classes. The telenovela nonetheless allows for a discourse of whitening through mestiçagem. Yet, potentially as Mônica is a nonwhite mocinha, her final feliz does not finish with exceptional wealth as it does for many mocinhas in other telenovelas, but rather with entry into the middle-classes and the ability to escape work as a domestic servant. Therefore, her skin color might be a barrier for inclusion into the white elite, but allows for a gradual branqueamento and class mobility. Alberto and Mônica did not have their own biological children, and therefore, Alberto, as a representative of the upper class, is expected to have children who reflect an image of his own whiteness. With Cemil, Mônica is granted entrance into the white middle classes in exchange for her reproductive labor and the whitening of future progeny.

When Mônica was a morena domestic worker, she was expected to meet productive demands of physical labor. When she marries Cemil, her body is placed with reproductive demands in order to fulfill her citizenship to the Brazilian nation through the gradual whitening of her children. Mônica's function as a virtuous morena rather than a hypersexual *mulata* relies on the idea of sexuality for the reproduction of whitened Brazilians rather than merely for sexual pleasure. Therefore, the morena figure has access to possible social uplift in a way that the *mulata* figure does not, precisely because the morena figure is presented as virtuous. These patriarchal discourses of racial progress rely on the purity of the morena figure as a path toward political and social citizenship.

Displacing Blackness:
Presenting a Multicultural Brazil

The lack of direct attention to Mônica's race in the telenovela is what allows the process of sexualized and gendered racializations to function. Rather than consciously seeing and recognizing difference, the telenovela ignores Mônica's visual distinction and the experiences, impacts, and institutions that undergird racial disparities. The darkness of her skin functions solely to reinforce the rags-to-riches morena ascendancy through marriage and sexuality, but it never questions or problematizes racialized socioeconomic distinctions. For example, when Alberto drops off Mônica in her low-income neighborhood, the camera lingers on images of idle Black women with dirty clothes and missing teeth and overweight shirtless Black men as children clamor for money as Alberto sits in his imposing SUV. As Alberto admits that he is shocked, Mônica waves off these inequalities by stating that people are used to living in these conditions. By neglecting intersectional oppressions and reaffirming motifs of white male saviors and mestiçagem, the telenovela legitimizes Black marginalization. The morena's upward mobility does not challenge the basis of white capitalist patriarchy.

In contrast, Mônica's Black friend Dagmar stands in as a figure of racialized difference. Dagmar's white boyfriend's racist mother, Tosca, repeatedly engages in racial insults and disapproves of the interracial relationship. Tosca's vitriol places Afro-Brazilians at the bottom of the social hierarchy, but also expresses disdain for Arab immigrants, whom she dubs "turcos" (Turks).[35] Overhearing the conversation, the police arrest Tosca for racism. In Brazil, racist hate speech is a punishable offense yet is rarely prosecuted. The telenovela critiques and punishes Tosca not for holding racist views but rather for expressing them. Here the telenovelas serve a pedagogical role, raising awareness of specific social issues, usually within a single telenovela. Starting in the 1990s, the TV Globo network worked actively with writers to strategically insert such "social merchandising" in the narratives. Often writers use the narrative to showcase characters suffering from an injustice and ideal model behaviors. However, this entertainment-education model must also be commercially successful, and the network must stand to profit from the message at hand.[36] Thus, as part of the pedagogical function of teaching audiences how to behave in the modern world, overt racism becomes a barrier in the global neoliberal order.

The telenovela does not address the suffering of those who are impacted by racism, but it again explains away racism as wrong only because it is verbalized.

After the arrest, community members gather to talk about the arrest in terms of its official recognition and punishment as a crime. Brazilian television, as an agent, in part, of the government, frequently engages in social merchandising such as Tosca's arrest. The object is to teach audience members about the punishments in place for racism. However, the incident only addresses overt racism and not inferential or institutional racism. By individualizing racism, the telenovela writers then demonstrate a dismissing of structural racism and the need for public remedies to remedy racism. Thus, these telenovelas largely manage Blackness in a way that does not threaten dominant national narratives around race. When Tosca's son visits his mother in prison, he tells her that she needs to learn that Black, Japanese, white, and Indigenous are all equal.

The telenovela places Tosca as an outlier to Brazilian multiculturalism and racial democracy. The morena, such as Mônica, and the celebration of multiculturalism repeat these tropes of connectivity. Tosca serves as a direct contrast to the *Belíssima*'s image of tolerance and harmony in São Paulo. Later in the same episode, Nikos, a Greek immigrant, recounts his time in Brazil to his fellow countrymen in Greece in terms of harmonious diversity: "Brazil is a very good country. São Paulo is a very large city. It has people from all over the world. Greeks, Italians, Japanese, Arabs, Jews, all live in harmony even Turkish. It's like an octopus. Lots of arms, each one comes from one part, but they all end together."[37] Like Dagmar's boyfriend's statements to his mother, this vision of São Paulo presents a harmonious view of multiculturalism in various ethnic components rather than the racial mixing and merging of mestiçagem. The telenovela thus reifies the image of tolerance and harmony in São Paulo while ignoring the actual racial hierarchy and its effects. Thus, the reliance on multiculturalism evades engagement with structural racism and depoliticizes difference. Thus, here the morena is included in a racial system that relies on acknowledging ethnicity and race, but ignoring racial violence and disparities, especially in regard to Afro-Brazilians. Through incorporation, Blackness can be managed and neutralized.

Especially salient in São Paulo, the Brazilian state's attempts to whiten the Brazilian population produced a multicultural society grounded in diluting Blackness. The recruitment and subsidization of European immigrants in the late nineteenth and early twentieth centuries further linked whiteness with modernity, progress, and civilization. More than three million immigrants, primarily from Portugal, Italy, Spain, as well as large numbers of Japanese, Syrian, Lebanese, and European Jews came to Brazil. São Paulo was the main destination of European immigration. Through immigration, Brazilian elites hoped that the mixed Blackness would be further diluted. As Oliveira Vianna's introduction to the 1920 census, he proclaimed that Europeans were "influencing powerfully the reduction of the index of Blackness (*nigrescência*) of our people."[38] Hemispherically, immigration policies, both in terms of incentives for certain racialized groups and the exclusion of other groups, demonstrate understandings of belonging and which bodies are desirable. Yet, the local is also important to consider as the concentration of immigrants in particular regions, such as São Paulo and other parts of southern Brazil, also implicitly tie in notions of modernity and development with race. As São Paulo remains Brazil's economic engine, it maintains its regional identity built on whiteness and modernity within a nation that emphasizes racial mixture. Epitomizing the vision of Brazilian progress, modernity, and whiteness, São Paulo's opposite is Blackness and backwardness.

Mônica's function as the morena gives the telenovela a vision of mestiçagem through her physical appearance and her marriage to Cemil. At the end of the same episode, Mônica attends the celebration of Cemil's parents' fortieth wedding anniversary, evidently pregnant by Cemil. His large extended family consists of Arab, Greek, and Jewish relatives, reflecting a multicultural picture of Brazil that contrasts with Alberto's single-ethnicity family, and presents an image of diversity, tolerance, and acceptance. Immigrant groups such as Arab and Jewish immigrants have had to negotiate to be in the desirable white category.[39] Nonetheless, they are not part of the Blackness that the Brazilian state had hoped to ameliorate, and Cemil's biological father is Greek, which is considered unassailably white. Unlike Mônica's family with the allusion to her nonwhite mother, *Belíssima*'s ideal modern multicultural family protects whiteness through diversity discourses and images. This emphasis dehistoricizes and renders invisible the racial inequalities. Within mixed families, the disproportionate affection and privileging of children with lighter skin and straighter hair demonstrates how the family itself fortifies racial hierarchies.[40] The emphasis on racial mixing by the children of and union of women of African descent with white men assures the whitening of the nation while maintaining white patriarchy.

Belíssima's focus on first- and second-generation immigrants in São Paulo also harkens back to early twentieth century ideas that encouraged European immigration to remake Brazil as a whiter nation through just such intermarriages as Mônica's to Cemil. Thus, the narratives of European immigration and intermarriage link to paintings, such *A Redenção de Cam*, in which Blackness will be diluted through the reproduction of mixed-race women and European men. The telenovela commodification of the morena body thereby protects white supremacy and bolsters white male authority through an emphasis on

Mônica (Camila Pitanga) celebrates her pregnancy along with other
expecting couples in her family in *Belíssima* (2005–2006).
Courtesy of TV Globo.

her reproductive ability. Rather, the telenovela's construction of mestiçagem
presents the potential of an imagined racially unified nation in the early 2000s,
when increasing contestations to racial democracy emerged.

Paraíso Tropical: The *Mulata*,
Eroticized and Devalued Blackness

In *Paraíso Tropical*, Olavo and Daniel both vie to be the designated successor to their childless employer, Antenor Cavalcanti, taking control of his vast
hotel business when he dies. In the course of the telenovela, Antenor decides
to try to produce an heir with his white girlfriend. Olavo has no scruples and
launches various plots against Daniel and Antenor. He is involved with Bebel,
a *mulata* sex worker played by Camila Pitanga. Bebel loves Olavo and hopes
he will rescue her from prostitution. They try to convince Antenor that he has
fathered a child with Bebel and to use this to gain power over him, although
the child is Olavo's.

The *mulata* figure, as represented by Bebel, is the object of both Antenor's
and Olavo's desire. She is simultaneously a danger displayed by her scheming, a
potential proof of racial democracy, and a threat to the whitening of the nation.

From Xica da Silva, an iconic historical figure famous for rising from slave status to slave owner and immortalized in literature, film, and a 1996 telenovela, to Bebel, the colonial and postcolonial narratives of the *mulata* rely on the use of sexual relationships between *mulata* mistresses and white wealthy men. As the moral white women's opposite, *mulata* figures typically appear as sensual seductresses like Bebel, who pursues sexual relationships with white men for ambition or merely for her own insatiable sexual desire. In *Paraíso Tropical*, Brazil is a sexual paradise filled with available women, a natural paradise of wild beauty, music, happiness, exoticness, and racial mixing. Bebel, as a *mulata* figure, symbolizes Brazil itself as an exploitable sexual paradise. At the same time, the telenovela demystifies this tropical paradise by displaying sex tourism and middle- and upper-class discontent.

With the title and imagery of a tropical paradise, the series opening pans over images of Rio de Janeiro and lush green landscapes. Antenor's hotel business, the Grupo Cavalcanti, representing the forces of global capital centralized in Rio de Janeiro, comes into conflict with Northeastern Bahia when Daniel seeks to restrain brothel activities and sex tourism in Brazil. The telenovela's focus on domestic sex tourism offer a darker internal vision of Brazil. At the same time, it reinforces stereotypical hypersexual images of women of color through the role of Bebel. As the Brazilian government began to advertise tourism abroad in the 1960s and 1970s, the sexually available *mulata* became a national product for the marketing and image making of Brazil abroad.[41] While criticism regarding sex tourism promotions led governmental tourism agencies to focus on the natural beauty and landscape of Brazil rather than on the sexual availability of women since the 1990s, the tropes persist in cultural products like *Paraíso Tropical*.[42]

Paraíso Tropical opens in Bahia and later moves to Rio de Janeiro. Most telenovelas are set in Rio de Janeiro or São Paulo, so the setting in Bahia seems notably exotic. Bahia is often celebrated as the locus of Afro-Brazilian traditions and revered as the birthplace of Brazil and its African heritage.[43] It is often used for nationalist purposes cultivating the idea of authentic Black origins, racial harmony, and racial mixing. By using Bahia in the beginning of the telenovela, *Paraíso Tropical* bolsters nation-building narratives.

The image of Bebel as the sexual *mulata* is tightly linked to the idea of Brazil, and to Bahia in particular, as a sexual tropical paradise to be enjoyed and consumed. *Paraíso Tropical* offers Bebel's body as part of the natural pleasures from Brazil, harking back to colonial imaginaries of Brazil as a sexual paradise of beautiful *mulata*s. While the telenovela exposes sex tourism, it does not reveal Bebel's history or delve into the colonial legacies and structural racism that leave women like Bebel with few options. Instead, it suggests Bebel is a product of a tropical paradise. As Kia Caldwell notes, "recent decades have witnessed the *mulata*'s transformation from being a source of national pride to being both an export item and source of tourist revenue . . . the term *mulata* has become synonymous with prostitute for many European men who travel to Brazil for the purposes of sexual tourism."[44] National narratives of the eroticized *mulata* influence these transnational narratives and imaginations. The *mulata* has often functioned as the mythic proof of racial harmony for both internal and external consumption. Bebel epitomizes the *mulata* and reinforces the nationalist and transnational image of Brazil as a racial democracy and racial sexual paradise.

Performing Race through Sound and Sexuality

Bebel was not specifically written as a *mulata*, and the first choice for the role was Mariana Ximenes, a white blonde actor.[45] However, Pitanga's eventual casting led inexorably to the subtle naming of the traces of African descent in the telenovela through performance, narrative tropes, and sound. Subtle cues and markers that draw from narrative tropes, and sensibilities such as performance, sound, and corporality, mark all of Pitanga's roles as mixed-race Black. While Pitanga plays a morena in *Belíssima*, and a hypersexual *mulata* in *Paraíso Tropical*, Blackness and mixedness function in both as tropes. As E. Patrick Johnson writes, Blackness is "contingent, malleable, performative," rather than a biological fact, and the performance of both figures relates to histories of social relations.[46] Pitanga's body reflects denotations of race and colonial history, even when race is not explicitly marked. *Paraíso Tropical* displays hemispheric ideas of mixed Blackness through Bebel's body such that even when the narrative does not overtly claim Blackness, Pitanga's portrayal of Bebel manifests the performance of race.

The production of hypersexuality and the body relies on racial cues. While whiteness is associated with respectability, brownness as signifying an exotic brasilidade is commodified, embodied, and performed. As Mireille Miller Young notes, as Black women put hypersexuality to work within the context of U.S. pornography industries, Bebel here uses her exotic brown body and its association with Black sexuality as a corporeal resource.[47] When the viewer first encounters Bebel, she is wearing a beaded fringed skirt and dancing to vaguely Middle Eastern music as part of a strip tease for male clients at the brothel in Bahia where she works. This use of music and notions of sensual Middle Eastern belly dancing exoticizes Bebel for a clientele that includes Brazilian and foreign tourists.[48] The telenovela uses a colonizing male gaze and deploys exotic imagery in order to market Bebel as a sexual object of desire to the audience. The space of the brothel reinforces colonial racialized and gendered hierarchies in which white male buyers purchase a woman of African descent. The camera's gaze objectifies Bebel's body not only as a sexual object but also as an exotic object of racial difference. Bebel stands as a gendered brown body that is both different and familiar, and her sexualization evokes the *mulata* figure.

The music linked to Bebel furthers this Black hypersexuality and sonically affiliates Bebel with the *mulata* figure. Every character besides Bebel has an English song associated with them on the international soundtrack. The first is "Vatapá" by Danilo Caymmi and the second is "Não Enche" (Don't bother me) by Caetano Veloso. Both of these songs are upbeat and have a pronounced Brazilian rhythm, while white characters are associated with more subdued melodies. Both songs invoke historical Brazilian national identity and samba specifically, which have exalted the sensuality of the *mulata* since the broad nationalization of samba in the 1930s.[49] "Vatapá," in particular, cites Bahia itself and the locale's status as the site of Brazil's African heritage, with lyrics such as

> Quem quiser vatapá
> Que procure fazer
> Primeiro o fubá
> Depois o dendê
> Procure uma nêga baiana
> Que saiba mexer
>
> (Whoever wants *vatapá*
> First the fubá
> After the dendê
> Look for a Black Bahian woman
> Who knows how to stir.)

Vatapá is a dish local to Bahia, and the image of a dark-skinned Bahian woman in a white dress selling *acarajé* and *vatapá* has become ubiquitous in tourist brochures and popular imagery. The song serves to reinforce the mythologizing of Blackness and racial democracy in Brazil, because Bahia is regarded as one of the birthplaces of racial mixing. Caymii names the ingredients for making *vatapá*, emphasizing the importance of a Black Bahian woman, a *nêga baiana* (*nêga* is a colloquial variation of "negra"). The ubiquitous image of the *vatapá* or *acarajé* vendor has conferred a sense of authenticity on the cooking of Bahian women, and the *baiana* (literally a woman from Bahia but popularly imagined as linked to Afro-Brazilian street food vendors, Candomblé, and samba) is a symbol of Bahia and its connotations as the birthplace of Brazil and tradition. *Vatapá* has

African roots, as the inclusion of *fubá* and *dendê* oil suggest. Thus, the song's association with Bebel emphasizes her *brasilidade*. Bebel's body stands in for the lack of mobility in favor of an emphasis on her body as the holder of Brazilian tradition as demonstrated by race. The song notes her authentic Otherness, as does her colorful costuming and playful vocabulary disassociated with the white urban modernity of Rio de Janeiro and São Paulo. By associating Bebel with *vatapá*, the telenovela claims African roots for her.

Caetano Veloso's "Não Enche" emphasizes Bebel's suspicious character. The lyrics include words such as *perua, piranha, harpia, aranha, pirata, malandra, vagaba,* and *vampira,* which invoke prostitution, gold diggers, and loose and untrustworthy women. The upbeat and highly rhythmic nature of the song masks the strongly gendered language. Caetano Veloso's male voice addresses the female subject in a denigrating manner, warning others of the dangers associated with involvement with a woman like Bebel. While *Paraíso Tropical* features other female villains, all of whom are white, none of these characters have songs with such negative imagery associated with them. This reflects, in part, the normalization of the use of denigrating, gendered language for women of African descent. "Não Enche" typically plays when Bebel is engaging in sexual activities, dancing, or attempting to attract male attention. The camera's focus on Bebel's body and the song's lyrics relegate Bebel's body to a commodity with the mythologized traits of her racialized sexualized *mulata* archetype.

Bebel's African origins haunt the telenovela with a hypersexuality mapped onto the mixed-Black body. In particular, there are multiple meaning associated with the line "Que sabe mexer" (Knows how to stir) in "Vatapá." *Mexer* is also associated with the bodily movement of dancing and swaying. The camera often focuses on Bebel's swaying hips as she dances or walks. Bebel sways her hips when she seeks male admiration, as in a scene when she seeks the attention of Jáder, a prospective client. In such scenes, Bebel evokes the myth of the racialized sexualized *mulata* who expresses her power through corporal performance. Although the music is not diegetic, Bebel appears to respond to its rhythms, which naturalizes Bebel as part of Brazil's tropical nature, landscapes, and Afro-Brazilian influenced music.

As the camera traces Bebel's hips and buttocks, the audience sees Bebel from Jáder's point of view, an object of desire. Here the camera participates in what Laura Mulvey identifies as the means by which film transforms the body from a subject into an object of desire—fragmenting it into eroticized parts, and thereby dehumanizing it.[50] The verb *mexer* also conveys blending. Therefore, *mexer* is linked to the mythologized sexual pleasures of miscegenation that have constituted the Brazilian nation.

The literal and figurative incorporation of darker bodies into the dominant Brazilian lighter body enables nation building through the telenovela, touching off a process that is modeled symbolically through sex and eating, the song "Vatapá" suggests. The telenovela uses Pitanga's body to sell access to pleasure and to the idea of the Brazilian nation that is associated with memories of miscegenation. Thus, it enacts what bell hooks describes: "When race and ethnicity become commodified as resources for pleasure the culture of specific groups, as well as the bodies of individuals, can be seen as constituting an alternative playground where members of dominating races, genders, sexual practices affirm their power-over in intimate relation with the Other."[51] While Brazil promotes the idea of a united multiracial body as nation, the idea of Otherness still remains. The othering of the Black body occurs through the exotification of the Black body in Bahia, known as the Blackest region in Brazil. Bebel's differentiation from the other white characters are linked to the song, her body, her sensual movement, and her racial origins.

Failures of Social Ascension: Consumerism and Becoming a "Mulher de Categoria"

Within the realm of who is marriageable and, thereby, respectable, white femininity is ideal. At the very least, a morena, must possess remarkable qualities that demonstrate she can be whitened and is thereby marriageable to a white man. In *Paraíso Tropical*, Bebel does not display the marriageability of the morena and instead falls into the *mulata* trope. Although Olavo falls for Bebel, taking their relationship out of the context of the brothel, their relationship still falls into a pattern of concubinage. Olavo continues to call on Bebel for sex on demand. Olavo gives Bebel a taste of an upper-class lifestyle, spurring her desire to enter that world, and she attempts to dress, behave, and talk like women of the elite class. Yet, despite her efforts, her lack of knowledge of mannerisms and social cues as well as her nonstandard grammar give her away. For example, her mispronunciation of "mulher de categoria" (high-class woman) as "mulher de catiguria" gives away the fact that she was not born into high social standing.

Bebel's desire to be a "madame" (lady) or a "mulher de categoria" intersects with ideologies of class and race. While presenting Bebel as sensual and sexually desirable, the telenovela rarely labels her as beautiful, in keeping with the cultural association of beauty with proper white femininity and upper-class conduct and sensuality with Blackness. In order for Bebel to move from *gostosa* (which literally translates as tasty, but often means sexually desirable) to a woman who is *linda* (pretty) like Vivian (Olavo's fiancée), she must demonstrate that she can acquire the customs and taste of the upper class. As Pierre Bourdieu argues, the powerful decide what is tasteful in terms of dress, style, music, and language.[52] In Brazil, where the upper class is predominantly white, cultural notions state that working-class and Afro-Brazilian culture lack taste and exist, pathologically, outside of the modern civilizing Brazilian imaginary. Unlike the morena figure of Mônica in *Belíssima*, Bebel struggles to conform to these standards. Although Mônica had to learn these upper-class customs, the telenovela shows that she gradually and naturally could fit into a higher economic class. The excessive *mulata* body and sexuality need to be repressed in order to become palatable in an upper-class white world. Bebel, as a *mulata* instead of a morena, cannot thereby assimilate into the ideal national body politic.

Consumption plays a significant role in Bebel's attempt to demonstrate that she has enough potential and knowledge to enter into a higher class and to surmount racialized and gendered class–based discrimination. Here *Paraíso Tropical* enacts an important role common in Brazilian telenovelas, which is the creation and broadcasting of the idea of the consumer-citizen. As Heloísa Buarque de Almeida argues, telenovelas serve the purpose of promoting not only consumption but also the desire for consumption. The desire to consume certain goods matched with economic ability becomes a central part of participating in Brazilian society as a consumer.[53] Armed with Olavo's authorization to spend money on goods in the shopping mall, Bebel taps into Brazil's consumerist desires and the idea that money whitens in Brazil.

For Bebel, consumption becomes a means to attempt to gain a higher social status despite her marginalization in dominant society. Thus, as people of African descent have historically been shut out from paths to wealth, Bebel's ability to purchase whatever goods she wishes is a form of resistance to this racialized consumption. Rather than focusing on social inequalities as a problem, the telenovela individualizes Bebel's struggle to ascend into a higher-class status. However, when entering the store, Bebel wearing a denim miniskirt and midriff-baring top marking her as low class and accompanied by her Black friend, Tatiana, Bebel is already racialized and classed as not belonging. The saleswoman treats her disrespectfully and tells Bebel that she must have entered the wrong store. As Néstor García Canclini indicates, the contemporary subject utilizes the rituals of consumption to enact citizenship.[54] Teresa Pires do Rio Caldeira points out that the consumption of luxury goods by the lower and working classes threatens the boundaries between social classes.[55]

Bebel is denied the satisfaction of citizenship through consumption, but Olavo brings Bebel back to the same store with him and demands that the saleswoman who insulted her the day before treat her with respect. Bebel is wearing similar clothing, which suggests women of color may always be excluded from consumerist settings such as this expensive store. After having the saleswoman bring out many items, Bebel decides that she does not want to purchase any of the goods and thereby, asserts her position of choice and of power. However, only a white man could confer this position on her.

While Mônica in *Belíssima* demonstrates this consumer citizenship through white men, Mônica, in contrast to Bebel, is already respectable and hence, a morena, not a *mulata*. Thus, Bebel has only herself to blame for her disposability while the morena emerges as a figure of racial and sexual discipline, the capacity to whiten, and the promise of capital. In *Paraíso Tropical*, disciplinary power is enacted through normalization and respectability. Determined to acquire *categoria* (slang for high class and quality), Bebel hires Virgínia to give her etiquette lessons. In comedic scenes, Bebel learns which silverware to use, how to hold her dining utensils, and how to chew properly at a formal dinner. Bebel is constructed as a character that audiences are meant to laugh at, whereas Mônica is a character that audiences are meant to empathize with and understand.

Yet, these scenes not only trace Bebel's narrative arc as she strives to assimilate to upper-class manners, but educate the viewers themselves. Telenovelas frequently function to create codes of behavior in Brazil, bringing the Brazilian masses to upper-class etiquette and into the matrix of Brazilian society.[56] Just as when Vivian, the sex worker in the Hollywood film *Pretty Woman* (1990) accompanies the wealthy businessman Edward to the horse races, Bebel is the sensation of the party. Like *Pretty Woman*, the telenovela alludes to the *Pygmalion* (1913) and *My Fair Lady* (1956) concept—if Bebel dresses in designer clothes and takes etiquette classes, she will exude beauty and class and therefore will be presentable to high society. Yet Bebel, through rehearsed social phrases taught by her etiquette coach, demonstrates that her social status is an artificial performance and not innate. At the party, she attracts the attention of Urbano, a wealthy businessman, thereby igniting Olavo's jealousy. The telenovela suggests that beauty and categoria can potentially be learned but never naturalized, and Bebel can obtain upper-class status only through the sexual economy.

Thus, Bebel's use of her relationship with Olavo to gain mobility narrates exchanges between white wealthy influential men and young women of color who trade their sexuality for financial wealth. As Donna Goldstein argues, the white enslaver in Gilberto Freyre's narrative of interracial sex is reinvented as the *coroa* (a wealthy white man) and thus codifies the fantasy of interracial sex and sets up contemporary paradigms of the sexual economy. This coroa fantasy presented as a color-blind racial democracy translates interracial sex as a lack of racism. Black and brown women pursue these fantasies to enact their own sexual commodification.[57] While Bebel's strategy of upward mobility opens up a space of agency, it ultimately relies on her sexual desirability. Furthermore, Bebel's access to this beauty and categoria is not inherent but rather temporally performed. Thus, material luxuries and etiquette classes cannot ultimately contain or discipline the *mulata* body. Bebel's later demise in the telenovela and her continual sexual exploits and manipulation delink her from whiteness and solidify her role as a *mulata*.

Audience Affect: Not the Mocinha's Fairytale

The popularity of Bebel's character soared far beyond TV Globo's expectations, with audiences calling for further development of Bebel in the script. This popularity evidences the character's affective implications, as the potential for subaltern spectatorship demonstrates their value. The writers who had scripted Bebel as a villain bowed to the pressure of viewers who sympathized with the *garota de programa* (an oblique term for prostitute, literally translated as a date girl). Audiences identified with Bebel's low economic status, vulnerability, and ambition to climb out of her economic situation. They aspired to her success through attracting a wealthy man. Donna Goldstein's research finds that lower-class women of African descent internalize such narratives, since the fantasy "plays with the ideology of whitening [and] illustrates a perfectly ambiguous romantic relationship in which women expect to gain materially while they play out the sexualized role of *mulata*."[58] The telenovela capitalizes on the affective desires and investments in the promises of upward mobility and racial democracy.

Bebel, in part through the physical appearance of Camila Pitanga, constructs sentiments of belonging through mestiçagem. The show's website on Globo identifies a crucial point of identification with Bebel: Camila Pitanga's phenotype is associated with affective notions of Brazilian unity. "Inside and outside the studios, inside and outside the country, Camila Pitanga is adored by everyone, all ages, all classes and social levels. . . . The color of our people, the color of our beloved country. She became a national sensation, reference for the Brazilian woman. For the scriptwriter, Ricardo Linhares, the success of Bebel is due precisely to this—'She is the face of Brazil.'"[59] For audiences, Bebel emerged as the literal representation of Brazilian identity and mestiçagem. Audience adoration can be read as part of their desire for social and cultural citizenship through visibility on television.

Bebel (Camila Pitanga), initially represented as a villainous sex worker with a minor role, soon became a fan favorite in *Paraíso Tropical* (2007) and catapulted Pitanga into stardom. Courtesy of TV Globo.

The fantasy of *mulata* mobility and the aestheticization of *mulata* sensuality also became forms of affective capital. Viewers began to imitate Bebel's style of dress and her colloquial linguistic mode. Although telenovelas often popularize fashion trends across Brazil, they typically funnel the fashions popular with the elite classes to cheaper imitations for the lower classes.[60] In contrast, the fashion popularized by Bebel comes not from an imitation of the upper-classes, but through an imitation of marginalized sexualized women. As an *O Globo* article notes, "numa trama cheia de gente muito chique, é a prostituta que está ditando moda" (in a story full of very chic people, it is a prostitute who is dictating fashion).[61] The distinctive fashion that Bebel uses in the early episodes is also a mark of a small amount of agency both for her character and for viewing audiences. However, Bebel effectively whitens herself as she tries to become part of Rio de Janeiro's high society through Olavo and wealthy white patrons, embracing designer fashion without markers of local Brazilian elements or of Afro-Brazilian culture, and wearing her hair straight. Although Bebel's signature styles rely on the notion of a *mulata* aesthetic, her character repeatedly attempts to assimilate to white upper-class norms. Yet, her increasing audience popularity was perhaps because of, rather than despite, her continuous failure to meet these norms. Unlike, Mônica, Bebel ultimately does not succeed. Her excessive *mulata*ness continues to seep out and she cannot pass as a respectable "mulher de categoria." Her continuous failure demonstrates the untenable mark of Blackness in modern Brazil. Yet, this same failure also heartened her to audiences. Her brazen sexuality and her inability to imitate upper-class feminine respectability endeared her to audiences, particularly working-class women. Her failure demonstrates the exclusionary practices of racial democracy. For women prevented from full citizenship, Bebel presents a recognition of their humanity.

Containing Blackness: Sexuality and Nonreproductive Labor

Descending from hemispheric and Brazilian *mulata* narratives of concubinage dating from slavery, Bebel relies primarily on white patrons to sustain herself financially. Using her body as a form of capital in a libidinal economy, Bebel's *mulata* eroticism is a commodity yet also the means through which she attempts to attain mobility and citizenship in the white-dominated Brazilian sphere that excludes her. With the help of one of her clients, Jáder, she leaves Bahia in hope of a better life in Rio de Janeiro.

Bebel idealizes the glamour of Rio de Janeiro that she sees on television and, like many northeastern migrants, she hopes to find upward mobility. However, when she arrives in Rio, she is forced to become a sex worker and Jáder becomes her pimp, while she continues to have sex with him. She attempts to convince Jáder to include her as one of his "garotas para executivos" (girls for executives), which resembles more of a high-end escort service. Pointing out her hair and clothing, he refuses: "top de linha são universitárias . . . educadas e não uma quenga vindo do interior, que tem cheiro de rua, não sabe falar, nem pegar num talher . . . tem que ter categoria" (the top of the line are university students, educated and not a worthless prostitute from the interior that has the odor from the street, that doesn't know how to speak properly).[62] Bebel tricks Jáder and switches with a woman that he usually sends for Olavo. Jáder verbally and physically punishes her for this, threatening to push her out the window, and then he locks her in the apartment. Bebel's imprisonment evokes master-slave relationships in which the control of her body, mobility, and sexuality are under patriarchal rule.

While furthering the fantasy of finding a wealthy man to help her escape her social position, Bebel is also highly aware of her differentiated racial and class status. She frequently refers to her distinction from Olavo's experience of white blonde women, referring to other escorts and his fiancée, Alice. He often calls Bebel "cachorra" (hot bitch). Their relationship eroticizes race, and he finds Bebel more sexually attractive than his white girlfriends. The comparisons between the hypersexuality of Bebel and the refinement and upper-class status of Alice desexualize Alice. As Alice does not sexually satisfy Olavo, she furthers the association of whiteness solely for marriage and the *mulata* for sex. As Alvaro Jarrín argues, whiteness is defined by its opposite—the eroticized *mulata* and, furthermore, this whiteness distinguishes itself from nonwhite bodies through an emphasis on beauty enacted through proper discipline and regime rather than the natural excessiveness of the *mulata*.[63] Coping with her oppression, Bebel also refutes hegemonic ideals of white beauty and flaunts her superiority and comments to Olavo, "Ah, bem que dizem, né, que branca azeda pega ruga cedo. Falta de melancholia" (They say that white skin gets wrinkles early. A lack of melancholy).[64] However, Olavo ridicules her and points out it is *melanina* (melanin) not *melancolia* (melancholy). The telenovela's framing of Bebel's linguistics as odd, infantile, and humorous consistently undercuts her small displays of agency and excludes her from a shared Brazilian modernity.

Stemming from tropes of the impulsive, manipulative, and jealous *mulata* of *O Cortiço*'s Rita Baiana, Bebel reifies the *mulata* archetype that wishes to break up white heterosexual unions. Bebel sets up a plan to sabotage Olavo's wedding. She hires Betina, a white garota de programa, to seduce him and arranges for Alice to find them and call off the wedding. When Olavo learns of her subterfuge, Bebel kneels and begs for forgiveness from Olavo. Meanwhile, Urbano, Bebel's other lover, finds out about Bebel's plan and falls for Betina instead. Urbano and Betina leave for New York together while Bebel is forced to go back to the street as a sex worker. While Bebel is punished, Betina's Cinderella fairy tale comes true with Urbano. Although Bebel loves Olavo, as both romance and upward mobility are coded as white, only whiteness can be rewarded.

As a *mulata*, Bebel demonstrates the biopolitical management of race so that her reproductive capacities, as a harbinger of undesired Blackness, are controlled. Bebel subsequently learns she is pregnant with Olavo's child. However, her small signs of joy are mitigated by Olavo, who does not share Bebel's rejoice and schemes to use her pregnancy for his own ends. Instead of the morena's reproduction as a beacon to the whitening project of the nation, Bebel, as a *mulata*, represents a Blackness that is wanted only for its sexual availability and not reproduction. Olavo sends her to seduce his boss, Antenor, so that they can pass the child off as his and make certain that Antenor will pay for the baby's support. Olavo falsifies a DNA test performed during the pregnancy, and Antenor makes Bebel his virtual prisoner enclosed within a private residence so he can monitor her behavior to maximize the baby's health. Bebel willingly participates in Olavo's manipulations and trickery, which gives her a small degree of agency, but she must rely completely on her ability to sexually please white men. Furthermore, Bebel's financial vulnerability does not offer her much choice. Yet Antenor does not see Bebel as a mother, but rather as the reproductive labor that will birth his child. At one point, he even pleads with Lúcia to help raise Bebel's child, but she rejects this proposal and temporarily leaves him. The raising of children for the nation is through a white woman or the morena.

The legitimacy of motherhood through adherence to respectable racialized femininity is maintained in telenovelas. Meanwhile, *mulata* sexuality, as associated with Blackness, immorality, and deviance, is punished for attempting to break social norms and the larger project of branqueamento. As such, the *mulata* is for sex, not procreation. During the pregnancy, Olavo dies, and Bebel is put in jail for helping him with illegal activities. As she attempts to escape the police, she falls and subsequently miscarries. Apprehending her in the attempt, the police officer says to her, "perdeu, piranha" (you lost piranha—a derogatory term for women). Subjecting her to this treatment, and the insensitive way the telenovela treats her miscarriage, points to the devaluation of *mulata* women. Descending from the colonial period, the linkages between sex work and race are already etched in the popular imagination and further, harking back to eugenics, both Black female bodies and sex workers are associated with degeneracy and deviancy. Female bodies of African descent are already marked as inherently violable and thereby are justifiably dehumanized. Hence, Bebel's miscarriage and her violent apprehension act as a form of disciplining of mixed Blackness and a management of racial boundary making.

White heteropatriarchy relies on the disposability of women of African descent and the legitimacy of white families. The narrative bestows on Antenor's white wife, Lúcia, the right to give him an heir. This narrative of juxtaposed miscarriage and birth allows for the telenovela to differentiate women fit to be mothers of the Brazilian nation and women who are excluded from the white moral ideal. Telenovelas fetishize motherhood as the pinnacle of respectability for women; therefore, denying Bebel this opportunity is significant. White men continue to lay claim to women's bodies, but the construction of a family including a whitened child, as representing the Brazilian nation, is now absent.

Like *O Cortiço*'s Rita Baiana, she is represented as responsible for the downfall of white men. While the men in Bebel's life have sex with her willingly, she receives all the blame in the narrative. Rather than an admonishment of Olavo and Antenor for cheating on their fiancées, Bebel bears the brunt of condemnation. As punishment for not adhering to codes of morality and for exerting her sexual power, Bebel is barred from the narrative of whitening. Bebel's racialized sexual difference becomes an unredeemable difference that positions her outside of the white upper- and middle-class standards. Her miscarriage and fall from grace in jail are violent but are justified by her *mulata* status. Furthermore, the death of an unborn child had already occupied a structural position of worthlessness due to Bebel's *mulata* Blackness. Unlike Mônica in *Belíssima*, Bebel does not have future biological progeny. Therefore, the future of the nation does not lie in the womb of the *mulata* figure.

The narrative presents a number of white female characters of higher moral status than Bebel. In addition to Betina, whose seduction of Olavo the narrative forgives, Paula and Ana Luísa provide this contrast to Bebel's sexual promiscuity. Paula moves to Rio de Janeiro from Bahia for love; Bebel moves for money, which she pursues through deceit and manipulation. Paula engages in premarital sex, but the narrative rewards her whiteness and goodness with marriage and upward mobility. Bebel, however, recognizes and acquiesces to the limits of her identity and the boundaries of whiteness. She knows her place in society, and while that place may be to serve, comfort, guide, or entice white men, it is never to occupy the space of a wife. Unlike the morena figure such as Mônica, the *mulata* as represented by Bebel does not fit into ideas of mobility through marriage.

Yet Bebel captured the public imagination in a way that Mônica did not. Bebel, who was originally a secondary character, stole the attention away from *Paraíso Tropical*'s main white mocinha, Paula. Many audience members rooted for Bebel's happiness despite her having been scripted as an immoral nemesis. Viewers demanded that the writers give Bebel a happy ending.[65] The writers delivered, but without liberating her from the impetus to be sexually desirable. Bebel embezzles millions from a corrupt politician, and in so doing becomes a national celebrity, as rich as she desired. However, she must use her wily sexuality to take advantage of the politician. The final shot shows Bebel under the assumed name of Sra. Francisbel dos Santos Batista. While dressed in a large white fur-trimmed suit with her hair straightened into a bun evocative of Evita, Bebel appears testifying in court against corruption charges. In a conflation of fiction and reality, Bebel's character is reminiscent of the journalist, Mônica Veloso, who was the mistress of Senator Renan Calheiros. As Bebel calls out to her photographer friends and smiles for the camera, "Não Enche" plays in the background one last time. Thus, the telenovela suggests that Bebel is still a gold digger. The charges she faces suggest that she is still of low moral value. At the same time, the telenovela's satiric scenes of Bebel in court present a critique of the Brazilian judicial and political systems. Bebel is no worse than many members of the elite occupying political office.

The telenovela writers foreclosed possibilities for Bebel by denying her motherhood and portraying her as corrupt even in the final scenes she appears. As an embodied *mulata* who engages in sex without procreation and who represents promiscuity and immorality, Bebel continues to threaten respectability. While ignoring the structural barriers and the regimes of whiteness that prohibit Bebel from entering into full citizenship, the narrative continues to differentiate Bebel as inherently other from the normative white mocinhas, such as Paula. Bebel's Blackness is ideologically and physically contained and situated only in the sphere of sexuality.

Bebel's potential agency is expanded and delimited within the tensions between sexual capital and Black female respectability. At the end of the court session, Bebel announces that she will pose nude in *Playboy*. Her body and sexuality are still paramount to her success, but she chooses to exercise them as power rather than being exploited by others. Furthermore, by telling the judge that it will be an artistic nude, which connotes glamour instead of sexual availability, Bebel distances herself from vulgarity. While the telenovela reinforces

Bebel as overtly sexual, the ending also possibly gives a new opening where it is not only the mocinha, a white good girl like Paula, who can achieve happiness. Rather, Bebel, through her own manipulation and planning, uses her femininity and sexuality to gain upward mobility. Pitanga's performance as Bebel offers opportunities for pleasure that may reinforce racialized and gendered oppression while also interfering with these same systems. Audiences, already rooting for Bebel, then might find pleasure in subverting a hierarchal class, race, and gender-based system. In one reading, Bebel's rise is one of liberation, a rags-to-riches narrative based on a neoliberal rhetoric of individualism, as the telenovela does not present the racial, class, and gender barriers to mobility. The erotics of racial performance and representation appropriates this trope of the *mulata* while countering dominant narratives. Nonetheless, Bebel never does escape the primacy of the *mulata* trope as an agent of pleasure whose social status depends on liaisons with white men.

Telenovela romance narratives have only recently begun to include Afro-Brazilian women at all as major characters with the first protagonists occurring both in 2009 with Camila Pitanga as Rose in *Cama de Gato* (Cat's Cradle) and Taís Araújo in *Viver a Vida* (Seize the Day). However, these romance narratives rely on foundational fictions of star-crossed lovers along with ideologies of social whitening and tropes of Black female sexuality. Gender and racial inequalities are naturalized while the telenovelas focus on the individual paths to mobility for these characters. Thus, for the *mulata* figure, the narrative emphasizes their eroticized and racialized physical attractiveness. For the morena figure, the narrative follows a racial self-transformation through branqueamento and marriage to white men. For both, only relationships with white men can provide economic gain. Corporeality, the use of flesh for reproduction or for sexual pleasure, informs how citizenship is constituted. Therefore, telenovelas also function as technologies of citizenship, which create a vision of proper citizenship according to racial, gender, and sexual norms.

Alternate Endings to Multiculturalism

Telenovelas like *Porto dos Milagres* (2001; Port of Miracles) and *Duas Caras* (2007; Two Faces) present a politics of renegotiation of Black pride rather than a whitening of the characters or a hypersexualization of the *mulata* figure. In contrast to *Paraíso Tropical*'s oversexed and desirable *mulata* and *Belíssima*'s morena, these telenovelas' mixed female figures become *mães de santo*—leaders of a *terreiro de candomblé* (religious community). Candomblé, an African-derived syncretic religion, has followers across racial spectrums, but it is most closely associated with Afro-Brazilian populations. As mães de santo leading Candomblé communities, they transcend the context of heteropatriarchy as there is no sex and marriage conjunction or sex and mistress linkage in their representation. Thus, the transformation of Andréia and Esmeralda from sexualized figures into spiritual figures helps strip the *mulata* from hypersexualization, further associates her with Afro-Brazilian culture, turning her into a leader. Furthermore, unlike samba or other Afro-Brazilian cultural forms, Candomblé has largely not been co-opted by the state as part of Brazil's multicultural identity. Instead, due to its centering of Black knowledge production, Candomblé is also a site of resistance to white hegemony and the incorporation of Blackness. Thus, the *mulata*, as an emblem of racial democracy, and her relationship to Candomblé in these telenovelas offers a form of resistance to racial democracy narratives.

This transformation also further associates the *mulata* with Afro-Brazilian roots. Andréia and Esmeralda stand out as nonwhite characters in *Porto dos Milagres* and *Duas Caras*, both of which came under criticism for their lack of Black characters. *Porto dos Milagres* was set in a small town in Bahia, a region with the largest population of African descent in Brazil. Although based on a Jorge Amado novel with numerous characters of African descent, the cast was overwhelmingly white. *Duas Caras* is based in a favela, and most residents of these neighborhoods are of African descent. While both of these telenovelas had more actors of African descent than most telenovelas, the majority of the casts were white. Aguinaldo Silva, the screenwriter for both *Porto dos Milagres* and *Duas Caras*, was a vocal critic of Senator Paulo Paim's proposal of a law to impose minimum quotas for the casting of Afro-Brazilian actors. Silva argued that to require that 25 percent of television parts and 40 percent of advertising parts go to Afro-Brazilians would limit creativity and that actors considered white were, like most Brazilians, actually *mestiço* (mixed).[66] While both telenovelas incorporate Afro-Brazilian cultural elements, *Porto dos Milagres* and *Duas Caras* ultimately privilege whiteness while using discourses and practices of mestiçagem to obscure this very privilege.

In both telenovelas, other desires and ambitions distract the *mulata* figure from Candomblé. In *Duas Caras*, Andréia, played by Débora Nascimento, is chosen as the samba queen for the upcoming Carnival procession. As samba is very much associated with the *mulata* figure, Andréia's performance suggests she is a *mulata*. Various men desire her in the telenovela, and her body is often put on display. As the samba queen, she ascends the pinnacle of brasilidade, sensuality, and desirability.[67] Dona Setembrina, the mãe de santo leader of the terreiro, repeatedly tells Andréia that her destiny is in the terreiro rather than the Sambódromo. Andréia resists, but when Dona Setembrina dies and Andréia breaks her leg right before her performance, she complies. Her transformation into a mãe de santo is her destiny chosen by the *orixás* (deities).

In *Porto dos Milagres*, Esmeralda, played by Camila Pitanga, relentlessly pursues the white fisherman, Guma, even to the point of breaking up his friendships and his relationship with his white love interest, the wealthy Lívia. Although she continuously rejects the advances of Guma's Black friend, Foninho, she uses him to buy material goods and dresses in hopes of attracting Guma. She tells Guma he has nothing in common with Lívia because she's a *branquela* (white girl) who did not grow up in Porto dos Milagres. However, she vows that if Guma wants a princess, she will transform into one by using Foninho to buy items for her. Like Bebel, Esmeralda attempts to fashion herself after a white woman in hopes of gaining her love interest's favor. Esmerelda, like Bebel, is a hypersexual *mulata* figure. Her white father often comments that he has suffered and that Esmeralda is like her mother and attracts too much attention from men. Audiences can infer that Esmeralda's mother, who never appears, is Black and that Esmeralda's passion, desire, and manipulation follow that of her mother.

While Foninho and Guma vow never to have a woman come between them, the triangle with Esmeralda is part of the idea of a racial brotherhood linked through the sexuality of the *mulata* figure. She also thereby represents the manipulative *mulata* seductress. Guma cheats on Lívia, and Esmeralda alleges that she is carrying Guma's baby, which causes a temporary breakup. At the end of the telenovela, Guma is in a terrible accident and Esmeralda promises that she will return to the terreiro if only the deity Iemenjá allows Guma to live. He recovers and Esmeralda, like Andréia, devotes herself to Candomblé and eventually becomes a mãe de santo. Esmerelda then replaces Mãe Ricardina, a very dark-skinned mãe de santo (played by Zezé Motta). Thus, her devotion to Candomblé makes her Blacker, but the face of Afro-Brazilian culture becomes whiter.

The characters of Andréia and Esmeralda begin as typical *mulata* characters as associated with erotic desire but end the telenovelas as mães de santo. As mães de santo, both characters are no longer a sexual threat to white men, white women, or the sanctity of the nation. Their immersion into Candomblé implicitly prevents them from becoming mothers of whiter children and contains the danger of their unbridled sexuality. Yet, their paths perhaps offer an alternative for the *mulata* figure as part of a politics of Afro-Brazilian affirmation as they become spiritual and community leaders. Furthermore, mães de santo, literally translated as "mothers of saints," perhaps suggests procreation. However, this idea of procreation is not rigidly heterosexual and does not adhere to a patriarchal model. Procreation here means the further dissemination of Afro-Brazilian culture. This idea of spiritual mothers, then, actually might leave a potential opening for the *mulata* to form oppositional subjectivities in relation to the nation.

Rather than represent racial democracy, the *mulata* as mãe de santo is a figure of Afro-Brazilian pride and mestiçagem, unrelated to racial democracy. Furthermore, the *mulata* as mãe de santo points to a possible source of feminist agency as Andréia and Esmeralda are no longer objects of desire, but subjects. Unlike their counterparts in *Belíssima* and *Paraíso Tropical,* they achieve agency outside of heteropatriarchal structures—outside the roles of the wife or the mistress. The mixed-race figure is not a vehicle of the nation. Through transformations into mães de santo, they become bodies outside of the nation-state. As in chapter 2's analysis of Pitanga's star text, disidentification with the *mulata* norm and a move toward Blackness unsettles dominant narratives of mestiçagem and racial democracy. The mixed-race figure is placed within historical dimensions of race and nation, yet the fate of the figure is not necessarily predetermined, as the resistant endings in *Paraíso Tropical, Duas Caras,* and *Porto dos Milagres* demonstrate.

Despite the high symbolic value of the mixed-race female figure of African descent in national discourse, the exclusion of women of African descent in telenovelas has also excluded these same women as participatory citizens of the modern nation. The mixed-race figure was largely rearticulated to fit hegemonic ideologies of racial democracy and mestiçagem that minimized structural racism and undercut resistance to these national racial paradigms. By the late 2000s, the recognition of the existence of racism, public debates on racial inequality, and the politicization of Blackness coincided with increased media visibility for actresses of African descent. *Belíssima* and *Paraíso Tropical* help facilitate both the further opening of Afro-Brazilian inclusion in the 2000s and yet help to reign in this inclusion. In TV Globo's *Cama de Gato* (2009–2010), *Insensato Coração* (2011), and *Babilônia* (2015), Pitanga had leading roles as her star power increased. From an office cleaner to a marketing executive to a waitress aspiring to attend medical school, Pitanga's characters display ambition along with a strong work ethic and moral compass. Nonetheless, these roles largely relied on contemporary social ascension through marriages with white wealthy men. In *Babilônia* (2015), Regina rises from her favela surroundings, becomes a successful model and restaurant owner, and marries Vinícius, a white lawyer. In *Insensato Coração,* Carol also marries her older white boss. Meanwhile, Regina's dark Black father is shown as a philanderer and Carol's Black boyfriend and father to her child is also unfaithful and sexually promiscuous.

Disassociating from Black men and marrying white men becomes a form of integration and, hence, containing feared masculine Blackness and safeguarding sexually desirable feminine mixed Blackness. Despite this opening, like the United States, conservative resurgence in the 2010s unleashed backlashes to affirmative action, social reforms, and the gains of Afro-Brazilians. These telenovelas in the mid-2000s then demonstrate an earlier media backlash to increased racial opportunities prior to the open political backlash in 2016.

As the purchasing power of Afro-Brazilians increased in the early 2000s from various economic, political, and social policies, the desire to attract and retain these audiences garnered a wider media visibility within telenovelas. Courting Afro-Brazilian audience members, Globo navigates the tension of including more Afro-Brazilian characters while reinforcing dominant tropes of the *mulata* and morena within the framework of racial democracy. Managing Blackness through the *mulata* and morena tropes, the telenovelas present a narrative of progress that is ultimately only a reworking of conservative racial democracy that ultimately centers whiteness as the ideal. Thus, the mixed-race female figure has and continues to act as a form of racial negotiation and underscores the particularities of mestiçagem as a strategy of managing Blackness.

This management of Blackness is connected hemispherically through representations of mixed-race women of African and European descent. Hence, even when these telenovelas are not necessarily broadcast in the U.S. English-language television market, these telenovelas, like the following U.S. media texts, encapsulate moments in both countries in which legacies of slavery and racial divisions are warped under auspices of racial harmony. Like Brazilian telenovelas, U.S. popular media manages Blackness through the disciplining of sexuality, the alignment of mixed Blackness with white unions, and the erasure of abject Blackness. In the United States, this tension operates as a containment of Blackness or mixedness as a move toward whiteness under the rubric of multiculturalism and postracism. The juxtaposition of popular media texts from Brazil and the United States illuminates the connective racial landscapes within the hemisphere.

4

Reinventing the Mulatta in the United States for the 2000s

Celebrating Diversity amid the Haunting of Blackness

In one of the most infamous sex scenes in Hollywood history, Leticia, a financially struggling death row widow grieving for the loss of her son, hysterically demands, "make me feel good." As she pulls up her shirt to reveal her breasts, she writhes against Hank, a racist executioner who killed her husband. Desperate for carnal entanglement, Leticia feeds into images of the Jezebel seductress unable to contain her sexual urges. With multiple angle shots, jerky cuts to a quivering bird in a cage, and Leticia's loud cries, *Monster's Ball* (2001) depicts a frenzied scene of brown and white skin intertwined. Described by film critics as "raw," "primal," and "graphic," the scene evokes arousal and discomfort as the audience becomes a voyeur. With Halle Berry as Leticia, Berry's star image reignites the mulatta figure as an emblem of carnal desire, tragedy, and racial taboo.

In *The L Word*, wearing a slim black suit while entertaining guests at her art gallery, Bette Porter tilts her head and smiles seductively as the audience takes in Tina's gaze. This seductive tilt brings eroticism to the fore, while Tina, white, blonde, and grasping the arms of her well-to-do boyfriend, tips off the audience through voice-over narration that she is about to take part in her first lesbian relationship. Tina appears as the epitome of white innocent femininity while Bette, with her dark eyeliner and crimson-red lipstick, appears as sensual and dangerous. Their encounters are told in flashback: Bette purposefully touches Tina's ear and notes that Tina almost lost her earring. The camera follows Bette's hands as she strokes Tina's neck and combs her hair back. After losing her earring again, Tina returns to retrieve it the next day, and Bette places her hands over Tina's, caresses her face, and kisses her. Quickly, the camera cuts to Bette kissing another woman, and the audience learns that Bette is cheating on Tina at the same time that Tina is retelling her romance. This scene draws in part from racialized fantasies of the mulatta as sexual seductress.

The film *Monster's Ball* (2001) and the television series *The L Word* (2004–9) are at the center of this chapter. Both exemplify how the depiction of mixed-Black characters and the casting of mixed-Black actresses in the United States have served to manage Blackness. As in Brazilian telenovelas, these two U.S. cultural productions reveal how the historical specter of the mixed-race figure continues to haunt the body politic, how understandings of mixed-race sexuality function as part of hemispheric and national racial narratives, and how concern over the place of Blackness has been inscribed on mixed-race characters.

Like the mixed-race figures in Brazilian telenovelas, the U.S. mulatta figure works within racial and sexual histories but is not necessarily beholden to them. Yet, despite the political immediacy of multiracialism in the early 2000s that focuses on race as a choice, the irrelevancy of race, and multiraciality as stemming from interracial love, the mulatta neither opts out of Blackness nor transcends it. Contradictory desires and attempts to incorporate and contain Blackness within narratives of mestiçagem, multiculturalism, and whitening are all strategies of controlling Blackness as part of hemispheric logics of racial management. Through these strategies, U.S. film and television, like telenovelas, usually contain Blackness, even as spaces of resistance occasionally disrupt these texts.

Both *Monster's Ball* and *The L Word* were produced in the early 2000s, an era when the notion of the extinction of race through racial mixing grew prevalent in the United States. The latest U.S. census had reported that over 6.8 million people self-identified with more than one race. Public discourse around this multiracial group suggested mixing might make race obsolete. For example, former Census Bureau director Martha Farnsworth Riche remarked that the 2000 census would be "the beginning of the end of the overwhelming role of race in our public life"; New America Foundation director Michael Lind pointed to Brazil's dismissal of racial categorization due to the high rates of racial mixture and suggested this might occur in the United States as well; and Census Bureau director Kenneth Prewitt commented that "as the classification system gets fuzzier and blurrier, we're going to have to re-create ourselves as a society without using a set of social policies which are based on race."[1] Noted

Harvard sociologist Orlando Patterson promised that because of racial mixing "by the middle of the next century, the social virus of race will have gone the way of the smallpox."[2] Envisioning the end of the utility of race, these media articulations anticipated the postrace rhetoric that emerged around President Obama's 2008 presidential campaign.

Neoliberals and neoconservatives of this era deployed multiracial figures, the growth of the multiracial population, and certain sectors of the multiracial movement as evidence for the needlessness of race-based public policies and the declining significance of race. As it has in Brazil, embedded structural racism privileging whiteness coincided with beliefs that racial mixture could end racial conflict. Similar to Brazilian popular culture and the use of the *mulata* as attestation to racial democracy, cultural expressions in the United States used mixed-race subjects, especially images of mixed-race women, as proof of racial progress despite the marginalization of African Americans. The diversity encompassed in *Monster's Ball* and *The L Word* left structural inequalities intact, and these visible evidences of multiculturalism operated alongside assaults on racial policies such as affirmative action programs.

In a post–civil rights context, media images of mixed-race Black women operate in a shifting terrain of an upwardly mobile Black middle class and an uneven distribution of capital, education, and opportunities for many other Black populations in the United States. This vision of multiculturalism becomes a tool for validating neoliberal social and economic policies so that the upper-class mulatta figure and the lower-class mulatta might both claim citizenship through interracial relationships and adherence to respectability politics. With the mulatta and fantasies of miscegenation, these media texts largely neglect Black feminist politics, fail to destabilize white norms, and render structural inequalities moot.

Refashioning the Mulatta and Diversity in the U.S. Media Industries of the 2000s

As in Brazilian telenovelas, the U.S. mixed-race female figure resides within the political economy of commercial production, inflected with U.S. sensibilities of diversity and inclusion. Yet while the U.S. culture industries present themselves as bastions of progressive values, their disproportionately white, upper-middle class, and male personnel belie this image. Even when they are present, people of color, women, and people from lower-class backgrounds have less power than others. As Herman Gray contends, the emphasis on media representation eases the compulsion to change labor, economic, and employment structures within these industries.[3] Thus, the stark structural inequalities prevalent in the United States mark the production of film and television.

From the 1970s to the 1990s, shifts in the production and consumption of Hollywood films opened up a model of specialization and niche group-focused films that has been referred to as Indiewood, a hybrid form that combines Hollywood and independent film aesthetics and sectors. By 2000, most major studios had subsidiaries devoted to independent cinema of this type.[4] While Lionsgate, which produced *Monster's Ball*, was not connected to major media conglomerates at the time of the film's release, it was very competitive in the market for producing and distributing films.[5] From 1994 to 2004, the U.S. media industry consolidated into six major transnational conglomerates: Viacom (which owns Showtime's *The L Word*), Time Warner, General Electric, the Walt Disney Company, CBS Corporation, and News Corporation. Despite a small number of nonwhite, female, and queer directors, producers, and writers, white men dominated employment and comparative earnings industry-wide. Meanwhile, women and minorities remained drastically underrepresented in the culture industries compared to their share of the U.S. population and have largely been excluded from institutional power.[6] Partly as a consequence, neither independent film nor cable television necessarily presents a platform for marginalized voices, nor do they challenge national and hemispheric racial narratives that devalue Blackness.

Both *The L Word* and *Monster's Ball* emerged in a period in which film and television producers, studios, and networks strategized to appeal to particular viewerships while adopting expressions of neoliberal multiculturalism. As Sasha Torres notes, the 2000s upsurge of "gay-themed programming" such as *Queer Eye for the Straight Guy* reflects the television industry's "understand[ing] that minoritarian audiences, identities, and subjectivities have now become commodities to trade."[7] Viacom, which owns both Showtime, creator of *The L Word*, and Black Entertainment Television, can profit from the marketing of these minority identities. Television networks tend to target groups with relative privilege and thereby do not necessarily promote the radical reordering of representations. As Jane Arthurs observes, cable channel audiences directly purchase unbundled, such as Showtime and HBO, bring "the audience into a different economic relation to the product [that] . . . allows for a pluralism that recognises previously marginalized cultures, albeit by their ability to pay."[8]

Premium cable television is directed at a demographically desirable high-income, college-educated, active internet user audience. *The L Word* took a new tack by becoming the first series to feature more than two major lesbian characters. With the series focus on white, upper-middle class, and femme characters, Candace Moore calls this strategy a "bivalent lure" to attract straight audiences as well as queer ones.[9] Gary Levine, Showtime's vice president for original programming at the time, admitted as much when he described the show's appeal to heterosexual men as tantamount to that of pornography: "Lesbian sex, girl-on-girl, is a whole cottage industry for heterosexual men."[10] Similarly, Robert Blatt, president of entertainment for Showtime, commented on the casting of actresses such as Jennifer Beals: "Ultimately, we want people everywhere to buy it. So yes, the women are all attractive and we make no apologies about that."[11] While *The L Word* widened the span of identities onscreen, it used a male gaze to link attractiveness with traditional images of femininity and its marketing reinforced white homonormativity.

As in Brazilian telenovelas, U.S. media representations of people of color have increased in visibility, yet these representations generally remain embedded within racialized and gendered legacies that position the mixed-race female figure as a conduit for managing Blackness. Greater media visibility of women of color has not necessarily changed racial and gender hierarchies. As Herman Gray contends, nonwhite characters within cultural expressions often assimilate to white, upper middle-class culture.[12] In the early 2000s, events such as Halle Berry's Oscar win for her part in *Monster's Ball*, the first time a Black woman received the award for best actress, marked a signal of celebratory progress while eliding structural changes not only within the cultural industries but within larger civil society. Television series such as *The L Word* demonstrated the potential of new programs to reorder and critique privilege and to the ways in which these programs also reinscribe hierarchies.

By the early 2000s, the use of the mulatta figure gestures toward promises of diversity while evacuating social, cultural, and political transformation. Scholars such as Ralina Joseph, Catherine Squires, and Caroline Streeter demonstrate that the mixed-race figures have not been dislodged from the U.S. understanding of race, but rather that these figures have been transformed to fit new social, cultural, and political conditions in a post–civil rights era.[13] The mulattas in *Monster's Ball* and *The L Word* maintain certain ideas of racialization through sexuality in different ways. While different forms than Brazilian telenovelas, *Monster's Ball* and *The L Word* contain elements of melodrama with love as a central storyline, exaggeration, mise-en-scène, narratives, characters, and tropes designed to elicit sympathy and revulsion. From the very first U.S. film, *The Birth of a Nation* (1915), to iconic melodrama films such as *Imitation of Life* (1959), the mulatta figure represented a threat to family and nation through her hypersexuality and mental instability. White female sexuality, defined against the image of hypersexual Black women, functioned to further pathologize Black sexuality and uphold white sexuality as the ideal. As the mulatta figure possesses the blood and, thereby, the traits of Black female sexuality, she is also assumed to display promiscuity and sexual availability while simultaneously showcasing exotic beauty through her physical features.

In a post–civil rights context, the mulatta figure allows for different forms of identification, especially in terms of class and sexuality. The mulatta body functions as a shifting signifier of race, gender, sexuality, and national belonging. The mulatta as represented by Leticia in *Monster's Ball* is still prone to tragedy and to tropes of Black pathologies. While the educated and upwardly mobile mulatta as portrayed by Bette Porter in *The L Word* allows for class mobility, the resignification of the mulatta also allows for Blackness as a form of disruption into white normativity. Film and television allow for adjustments of phenotypical meaning based on how the viewer reads race either on or off the body. The mulatta then is raced differently based on how subjects are moralized or pathologized. While earlier tropes of the tragic mulatta and the hypersexual mulatta linger after the civil rights, feminist, and gay rights movements, the use of the mulatta as a symbol of racial progress reveals and evidences racial and gender anxieties rather than the eradication of racism and sexism. The illusion of the inclusion of Blackness operates alongside the occlusion of racial and gender disparities. The mulatta haunts and troubles the articulation of progress and liberal multiculturalism while surfacing the presence and prospect of increasing nonwhite identities. Therefore, while the aesthetics of mixed-race Black representations signal political, social, cultural, and demographic shifts, the containment of Blackness and the centrality of whiteness are still paramount.

Descending from colonial tropes of mulatta hypersexuality as a transgressive threat to the nation replayed in films such as *Imitation of Life* (1959), the mulatta in the 2000s conducts self-governing behavior in a normalizing discourse that values whiteness. In a neoliberal era, she represents a simultaneous disavowal and desiring of Blackness. As ever, the mulatta's sexual desirability is evidence of her lack of virtue. Mulatta sexuality comes into the text as enticing and titillating but in need of discipline. Blackness is only acceptable within a contained space that maintains concepts and desires of eroticism.

While neither Leticia in *Monster's Ball* or Bette in *The L Word* claims whiteness, both represent the anxieties and desires of an acceptable Blackness that can be brought into civil society or contained. Both allow for a liberal cultural interest in race without actually addressing racial inequalities. The fascination with the light-skinned mulatta, then, reproduces an abjection of Blackness or an acceptance of Blackness under the terms of assimilation and the maintenance of an exotic but safe sexual desirability. Ultimately, the mulatta figure becomes the vehicle of white redemption. Her body is inscribed within the politics of multiculturalism while simultaneously revealing anxieties surrounding racial differences.

Monster's Ball: The Suffering and Tragedy of the Mulatta

Monster's Ball exposes how contemporary film falls back on historical memories of miscegenation, with the mulatta as the representative and expressive figure. As in Brazil, she represents sexual deviance and occupies a state of relative stasis, rather than mobility, when connected to Blackness. Haunted by colonial legacies of slavery and ongoing formations of white supremacy, the mulatta in the early 2000s engages histories of racial and gender violence alongside hopes of racial progress. Carrying the weight of hemispheric traumas and erotic desires, the specter of the mulatta figure lingers over *Monster's Ball*.

Although Halle Berry cannot be conflated with the character she plays, her casting nevertheless influences the reading of the film. Although the script never explicitly identifies Leticia as mixed-race, viewer knowledge of Halle Berry's mixed heritage and tropes of hypersexuality all come into play to produce an image of the mulatta figure as a form of sexually deviant multiracial Blackness. Following historical representations of oversexed mulatta Jezebel archetypes, Leticia's sexuality is pathological. Though Berry delivers an extraordinary performance, the historical context of Berry's star image and the role of Leticia does not absolve the lingering Jezebel mulatta imagery within these exchanges.

Monster's Ball narrates the relationship between Leticia, an African American woman, and Hank, the white corrections officer who, unbeknownst to her, presided over her husband's execution. The film's setting in post–civil rights Georgia displaces characters' white supremacist ideologies as characteristic of an underdeveloped, racist South rather than as part of national and hemispheric structural racial inequalities and histories of racial violence. At the beginning of the film, Hank, a widower, follows the racist attitudes of his father, Buck. He often chastises Sonny, his own son, for failing to share these attitudes. Both Hank and Leticia lose their sons—Hank to suicide and Leticia to a fatal car accident. The relationship is thus set within multiple deaths, poverty, and family disintegration, as well as deception, as Hank does not tell Leticia that he executed her husband, Lawrence.

Leticia is a tragic sympathetic character for white audiences as she appears to be a victim of the circumstances of her birth. Unlike the tragic mulatta figure, who must accept her fate as Black or accept death, Leticia's tragedy does not result from her passing, but stems from having already been immersed in the Black world. The death of her husband and son, her abuse of alcohol, and her poverty are all derived from her Blackness. The film implies the Black men in her life have created her suffering by their actions, due to her husband's criminality and her son Tyrell's obesity. The Black male characters are coded as symbols of pathology in spheres of criminality, violence, and degeneracy. Lawrence and Tyrell thus conform to the ideological legacy Patricia Hill Collins describes: "a heterosexuality [constructed] through the images of wild beasts, criminals, and rapists."[14] These Black male bodies threaten Leticia's potential for happiness and her incorporation into civil society.

Lawrence and Tyrell suffer offscreen. The day before Lawrence's execution, Leticia tells him that she is only in the visiting room because she wanted Tyrell to be able to say goodbye to his father. Later, Leticia beats Tyrell for stealing candy and forces him to step on the scale after eating too much. Tyrell's body is literally a representation of excessive Blackness as his surplus of Black skin and body mass seems to envelope Leticia. His excess Blackness appears as a grotesque materialization of Black pathologies. Tyrell's dark Black heaviness runs counter to Leticia's slim caramel beauty. With Lawrence as a criminal figure put to death by the electric chair and Tyrell's body stigmatized by his weight and his dark skin, *Monster's Ball* reveals which bodies must remain excluded from national belonging. Leticia can survive in a nation that puts Tyrell and Lawrence to death, although she is not necessarily a citizen equal to whites.

Monster's Ball posits that only some bodies, and certainly not the dark Black abject bodies of Lawrence and Tyrell, can be part of national belonging. However, Hank's white body does belong, and in fact it represents the state through his role as a prison guard and executioner. Leticia's body is on the margins of national belonging, but the death of abject Blackness must precede her incorporation. Leticia's suffering comes in part from her detachment from civil society and her tethering to Blackness. After the deaths of her husband and son, Leticia does not appear to have any connection to Black communities, neighbors, family, or friends. While the film revolves around Hank's relationship with his family, the audience learns very little about Leticia. While Hank, as a white savior, redeems himself from familial racist practices, Leticia conforms to the figure of the tragic mulatta through her isolation and grief.

Hypersexuality and Excess in the Mulatta Figure:
Fetishizing and Pathologizing Blackness

Leticia's failure to save her son from the consequences of Black masculinity in the United States devalues her motherhood, and she becomes interpellated into a hypersexualized mulatta. As Leticia grieves over Tyrell, she recounts to Hank that he was a good kid and that she was a good mother. Her self-assurance of good mothering is an attempt to justify her grieving status because Black women have historically been positioned within the cultural imaginary as inadequate, bad mothers. Black motherhood is always suspect in part due to the devaluation of Black women and to the association of Black femininity with improper sexual mores. Just as with Brazilian *Paraíso Tropical*'s *mulata* figure, Leticia is posited as undeserving of motherhood and, like Bebel, she loses her child in punishment. Distraught, Leticia repeatedly explains that she told her obese son that he "can't be like that in America and a Black man." Hank responds, "I'm not sure what you want me to do." Quickly unclothing herself, Leticia screams in reply, "I want you to make me feel good."[15] Hank promptly has sex with her.

Recasting Leticia's pain into a scene of sexual frenzy, *Monster's Ball* reinforces the myth of the eroticized mulatta. The camera focus on Leticia's nakedness makes her body available to viewers and recalls other images of mulatta women as erotic objects of pleasure. The beauty of the mulatta, supposedly derived from the taboo miscegenation that created her, serves as proof of her sexual availability. The exotic and erotic allure of the mulatta stems from representations of her body as the source and product of taboo interracial desire. By signifying the transgression that produced her, the mulatta's body invites future reenactment of this taboo. Furthermore, her sexual availability serves to racialize her as Black. Leticia's call to "make [her] feel good" stimulates the effect of desire and intimacy across the color line while gesturing toward a violent forgetting of white patriarchal power. Leticia's solution to her suffering is found through Hank. This scene suggests that miscegenation can undo centuries of white supremacist culture. The scene's graphic nature also renders Leticia's sexuality as primitive. Leticia, as linked to Berry's racialized star persona, symbolizes the embodiment of miscegenation while she simultaneously participates in interracial sex with Hank. Against the backdrop of U.S. legal definitions of whiteness and blackness, Leticia is within the boundaries of black racial categorization. As opposed to her relationship with Lawrence, Hank and Leticia's onscreen explicitly graphic sexual relationship interplays an imagining of racial difference and eroticized racial fantasy. As a mulatta Jezebel figure, Leticia displays dangerous oversexed behavior that marks her as deviant. Her undisciplined and unruly sexuality diverges from normative white female sexuality.

The spectacle of carnality feeds into longstanding fantasies of racial mixing. As Black female bodies have been represented as sexually available and complicit in their own sexual exploitation, *Monster's Ball* follows a pattern of slavery-based memories. The relationship between Leticia and Hank cannot be read outside of these historical memories and narratives. With Leticia's lack of financial resources and dependence on Hank, the relationship evokes the racialized economy of slavery and the sexual economy of mulatta concubinage. The historical specter of the mulatta figure looms large. Leticia does initiate sex, which obscures the uneven relationships of power between her and Hank. By showing Leticia as the seductress and initiator, the film makes it appear as if Leticia has power over Hank, in spite of the social, political, and cultural inequalities between them.

Like the *mulata* figure in Brazil, the mulatta figure in the United States is historically rooted in the perpetuation of interracial sexual exploitation and abuse. As Saidiya Hartman argues, slave women have been depicted as responsible for their own sexual exploitation through the "discourse of seduction" that positions slavery as a relationship of mutual desire and slave women as the agents of the rape perpetrated on them. The discourse of seduction eradicates relations of dominance by representing women as seductresses who possess excessive sexual power and who will initiate sexual encounters.[16] In the scene's climatic moment, Leticia moves from victim, subjected to poverty, the death of her family, and racial and gender inequalities, to seductress. Hank, arguably the very agent of her oppression as her husband's executioner, becomes her savior.

Leticia's sexuality is represented as excessive and grotesque, which reproduces the notion of the hypersexual mulatta figure. The scene's use of excess and hysteria also evokes the hysterical, mentally unstable, and sexually lascivious mulatta responsible for racial and sexual degeneracy.[17] Her repeated cries of "make me feel good," moaning, and physical agitations signify physical and psychological hysteria. Early twentieth-century medical discourses and popular film and literature associated the mulatta with inherent pathologies and weaknesses. Due to her mixed blood and internalized racial conflict, the mulatta's hysteria is presumed to come from the womb. Leticia, traversing myths of female hysteria, Black irrationality, and mulatta mental incoherence, presumably needs a white male to control and heal her unstable racial and sexual identities.[18]

Yet Leticia's hysteria suggests racial and sexual trauma. As Elin Diamond notes, "hysteria in feminist discourses has become meaningful precisely as a disruption of traditional epistemological methods of seeing/knowing."[19] The moments following Leticia's screams of "make me feel good" in which she becomes hysterical destabilize the idea of stable homogenous and separate racial communities. The notion of a fixed racial identity or community disintegrates as the cognizance of the racial mixing that produced Leticia's physical features and the interracial sex that Leticia and Hank are performing become blurred. This awareness later in the film moves from hysteria to resignation and stupor after Leticia realizes that Hank is also Lawrence's executioner.

The trope of depravity from the unnatural mixing of the races manifests in Leticia's body and in her sexual relations with Hank. However, it is the excessive nature of Black female sexuality that grabs the viewer. The scene positions Leticia as tragic, desperate, dangerous, and sexually alluring all at once. With her sexuality exposed, Leticia is positioned as a threat that needed to be controlled. Leticia embodies the excesses of the desire and repulsion of mixed Blackness. Only the disciplining of the Black body can restrict this threat.

Although Leticia does not necessarily become whiter through becoming closer to Hank, her cutting off of Blackness, especially the criminal Blackness that Lawrence represents and the grotesque Blackness that Tyrell represents, distances her from the margins of society. With the U.S. moral panics of the 1980s and 1990s linking Black criminality and poverty with the absence of Black fathers and the deviance of Black welfare mothers, Blackness itself is at fault rather than the structures of racial violence, poverty, and incarceration.[20] Tyrell does not grow up to become the imagined Black criminal associated with Black fatherless households. While he is not executed or disciplined by the carceral state, the looming deviance and grotesqueness of Black masculinity determine his death. Like the excess of Tyrell's body mass due to his lack of ability to moderate his eating and Leticia's inability to manage him, Leticia's excessive sexuality are also tied to the decadence and absence of restraint in the Black body. As Leticia appears out of control sexually and financially, Hank, appearing as the white patriarchal authority, is the only one who can potentially regulate her. Leticia's economic dependence on Hank precludes her from independence. Her sexual relationship with Hank also simultaneously becomes a financial relationship. Marginalized by both historical legacies of slavery and neoliberal structures, Leticia emerges as a mulatta figure who requires Hank's privileged whiteness for material and physical survival.

The Mulatta as a Commodity

As a sexually available mulatta, Leticia resides within the racialized sexual economy with roots in hemispheric slavery and practices of concubinage. With Leticia having no car and being evicted from her home, Hank gives her Sonny's car and invites her to live with him. He shows that he is able and willing to financially care for her because he desires her. She is in no position to refuse his help and therefore in no position to refuse sex. The conflation of the financial and sexual relationships between Leticia and Hank evokes historical cultural memories of plaçage, in which relationships, often lifelong, were established between white men and mulatta, quadroon, and octoroon concubines. Like Bebel in *Paraíso Tropical*, Leticia is desired and provided for financially, but as a subordinate to her white patron.

While the film does not prescribe marriage as a heteronormative form of national belonging, Leticia's role as a mistress does not give her much agency. Without recourse to legal protections, she depends on Hank's willingness to continue to financially support her. As in Brazilian telenovelas and other cultural constructions, a mixed-race woman is tied to a white patriarchal figure and colonial constructions of female sexuality. Unlike the male neocolonial figures in Brazilian telenovelas, Hank overtly reveals his racial prejudices. While Hank quits his job and places his racist father, Buck, in a nursing home, Hank does not acknowledge his role in reinforcing racist practices. Instead, the film places his redemption by sexual intercourse with a nonwhite woman. This evidence of racial prejudice makes the film's framing of Hank's redemption even more compelling for a liberal multicultural project.[21]

When Hank buys a gas station and names it after Leticia, he publicly signals his ownership of her. Like Bebel's in *Paraíso Tropical*, Leticia's racialized, gendered, and sexualized body is represented as a commodity and, thereby, as exploitable. Leticia's race, gender, and sexuality are not valued as part of her self-identity but are valued as an article of trade. Like gasoline as a commodity, Leticia's body becomes an item of exchange in a capitalist market. Leticia's rendering into a commodity also evokes the familial separation needed to cement her relationship with Hank. By severing her bonds to Tyrell and Lawrence, the narrative makes it easier to mark her as a commodity. The decimation of these familial bonds then also blunts the lines of affect between Leticia and her family of origin, who never appear. The interminable loss of Tyrell and Lawrence sever her ties to Blackness. Like the Brazilian *mulata*, the hypersexuality of the U.S. mulatta figure creates the spectacle of an interracial erotic love narrative. However, the narrative must displace Black men in order for this erotic narrative to take place. The hope for a U.S. multiculturalism through interracial sex gets its expression in Leticia's severance from abject Blackness and transformation into an erotic mixed-Black commodity.

The consumption of Blackness is significant for the formation of Hank as a white male subject. Blackness, however, must be contained and literally imprisoned in Lawrence's case or eventually extinguished, as in Tyrell's. Given the racialized nature of capital punishment in the United States, Lawrence's state execution presents the literal death of Blackness. As Hank tells Sonny that executing another man will make him into a man, masculinity is associated with dominance and the witnessing and consumption of the Black body's death. As a mulatta figure, Leticia is a potential mediation point. For example, during Lawrence's execution, the film sets up a mise-en-scène between Hank and Lawrence and Leticia at home with Tyrell. As a specter of the mulatta object of exchange, Leticia can only be fully transferred over to white notions of multicultural belonging with the death of Lawrence and Tyrell. Lawrence's Blackness and his own admission that he's "a bad man" exclude him from civil society. Tyrell's obesity also renders him as socially abject. Both men were already sentenced to a form of social death that reestablishes Hank's white male subjectivity.[22] As a mulatta, Leticia can escape social death but must bear a rupture with Blackness.

The consumption of Black female sexuality is also linked to the formation of white masculinity. When Leticia pawns her wedding ring to buy a white cowboy hat for Hank to replace the hat stained by Tyrell's blood, she exhibits a small amount of agency. Yet this agency is tied to again removing ties to her Black husband and replacing her attachments with Hank as a white male hero, represented by the white hat. When Leticia encounters Hank's father, Buck, he remarks, "Yep, I had a taste for nigger juice when I was Hank's age. He's just like his Daddy. You ain't a man till you split dark oak." Buck's comment reveals a mixture of sexual desire and antipathy for African Americans. Black coal, like the gasoline the station named for Leticia will sell, is a staple fuel and a vital commodity. Buck degrades Leticia as a mere object of consumption and highlights the sexually precarious status of Black women. The sexualized Black woman is key to Buck's sense of masculinity and to white male supremacy.

Buck's treatment of Leticia demonstrates that interracial sex is not necessarily the answer to racism. As a mulatta figure, Leticia is presumably the product of interracial sex such as Buck describes. She is also the materialization of Buck's desires and dominance. The scene suggests Hank may be reproducing the arrangement his father describes. When Buck crudely assesses that "you ain't a man till you split dark oak," he reveals that miscegenation is crucial to white masculinity. Buck's earlier remark about two young Black boys playing by his house—"There was a time when they knew their place. There wasn't none of this mixing going on"—becomes clearer in this scene. "Mixing," apparently, does not refer to interracial sex, at least if it occurs between white men and Black women. However, the affective relationships that Black–white relationships and friendships might threaten the dominant order. Buck's denigration of Leticia codes Leticia's relationship with Hank as merely sexual rather than affective. His indirect reference to Leticia as "nigger juice" places her within the frame of the Black body rather than in an idealized in-between liminal space. The presence of Leticia as a mulatta figure is a way to access not only interracial sex but prohibited intimacies and alliances. Buck's comments serve as a reminder of the South's interracial heritage of Black female exploitation with Leticia's mulatta body as the physical record. Her light skin and phenotypical features allows for the inscription of interracial desires onto her body.

Buck's racist language usurps Leticia's attempt to assert her own agency by way of consumption. When Leticia pawns her wedding ring for a white cowboy hat, she is trading her past with Lawrence for a new future with Hank. The symbolism of the white cowboy hat, with its association with white masculinity and the regulation and conquest of the American frontier, reinserts Hank in a position of authority and places him in the position as a white savior and conqueror for Leticia. Given Leticia's lack of money, she uses the resources that she does have to demonstrate some independence and power. This gift is one of the few financial transactions in the movie that do not depend on Hank. The transaction does not rely on Leticia's body as part of the exchange but requires detaching the intimate embodiment of her relationship with Lawrence. Yet, Buck's behavior denies Leticia any satisfaction from the purchase. She enters the house to find Hank and give him the hat, but she only meets Buck, who tries it on and says eventually that he will see that Hank gets it. The interactions with the hat symbolize generational patterns of celebrated sexual expressions of white patriarchy. Consumption here is not a form of empowerment and does not displace racial, gender, and sexual hierarchies. Buck denies Leticia the opportunity to have Hank see her giving away anything other than her body. Thus, the mulatta figure remains a commodity rather than a consumer. She remains in a subservient position due to her financial dependence on Hank. Leticia lives on the margins of civil society and is refused social equality with whites. Whereas in Brazilian *telenovelas*, the path toward mobility, inclusion, and potential citizenship comes through consumption, the U.S. mulatta in *Monster's Ball* cannot gain independence through buying goods.

Rather than Leticia consuming the idea of Hank through the white cowboy hat, Hank consumes Leticia. This consumption is associated with both sex and eating. After a scene with Hank in which he performs oral sex on Leticia, Hank says that he is going out to pick up some chocolate ice cream because "it just feels right." By correlating Leticia's darker body as edible, the film constitutes Leticia as devourable racial difference. As Mia Mask notes, *Monster's*

Ball epitomizes bell hooks's description of "eating the Other" in this scene.[23] hooks explores the commodification of race in a "white supremacist capitalist patriarchy" so that the Other is eaten and the white self is satisfied with the consumption of the Other through food, music, tourism, or, in Leticia's case, literally her body. hooks maintains such commodification makes the culture of specific groups, as well as the bodies of individuals in these groups, an alternative playground where dominant members of society affirm their power in intimate relations with the Other.[24] Hank's white male privilege and Buck's reference to his past penchant for "nigger juice" demonstrate this delving into the Other as an alternate playground as a reaffirmation of domination.

The consumption of Blackness, marked as desirable and as abject, facilitates Hank's later redemption and procures a progressive white subjectivity for audiences. The mulatta, imagined as a sexually consumable woman, serves the purpose of the subordination of Blacks, the suppression of claims of equality in a post–civil rights context, and the reconceiving of histories of racialized sexual violence as exotic pleasure. The consumption of the mulatta, juxtaposed against explicit racism and interracial mixing, sets up the postracial discourses of the mid-2000s.

Purging Abject Blackness

In *Monster's Ball*, interracial penetration requires the expulsion of abject Blackness in order to stabilize white patriarchal society. After the first sex scene between Hank and Leticia, Hank wakes up and sees Lawrence's picture in the background. He immediately vomits, echoing his son's vomiting at Lawrence's execution. While Hank was already cognizant of Leticia's relationship with Lawrence before having sex with her, he did not disclose his own relationship with her husband. The photograph forces an encounter between Hank and the ghostly reminders of Blackness. In this scene, the internalization of racial difference, as represented by Lawrence's Black masculinity, is a form of consuming and rejecting abject Blackness. Lawrence's image invokes the undesirable parts of Leticia's Blackness. Once Leticia is dependent on Hank, her mulatta symbolism dilutes this abject Blackness. By "eating the Other" and killing the abject, Hank obtains the erotic mulatta. However, she does not become white. Rather, the sexualized mulatta feeds appetites of white desire for domination and intimacy under the guise of liberal benevolence.

While stories of the tragic mulatta of nineteenth- and early twentieth-century popular culture often end with the mulatta committing suicide or succumbing to death, Leticia chooses survival over death. While Hank is out buying ice cream, Leticia finds one of Lawrence's drawings of Hank in Hank's house. Realizing that Hank played a part in the execution of her husband, Leticia gasps, cries, and pounds a pillow. Horror evaporates into resignation. Leticia's discovery solidifies Hank's identity as a dominant white male. Through an ideology of neoliberal multiculturalism, the film presents raced and classed divisions as individual rather than structural. As Aimee Carrillo Rowe argues, *Monster's Ball* operates through fantasies of miscegenation as a white masculine redemption narrative that shifts racial conflicts to the realm of interpersonal relations and individual racial healing rather than addressing structural racialized inequalities.[25] Instead, the film relies on a notion that interracial intimacy through the mulatta can serve as racial reconciliation and solve racial, gender, and sexual domination.

Accepting what the relationships can financially provide for her and the precariousness of her circumstances, Leticia enters a state of stupor. Rather than displaying expressions of emotion or repressing her knowledge, Leticia resigns herself to her position as the passive mulatta body. Sitting outside with Hank as he feeds her chocolate ice cream on a white spoon, she metaphorically eats the mixed Blackness that Hank projects onto her. As Leticia looks into the distance, the viewer sees her vision of his wife's and son's tombstones—the relationship depends on their deaths as surely as it depends on the deaths of Lawrence and Tyrell. Yet, the interlocution of the mulatta figure relies both on Hank's redemption from his racist past and parenting failures to become a better more palpable kind of whiteness for civil society and the vacating of Leticia's Blackness to a state of numbness. *Monster's Ball* reaffirms the value of whiteness while devaluing Blackness. This desire for the white hero redeemed from his racist past emerges as a key component of the future postracial discourse of the 2000s. This redemption relies on the exploitation of the mulatta body and neglecting structural racism to create a future postracial landscape. *Monster's Ball* sets up other critically acclaimed and Oscar-winning films, among them *Crash* (2004), *The Blind Side* (2009), and *The Help* (2011), that feature white-savior motifs and the overcoming of racial and class barriers.

The film's southern setting is resonant with U.S. colonial legacies, reinforcing the mulatta body as a site of suffering. It repurposes the suffering sexual mulatta to stage an anti-Blackness that upholds white patriarchy as symbolized by Hank. Therefore, the redemption of civil society and the resolution of racial strife depend on the use of the mulatta figure as a haunting object of Blackness. Just as Brazil's discourse of mestiçagem and racial democracy rely on the *mulata*, the U.S. hope for multiculturalism here depends on the mulatta figure and interracial heterosexual union. However, this interracial union, with its emphasis on

Leticia (Halle Berry) and Hank (Billy Bob Thornton) sit on the front steps after Leticia discovers Hank's role in the execution of her husband in *Monster's Ball* (2001). Courtesy of Lionsgate Films/Photofest.

interpersonal relations, fails to challenge the institutional structures of white privilege and Black disenfranchisement. Cinematically, *Monster's Ball* reworks understandings of racial histories, inequalities, and interracial unions with a reinvestment in the production of white dominance.

While the mixed-race Black male is integral to the idea of national reconciliation and social change in the political sphere, the mulatta continues as a central figure of interracial intimacy in the cultural imaginary and both precedes and undergirds the hope of a postracial future. Unlike the Brazilian telenovela *Belíssima, Monster's Ball* does not end in interracial sex as a means of reproducing whiter progeny for the nation. At the end of the film, the couple is childless—Leticia was already not a redeemable mother due to her Blackness and Hank's redemption relies on the death of Black men. Here, Leticia, like Bebel in *Paraíso Tropical*, acts as the sexually depraved mulatta incapable of fostering respectable morality. As Hank and Leticia gaze into the dark distance, the camera pans upward to the starry sky and suggests that the couple has been elevated. The spectacular fantasy of the mulatta, hinging on racial desire, hysteria, and lurid danger, works within promise and failings. Hence, the mulatta in *Monster's Ball* manages Blackness through the erasure of abject

Blackness and the control of mixed-race Blackness. *Monster's Ball*, like Brazilian telenovelas, relies on the reimagined evocation of gendered and racial fantasies on the mulatta body. Yet, wishing for redemption while maintaining power structures and neglecting historical precedents, only reinforces white patriarchal hegemony.

The L Word: Upward Mobility, Consumer Citizenship, and the Mulatta

The L Word's mulatta figure acts as a site of desire and anxiety surrounding racial mixing and racial identities in a post–civil rights era, yet unlike Leticia, Bette represents an upwardly mobile educated Black elite and appears as a contemporary materialization of W. E. B. Du Bois's "talented tenth" and the successful uplifted "New Negro."[26] As such, Bette feeds into a white liberal management of race that simultaneously counters white supremacy while excluding most of the African American population.

After the civil rights, women's, and gay rights social movements, Leticia and Bette represent the asymmetrical class axes of power that uphold racial, gender, and sexual difference while at the same time marginalizing racialized and sexualized deviant populations because of their inability to assimilate and accumulate capital. While Bette potentially has a claim to citizenship through her upper-class consumerism, Leticia's abject sexualized Blackness does not have a place of belonging without the purging of this abjection.

Unlike Leticia in *Monster's Ball*, Bette is explicitly written as a mixed-race character. Jennifer Beals, who played her, requested that the writers frame the character as biracial. Ralina Joseph suggests Beals's racial framing of her Otherness and tragic mulatta tropes in the popular press inform the reception of the character she played.[27] Suspicion as to Beals's racial allegiances, her elite Ivy League education, and her association with the bourgeois all spill over into Bette's mulatta figure as a specter of passing and upward mobility. As noted in chapter 2, Beals's star image is rooted in the emergence of a racially ambiguous sensual dancing body in *Flashdance* as well as a passing mulatta figure in *Devil in a Blue Dress*. The notion of an erotic Blackness hidden by a visible whiteness influences Beals's portrayal of Bette.

Bette's contingent status of entry into national belonging and citizenship relies on adhering to homonormative class-based status and notions of African American class-based progress, yet her mulatta sexuality threatens her designation as a good subject. As Bette is the series' character who has most earned her class status with her education and ambition, she stands as a potential model of upward mobility and advancement in a post–civil rights era and demonstrates the possibility of and success for queer individuals and for people of color. Yet, the show's focus on her hypersexuality also reinscribes Bette into ideas of mulatta sexual deviance. While *The L Word* does not overtly ignore race and in fact sometimes foregrounds race, the show moves beyond the frame of mixed-race women as tragic victims. Thus, the show revises a tragic mulatta trope and replaces it with the contemporary flourishing independent mulatta flawed by her hypersexuality. Bette's inability to restrain herself sexually presents her not as a tragic mulatta who has no agency or is already sexually acted upon as in antebellum literature. Rather, Bette is the mulatta seductress who brings disorder until she can be tamed. Her character allows for an exploration of national identity and anxieties and desires concerning race, gender, sexuality, reproduction, and alternative forms of kinship.

Hemispherically, the mixed-race female figure operates within a discourse of consumer citizenship in which her exotic racial Otherness becomes a form of sexual capital and hence a way in which this sexual capital becomes reconfigured as form of empowerment through consumerism. While *Belíssima* and *Paraíso Tropical* and *Monster's Ball* presented mixed-race women as sexual partners who may attain money gains, status, and inclusion when linked with white men, *The L Word*'s Bette enters a neoliberal postfeminist area in which her empowerment expresses her sexual and financial freedom. While *Monster's Ball*'s Georgia setting evokes rural southern poverty, *The L Word*'s Los Angeles sets the stage for conspicuous consumption and U.S. westward dreams of prosperity rooted in U.S. imagery of the frontier and California as a land of promise. Furthermore, the South's associations with slavery and Jim Crow contrast with the image of a progressive California devoid of Black slavery legacies. Bette represents a new mulatta consumer citizenship uprooted from southern vestiges of slavery and sexual and financial dependence on men.

She presents the televisual relationships between gay consumerism and neoliberalism and African American consumerism and citizenship. She represents a merging of these two ideals of consumer citizenship with her biracial lesbian identity and cosmopolitanism. Much of Bette's belonging depends on her elite education at Yale University, her prestigious positions as a curator at the California Arts Center and dean of the California University of the Arts, her wealth, and her light skin. Like Brazilian telenovelas' linkage between consumption and citizenship, *The L Word* ties citizenship and consumerism together to paint an image of acceptance and advancement. Bette's beautiful home, prominent and expensive art collection, designer clothes, and luxury goods all showcase an educated upper-class lifestyle. Bette and her friends represent homonormative lesbian identities marked by consumerism and class. They hold disparate occupations and have varying educations and family backgrounds, but they rarely experience financial difficulty—and rapidly recover from any such hardship. Exercising material consumption presented as a form of empowerment, Bette embodies a neoliberal discourse in which racism and sexism are not major obstacles. She is a model citizen, and her very existence and her many accomplishments serve as proof of racial progress.

As an educated mulatta, Bette is presented within the referential scope of the New Negro identity and racial uplift, which has often only been open to lighter-skinned Black people. Historically, the Black elite has had to perform respectability and distinguishing themselves as what Kevin Gaines terms "bourgeois agents of civilization, from the presumably undeveloped Black majority."[28] By the 2000s, The L Word's Bette focuses on individual accomplishment rather than on uplifting the Black community. Her success revolves around the hopes prescribed by a neoliberal postracial context that emphasizes the needlessness of race. Thus, television articulates the social and political discourse of the early 2000s in which racism is articulated as invisible because the United States has moved beyond racial hierarchies and privileges. Showtime as a corporate network addresses this niche marketing as a way to deploy postracial politics that largely dismisses differences. Hence, television operates as a way to manage Blackness as what is leftover and obsolete in this moment.

Bette's embodiment of a light-skinned bourgeois who can pass for white assures greater potential for U.S. national belonging. While Bette and Leticia experience starkly different economic circumstances, both The L Word and Monster's Ball ignore social structures—The L Word never explicitly turns attention to the intersection of race and class in Bette's elite status any more than Monster's Ball recognizes that Leticia is mired within structural forms of racial poverty. Instead, Bette's education and workaholic ambitions support neoliberal ideas of an individual work ethic leading to success and financial security. Through racialization, sexualization, and class discourse, the mulatta as nonnormative is rendered visible within media texts as a site of struggle that challenges dominant ideologies of the nation. On a hemispheric level, these nonnormative bodies are part of larger relations of biopower. The imaginary of the mulatta as a nonnormative subject results in the abjection of class difference and her inscription as sexually deviant. This abjection obscures patriarchal and racial capitalism while focusing on sexual and class difference. Theorizing the production of difference requires an understanding beyond the nation-state to examine the role of media texts within the neoliberal organizing of hemispheric politics.

While Leticia, like the telenovelas' Mônica and Bebel, has sexual capital and experiences attachments to white men as the primary means of becoming consumer citizens, Bette is sexually and financially independent in a postfeminist and post–civil rights framework. While Bette is successfully integrated into a consumer citizenship, her role in sexual reproduction and her identity as a lesbian reconfigure narratives of the mulatta figure. Through her assertion of her mixed Blackness, Bette possibly represents the survival of Blackness, rather than the erasure of Blackness, in the shaping of a future postracial landscape as depicted on *The L Word*. Often misrecognized as white, she unsettles normative ideas of racial identity. Yet, these misrecognitions also manage her Blackness to mask white hegemony. *The L Word* suggests that Bette can be refashioned from a New Negro ideal to a postracial model through her elite education, career success, and consumerist lifestyle.

In contrast to the glamorous Bette, Kit, her Black half sister, is initially presented as a talented but failed and financially unstable singer who suffers from alcoholism. She potentially represents the abject Blackness that Leticia confronts in *Monster's Ball*. Like *Monster's Ball*, *The L Word* reinforces a neoliberal ideology that promotes personal responsibility to efface structural inequalities. Kit is completely left out of the consumer citizenship model at first. But she becomes the owner of the Planet, a lesbian-friendly café and nightclub, and become financially solvent. This requires Bette's help with a business plan and the financial support of both Bette and Ivan, a white gender-fluid person with a romantic interest in Kit. Kit's white love interest and her biracial half sister thus save Kit from her potential abject Blackness. Ivan's gender fluidity complicates the idea of a white male rescuer in a heteronormative context. At the same time, Kit contrasts with Bette, the affluent and light-skinned younger sister. This contrast, and concerns over Bette's racial status later in the series, demonstrate the connection between notions of Black authenticity and working-class Blacks. In a neoliberal era, Blacks who do not prosper are told to lift themselves up; if they fail, they are told it is their fault, not the result of racial structural inequities. This mode of racialized uplift fits in within neoliberal capitalism that emphasizes individual responsibility and entrepreneurship while ignoring struggles for social justice. Like *Monster's Ball*, *The L Word*, while set in glamorous upper-class Los Angeles, nonetheless attributes inequalities to a culture of Blackness rather than continuing legacies of institutional racism. Thus, the lingering notion of authentic Blackness is associated with depravity and poverty while the fantasy of a post–civil rights Blackness is equated with proximity to whiteness and the capacity to expunge abject Blackness.

Bette stands in as a potential marker of an acceptable mixed Blackness based on her class standing, yet she is not completely respectable due to her hypersexual behavior. Bette's mobility at first appears to align her with the uplift of the morena, Mônica of *Belíssima*, but her lesbian identity and hypersexuality complicate the notion of a national uplift narrative. Her sexual autonomy exceeds the national and hemispheric orders of heterosexual womanhood that structure the conventions of popular culture texts. Unlike Leticia, Bette has socioeconomic resources, is integrated within her community, and thus has a claim to citizenship. Although she does not encounter derogatory labels like "nigger juice," as Leticia does, her lesbian identity also complicates the tragic mulatta figure by placing her outside patriarchal heteronormative standards. It troubles a narrative of interracial sexual pairings with white men as part of racial erotic narratives and ideas of whitening and uplift. Therefore, Bette challenges the tragic mulatta trope that works within a white heterosexual framework. However, like Leticia, she remains a hypersexual figure.

Allure of Racial and Sexual Difference: Exotifying and Eroticizing Mixed-Race

From *The L Word*'s first scene, Bette initiates the series, sex, and queer reproduction with her own allure. *The L Word* opens with Bette and her partner, Tina, discovering that Tina is ovulating. Bette kisses Tina and says "let's make a baby."[29] Tina occupies the role of the maternal figure while Bette represents the sexual initiator. This very first reading contests white patriarchal visions of family formation. Queer racial mixing here undermines the idea of a pure white female sexuality that white men must protect. Rather than evoking the fear of an aggressive hypersexual Black male, *The L Word* contests the protection of white female sexuality with Bette as the mixed-Black sexual initiator. The subsequent scenes involve Bette pleasuring Tina before insemination because the fertility doctor has suggested that it will make Tina's body riper for insemination. Thus, it renders lesbian interracial sex as reproductive, placing the two women within an alternative to a normative family unit involving heterosexual sex. Race and reproduction here and elsewhere in *The L Word* present a complicating of the mulatta figure. Dissimilar to the traditional mixed-race hemispheric figures, Bette is not the physical childbearer who produces the future progeny of the nation, nor is she the physical threat of contamination. Unlike the Brazilian morena in *Belíssima*, Bette's sexuality is unfastened from heteroreproductive marital relationships and she is not a reproducer for the uplift of the nation.

The projection of queer desire and interracial desire come through the mixed-race figure nonetheless. Jenny Schecter, a Jewish neighbor who has just moved to Los Angeles with her fiancé, Tim, watches a couple having sex next door and assumes that they are Bette and Tina. Describing a dark-haired woman with a blond-haired woman in the pool, Jenny, as voyeur of both interracial and queer sex, finds the image of the women to be titillating and proceeds to have sex with Tim. While Jenny is not actually watching interracial sex, the ideas of both queer and interracial sex are layered together as titillating. Although Jenny is mistaken as to the identity of the women she has watched, the scene nonetheless constructs interracial sex as well as queer sex as enticing in part because they are taboo. As the product of interracial sex, Bette therefore represents forbidden sexual desire and fantasy much as other mulatta figures have.

The correlation between queer desire and interracial desire are implanted with the figure of Bette. At a party at Bette and Tina's house, already coded as a sexual and racial space of permissiveness, Jenny finds herself attracted to Marina, a European heiress and Kit's predecessor as owner of the Planet café. Played by Karina Lombard, an actor of American Indian and European descent, Marina's accent and cosmopolitanism evoke a sexual desire of queer and racial exoticism through the idea of the ambiguously tan foreigner. As Bette and Tina's house is already coded as a sexually and racially permissive, Jenny's desire is stimulated in this setting. Bette and Tina's space is coded as sexually and racially permissive because it heightens Jenny's desire. Like many women of color on the show, Marina is sexually aggressive. Jenny's attraction to Marina eventually leads to her breakup with Tim and her decision to seek a female partner. Racially ambiguous women often serve as a conduit of escape on the show. For example, when Helena Peabody, a British heiress, finds herself without a fortune, Catherine, played by Sandrine Holt, of French and Chinese descent, seduces her. Helena steals Catherine's money and lands in jail. She then flees prison with Dusty, played by Lucia Rijker, who is of Creole Surinamese and Dutch descent, to Tahiti. These narratives construct modern white lesbianism as awakened and reinvigorated through encounters with exotic racially mixed women. These nonwhite characters are presented as forms of desirable racial cultural capital while the core sexual modernity is presented through whiteness.

Furthermore, this exotic racial ambiguity is highly prized as desirable, enticing, and, in the vein of mixed-race female tropes, as dangerous to order. Hence, the racially ambiguous body is consumed temporally or disciplined as a rite of passage that allows white exploration of racial and sexual borders to prove one's cosmopolitanism and tolerance. They are ultimately disciplined or brought back into the fold to further reinforce white ideal femininity. In an article analyzing the show, Burns and Davies describe this process as "render[ing] the white (lesbian) body as the normative or model cosmopolitan sexual citizen" through "consumer and lifestyle practices that fetishize the raced lesbian 'other.'"[30] This neoliberal multicultural model that values and commodifies diversity presents white femininity as the progressive ideal and manages racial difference. Bette, as a subject who already exceeds racial and sexual norms, is included and appropriated as a racially ambiguous body that justifies white dominance.

The viewer learns that Bette has sexually initiated a number of white women who previously solely had heterosexual relationships, Tina among them. Here racial ambiguity resonates with sexual ambiguity.[31] Bette is the sensual and exotic mulatta, positioned within a spectrum of whiteness and Blackness, and thereby stimulates the desiring gaze of her admirers and the viewers. Numerous characters attest to Bette's sexual magnetism. She is dangerous and alluring and awakens queer sexual desire and interracial sexual desire. Her sexual identity and racial ambiguity combine to produce her allure and charm. For example, Phyllis, Bette's supervisor at the California University School of the Arts, confesses to Bette that she has feelings that she would like to explore. She begs Bette to take her to a party at the Planet. Bette becomes the vehicle for Phyllis's sexual exploration. Later, as Bette is considering resigning, Phyllis eventually confesses that she has always been attracted to Bette. She gushes:

> You've always been a beautiful role model to me . . . in a special way, and I will always be grateful . . . if I had svelte young blond co-eds throwing themselves at me, I would too. . . . To tell you the truth, I've had my own struggles with attractions to subordinates. . . . Now that you're no longer my employee, I feel free to make my confession. Bette, I've always found you wildly attractive. From the moment I saw you, tall, strong, brilliant, erudite, it was so difficult for me not to act on it.[32]

Similarly, Kelly Wentworth, a wealthy white divorcée, appears in the last season as Bette's old crush. Kelly had previously turned down Bette's advances but now repeatedly flirts with Bette and says that she was the one that got away. Rather than representing white women as sexually vulnerable, these women are sexually independent and actively desire Bette. Bette acts as a conduit for intensified homoeroticism. Queer desire and racial desire work in tandem to construct Bette as a sexually desirable exotic nonwhite body. As with *Monster's Ball's* Leticia and *Paraíso Tropical's* Bebel, Bette's desirability is constructed through a dynamic of racial and sexual Otherness. Thus, these historical ideas of mixed-Black sensuality and availability continue to propel the fantasies of interracial encounters.

As the desired and desirous mulatta figure, Bette both sexually pursues and is actively pursued throughout the series. Most of Bette's lovers are white. The main exception is Candace, an Afro-Latina contractor, who Bette hires to help install the controversial *Provocations* exhibition. Even the title of the exhibition thus associates Candace and Bette's relationship as a temptation of racial queer arousal and stimulation. With her dark-tan skin, Candace, played by Ion Overman, of mixed African American and European descent, evokes a desire of similarity of race and sex. When Bette cheats on Tina with Candace, her friends condemn her and Bette is shunned from the group. Bette's racialized erotic encounter disrupts the ideal of monogamy and the normalization of whiteness within the group. Furthermore, Bette's infidelity is presented as an innate promiscuity as Alice, for example, says a friend in the group, comments, "cause of the sex thing and Bette can't help it [seeking out sex]."[33] She implies Bette is innately promiscuous, aligning her within tropes of the hypersexual mulatta.

Candace breaks up the primacy of white social networks on the series. Prior to her appearance in the series, the women of color in the series had no apparent connection to Black communities apart from Bette's connection to Kit. Candace and Bette first meet in a predominantly Black music nightclub, the only majority Black public space that appears in *The L Word*. The hip-hop artist Slim Daddy (played by rapper Snoop Dogg) is the first to vocalize Bette and Candace's magnetism. He calls Candace Bette's "woman" even as Tina sits next to Bette. "I guess I'll dream about the two of you," he tells Candace and Bette. "Because I have that basic instinct."[34] Slim Daddy mediates Bette's attraction to Candace through a gaze both male and African American. Slim Daddy's projection of desire reinforces Bette's association with Blackness.

In this frame, Bette's desire for Candace is also a racialized desire for Blackness, for self, and for a reconfiguration of identity. The image of two brown queer bodies together reconfigures queerness outside of a white formation. Up to this point in the show, the absence of women of color in queer relationships with each other demonstrates uneven power dynamics between queerness and Blackness such that queer identity is most associated with whiteness. As David Eng argues, colorblind queer liberalism is constructed around gay white, middle-class communities as citizen-subjects while deeming racism as occurring in the past.[35] Hence, Candace and Bette potentially threaten the hegemony of whiteness and allow for Black female subjectivity in relation to queer desire. Candace and Bette are not readily racially identifiable, but their brown bodies together onscreen contrast with the whiteness of the depicted queer Los Angeles. Furthermore, the brown nonreproductive bodies seeking pleasure contrast with the assumptions or fantasies of mulatta sexuality predicated on sexual availability in a heterosexual frame or the idea of the mulatta as sterile. Here Candace and Bette are objects of each other's desires in mutual recognition. Centering queer desire of color with Bette and Candace challenges dominant media narratives of the mulatta figure as object of white male desire. Furthermore, Candace and Bette's relationship breaks the homonormative arcs of whiteness and monogamy as ideals of queer citizenship and undermines a politics of Black respectability.

Anxieties of Racial Difference: Accommodating Blackness without Disrupting White Normativity

The L Word manages anxieties of racial difference so that race is not constructed as a central issue unless, as Ralina Joseph argues, Bette plays her "race card" as a strategic choice when she needs to win an argument or gain an advantage. As Joseph notes, *The L Word* uses the race card to absolve itself from critiques centered on its lack of diversity, given that Kit and Bette are the only characters of color to appear throughout all six seasons of the series.[36] Whereas the show's characterization of Bette presents race as an individual choice that can be easily discarded, racism is never addressed, reinforcing notions that race is politically irrelevant. Meanwhile, gay discrimination is repeatedly addressed as a structuring matter in institutions and cultural and political life. Bette is framed as a subject whose concerns for belonging are primarily defined by overcoming structural LGBTQ discrimination while her racial identity is deemed as largely her own individual concern.

Although scholars, activists, journalists, and viewers have criticized the minimal presence of women of color in *The L Word*, José Muñoz writes that the presentations of Kit and Bette are more than "light multicultural window dressing." "The narrative," he argues, "does not try to contain or manage race. The race plots that these characters generate keep *The L Word* from slipping into a mode of neoliberalism in which race is sidelined."[37] Indeed, *The L Word* uses Bette's character to explore racial differences and tensions. However, these racial differences are managed through Bette as a mulatta figure, against what appears at first as an antiassimilationist queer landscape. The revised mulatta appears as a conduit to a seemingly progressive antiassimilationist queer landscape that maintains white privilege. The mulatta echoes the anticipation of symbolic progress while obscuring the limits of neoliberal multiculturalism.

Like Jennifer Beals herself, Bette can pass as white and sometimes does so unintentionally. The show presents the themes of racial passing and sexual passing as slippery and overlapping. Just as Deborah McDowell's unearthing of narratives of sexual passing within a novel concerning racial passing in Nella Larsen's *Passing* (1929) links discourses of racialization and sexualization during Jim Crow, *The L Word* details a surveillance of women of African descent and queer women in the 2000s. Using metaphors of closeting and passing, LeiLani Nishime demonstrates how the performances of race and sexual orientation unveil unstable identities and notes the 1990s push to conceal queer and nonwhite identities to conform to mainstream white heterosexual norms.[38] Historical vestiges of racial and sexual deviance alongside a politics of authenticity follow Bette's mulatta character into the early 2000s within a context of increasing queer and multiracial media visibility alongside state policies such as "Don't Ask, Don't Tell" and controversies over multiracial identifiers in the 2000 census. Highlighting sexual identity discrimination as the main issue of the present, the series largely relegates racism to an occurrence of the past and as a relic of individual identity rather than as a structuring force.

In contrast to earlier narratives such as *Imitation of Life* (1959), *The L Word* does not use passing to acknowledge how whiteness facilitates inclusion and opportunities and exclusion for African Americans. Yet, like *Imitation of Life*, in which Sarah Jane is presented as unable to accept her authentic identity, Bette is framed as performing as white. In a group therapy session, Yolanda, a Black woman, accuses Bette of trying to pass for white by failing to mention that she's African American yet "talk[s] so proud about being a lesbian." Historically, African Americans have had an awareness of racial ambiguity and the wide variety of phenotypes within African American communities. As Adrian Piper suggests, a woman like Bette, given her phenotype, can pass before African Americans as well as whites. Conveying racial identity consists of a mutual recognition of a Black racial identity. Therefore, African Americans who are racially ambiguous are expected to make their racial identity known. As Adrian Piper observes, individuals who can pass for white are subject to accusations of racial inauthenticity from whites. She points out that many African Americans place light-skinned Blacks before a suffering test of experiences of racism or are told that their Blackness was always innately detectable.[39] Thus, racially ambiguous people of African descent are consistently met with racial essentialism.

Unlike the passing mulatta figure of earlier narratives, Bette does not explicitly hide her Blackness. Yet, her failure to declare her Blackness causes other women of color to suspect her of opportunism. As Ralina Joseph argues, since others perceive Bette as white, when she declares herself Black it seems strategic rather than authentic.[40] Furthermore, Bette does not often acknowledge the privileges of her light skin and phenotypical features. Central to understanding

Yolanda and Bette's discussion are narratives of racial passing that presume a Black person is capable of and willing to deny her or his Blackness to pass for white. When Yolanda retorts, "But legally you're Black. Isn't that a fact?" Bette responds, "Well, that's the white man's definition of me, yes. The one-drop rule. So basically what you're saying is that you would like to see white America define me."[41] Yolanda's accusation and invocation of legal definitions of Blackness acts as disciplinary and surveillance technologies of racial ordering. With the specter of the mulatta, racial passing, and lesbian sexuality, Bette's mixed-race status intrinsically makes her deceptive. Bette rejects the imposition of racial boundaries rather than placing herself within a collective Black identity of solidarity.

Accusations that Jennifer Beals has also passed, refusing rather than affirming her Blackness, are critical context for *The L Word*'s presentation of Bette. As described in chapter 2, the press framing of Beals repeatedly mentioned her Black father, yet Beals did not publicly claim a monoracial Black identity. Yolanda says to Bette, "You need to reflect on what it is you're saying to the world while hiding so behind the lightness of your skin." When Bette tells Tina how much Yolanda's attack upset her, Tina responds, "We're going have some fun with her." Bette questions the "we," and Tina says that Yolanda upset her just as much as she upset Bette. Bette counters: "I don't think so Tina. It was my whole life she was attacking. My life."[42] Later in the series, Jenny makes a film based on the friendship group, *Lez Girls*, and the casting of a white actress to play the character based on Bette makes Bette visibly angry. She claims that a white actress could not possibly know how to play her. Again, she suggests that persons who have not embodied mixed-Black racial identity cannot understand it. Reading Bette's rebuff alongside Beals's racial star text, *The L Word* questions race as a performance rather than as an embodiment. In a post–civil rights era, this colorblind casting becomes code for assimilation to whiteness while negating the materiality of race.

Passing and being passed, with affective and material consequences, shapes *The L Word*'s postracial notions of national progress. The show presents Bette's Black invisibility as proof of the lack of ongoing racial discrimination. Thus, as part of U.S. multicultural discourses, the show implicitly celebrates the invisibility of racial identity as long as it is shrouded in near whiteness, which makes it color neutral. Long-term relationships between or with women of color on the series ultimately fail or, in Bette and Tina's case, are consistently in peril of dissolution. As Michele Elam notes, "because mixed-race has often been represented since the 1990s as hip testimony to American democracy, the corporeal resolution of racial diversity and national unity, it is also represented as a painless antidote to the centuries old process of passing. Passing, then, seems a particularly antique phenomenon in this 'mulatto millennium.'"[43] Announcing the possibility of racial passing and the existence of racism itself becomes irrational. After the group therapy facilitator reprimands her for confrontational behavior, Yolanda prompts, "Is this Black lady getting out of control? Why is it that whenever a Black woman has an opinion, she's being confrontational?" Thus, the show situates Yolanda as the accuser and an angry Black woman, who is stuck in the past and impeding national progress.[44]

Race and sexuality are constructed as domains of potential choice yet require constant policing. After Yolanda's accusations, Bette outs Yolanda as a lesbian in the therapy group. She tells her, "you're not exactly readable as a lesbian, and you didn't come out and declare yourself." Thus she draws parallels between racial passing and sexual passing. While both Bette and Yolanda accuse each other of privileging one social marker over the other, Bette does not acknowledge that her skin color affords her the privilege of passing as white, which Yolanda cannot. This asymmetry insinuates that race and sexuality must be performed. This scene evokes African American literature, such as that of Nella Larsen's *Passing* (1929), in which anxieties over racial and sexual passing converge and racial differences and sexual differences cannot be fully separated.[45] Maurice Wallace points to the distinction between white queer subjects, who can pass as heterosexual, and most people of color, who cannot pass into the dominant group.[46] As Bette's body is not readily legible sexually or racially, the mulatta figure is a source of racial and sexual anxieties in a post–civil rights era in which racial identities are contested, reconfigured, and reinforced.

In response to Yolanda's pressure to identify only as Black, Bette asks "why is it so wrong for me to move more freely in the world just because my appearance doesn't automatically announce who I am?"—she implies that race constrains more than sexuality. As Ralina Joseph suggests, Bette associates Blackness with a lack of freedom.[47] Bette's hedging of labeling herself as Black echoes strands of the 1990s and 2000s multiracial movement that pushed for a multiracial census category. As Habiba Ibrahim argues, "the multiracial phenomenon produced discourses about race that tacitly situated Blackness as outmoded and multiracial as emergent."[48] Thus, Yolanda is a harbinger of the past and Bette represents a potential successful glamorous future hinged on casting away monoracial Black identification. Bette's comments attempt to position her as beyond Blackness while ignoring her privileged position in a society marked by anti-Blackness. With the neoliberal emphasis on individual freedom and responsibility, Bette posits her own personal identity as paramount to group solidarities and racial and sexual oppression.

The L Word gestures to the continuing significance of race yet remains complicit in safeguarding neoliberal discourse by obfuscating continuing racial disparities and marking racial Blackness as oppressive. Thus, through Bette, *The L Word* furthers a multiracial fantasy devoid of political and social change. The parameters of color blindness along with the reconfiguring and questioning of racial identities is especially pertinent in regards to reproduction with respect to Bette and Tina's child. After the first insemination, from a white man, fails, Bette finds a substitute. Like the first donor, Marcus is an artist. When he arrives at Tina and Bette's door to deposit his sperm, Bette is not present. Visibly upset, Tina quickly excuses herself. As the viewer encounters Marcus for the first time, the viewer realizes that she is upset because Bette did not mention that Marcus was Black. His Blackness, as well as his height, size, and muscular features, rely on tropes of racialized physical virility to insinuate that he can succeed where his white predecessor failed. Colonial discourses about Black male physicality and sexuality reemerge in this scene. Again, Blackness is presented as a surplus to whiteness. Like mulatta excessive sexuality, Marcus's presence on screen evokes alarm of Black hypermasculinity and thus, the viewer is made to sympathize with Tina. Sensing Tina's discomfort, Marcus asks if Bette told her that he was Black. Tina confirms, saying, "No, not at all. But, she didn't not tell me because it doesn't matter, right?" Refusing to feign that race might not matter to Tina, Marcus responds coolly, "I can't answer that for you."[49] The scene between Marcus and Tina demonstrates assumptions of an investment in whiteness and anxieties of a liberal colorblind attitude.

Within assisted reproduction, racial similarity between mother and child is presumed and as white mothers are most likely to utilize these technologies, white racial selection is highly valued. Assisted reproduction technologies have been designed to increase reproduction of white women and has historically controlled the reproduction of Black women.[50] Thus, the threat of Black reproduction collides with the historical legacies of Black reproduction as a form of enslaved labor. Bette's mothering objectives refute the absolution of Black life as well as the commodification of Black reproductive labor. Withdrawing from reproductive labor yet engaging in mothering, Bette undoes the dominant social order of white heteronormativity. When Tina confronts Bette about her omission, Bette becomes upset. She claims that she and Tina had discussed having an African American donor to reflect their relationship. Tina pleads, "Look at me, Bette. I don't feel qualified to be the mother of a child who's half African American. I don't know what it means to be Black." Tina does not question whether she, as a white woman, will be perceived as part of the family but rather how a mixed-Black child will intersect in her idea of motherhood. Bette counters, "I think I can make a contribution in that department." Tina responds, "and don't you think, on top of everything else, to also have two moms, that is a lot of otherness to put on one child?"[51] The question privileges homonormativity over race. Mixed-Black racial difference is rendered as constraining the capacity to assimilate to white heterosexual norms. Tina's remark speaks to the illegibility of interracial and queer families and to the maintenance of white privilege.

The scene marks Bette as insensitive to Tina's presumed innocent whiteness and marks Tina as not as colorblind as she thought. Tina's liberal front hides conservative underpinnings that often express concerns about the children of both interracial and lesbian parenting. Her concern is a mask for her discomfort, as her privileged whiteness assumes that her children will suffer. The scene unravels fictions that interracial couples can fix racism and that queer people do not hold racist views. The use of race and sexuality together here suggests that Bette cannot possibly be part of a national belonging as she is implied to be other. Tina's remarks also insinuate that her interracial queer relationship with Bette is taboo and that she fears both hidden and visible Blackness. Tina's investment in white privilege is only unmasked through the racial flesh of birthing and mothering a child who may not resemble her own physical whiteness. At stake is also Tina's own whiteness, which giving birth to a daughter with phenotypical Black markers, would disrupt, while Bette, who is not visibly Black, does not threaten her partner's sense of white normalcy. Thus, Tina's rejection is also an intentional erasure of Bette's Blackness.

Hurt by Tina's reaction, Bette goes to Kit for comfort. Her sister sympathizes, but nonetheless says, "When she looks at you she doesn't see a Black woman or a white woman. She sees what she wants to see. Maybe she sees what you let her see. Maybe it wasn't that important before. Maybe that's what's worked best for you all these years, you getting all your pretty things, and you know putting together your pretty life, is that you let people see what you want them to see."[52]

Rather than absolve Bette for her complicity, Kit points to Bette's light-skin privileges and the racial and class advantages that stem from Bette's willingness to be read as white. She suggests, as Yolanda had in her accusations of passing, that Bette lacks cultural trust and that she sacrifices potential Black identification in exchange for success in dominant white society. Pam Grier plays Kit, and like Beals's star text, Grier's figures here. Grier played Blaxploitation film characters in the 1970s with a signature Afro hairstyle similar to Angela Davis's. She resides within a fantasy of Black authenticity and an insistence on Blackness rather than mixedness. Grier, like Beals, acknowledges her family's mixed heritage.[53] However, Grier is strongly associated as a Black heroine. The juxtaposition thus presents Bette as a possible race traitor who is complicit in the misperception of her mixed Blackness. In an allusion to conservative Black nationalism that called for racial unity and loyalty, Bette becomes a target of antipathy for her mixed Blackness and interracial intimacy with Tina.

Bette's character brings historical valuing of light skin and the denigration of dark skin as associated with the lower classes, visible Blackness, and the inequalities within the U.S. Black population according to skin color into tension. African Americans recognize how lighter-skinned Blacks are often seen as less threatening and are hired and promoted with greater frequency.[54] From Kit's suggestions and the incidents with Yolanda and Tina, Bette must come to terms with her Blackness by confronting her light-skinned privileged status. Her brief relationship with Candace becomes a reaction to accusations of assimilation. She seeks refuge and affirmation in Candace's skin as well as her activism and comfort in her own identity.

Eventually, Tina and Bette successfully conceive a child with Marcus's sperm. While Tina demonstrates a white female fragility and her assumptions of whiteness in her proclaiming that she wasn't prepared to carry a biracial baby, Bette repeatedly references that the couple had previously discussed an African American donor. While their therapist suggests that Tina's reaction comes off as a rejection of Bette's identity, Tina reiterates her love for Bette. Thus, the series suggests that interracial love and racial mixing can absolve racism. Thus, the use of insemination on *The L Word* destabilizes heterosexual reproduction and patriarchal privilege as continuing racial bloodlines. Rather, it is Bette's desire for a racially mixed child who will reflect her relationship with Tina that predicates this racial mixing.

The narrative disconnects heterosexuality with reproduction and biological kinship yet maintains notions of racial biological likeness. In 1990 media attention focused on the lawsuit of a white woman who was mistakenly inseminated with a Black donor's sperm instead of her white husband's; the media framed the mistake as a nightmare.[55] The episode's airing predates California's same-sex legal recognition in 2008 and federal recognition in 2013, yet the normative understanding of families underpinning the same-sex marriage movement also is at play in this scene in which queer families must look physically similar to nuclear heterosexual families. Indeed, in 2014, a white lesbian couple sued for emotional and economic loss of wrongful birth when the mother was also mistakenly inseminated with Black sperm.[56] Rather than focus on confronting racism, these lawsuits demonstrate anxieties of racial mixing, the loss of white privilege, and ideologies of anti-Blackness. The detachment of procreation from heterosexual sex potentially marks a shift from a patriarchal heteronormative model of kinship yet maintains racialization as a key component of the family unit. Unlike the Brazilian morena, Bette's place in the nation does not rely on her role as a heterosexual reproducer. However, as a partner with Tina, she is active in her choice of a Black sperm donor.

Bette's desire for her daughter to have Black genes potentially reifies the co-constructions of race and kinship. When Tina becomes pregnant from the insemination, Bette announces Tina's pregnancy to her father, Melvin (played by Ossie Davis). Melvin suggests he will not see the product of Tina's pregnancy as his grandchild, and Bette emphasizes that the donor is African American. Melvin responds, "And because of all of this I'm supposed to feel closer to this child? Because all of us Blacks are somehow connected? We can be traced back to some tribe in Africa where we were beating drums? That is absurd. You are an Ivy-Leagued woman. How is this logical?"[57] He calls his and Bette's connection to the baby "a fiction of [her] own invention." Melvin rejects an essentialist idea of race that is rooted in biological inheritance and denaturalizes racial identity as biological. He cannot see the baby as carrying on a familial legacy. He also implies that Bette is reifying an archaic idea of race. As Ralina Joseph argues, Melvin's critique points to the precariousness of communities and kinships based on ideas of biological sameness.[58] However, his denial of a connection also reinforces stereotypes of Black male homophobia and detaches class privilege and entitlement as protection from discrimination. Likewise, Kit's Black son, David, in the company of adoption lawyers with influence over Bette's claim on the coming baby, suggests Bette will not be a good mother because she is a lesbian. Both of these incidents code liberalism and tolerance as white. As a result, Bette and Tina must seek out alternate forms of kinships and communities.

The L Word also puts into play notions of kinship and identities that stem from common experiences based on racial heritage and phenotype. When Tina and Bette separate, Tina begins a relationship with a straight white man. She threatens to ask for full custody of their daughter, Angelica. Bette kidnaps the baby and seeks full custody. Bette represents a mothering that is not a reification of the reproductive figure of the mother herself but as a set of practices and tasks. Hence, Bette exceeds the conditions of the mulatta as a reproductive or nonreproductive figure. In spite of Tina's claim to Angelica, Bette absconds with Tina's status as a birth mother and rejects Angelica following Tina's racial status. This invocation of the family reverses the material institutionalism of the family and places Bette's mothering as a form of freeing and humanizing Blackness. Echoing Tina's own reservations that she put aside, she asserts that Tina will have no idea how to raise a biracial daughter: "Tina may have given birth to her, but really, Angelica is the mirror of me. I know what she's going to experience as a biracial girl growing up in a divisive world. I'm the one who's going to be able to give her a sense of belonging. I do not want my daughter growing up in a house where she feels like an outsider because everyone else is white. She's going to get that enough as it is in the world at large, and I know—I know what that feels like."[59] Here Bette posits that whiteness disqualifies Tina from being a proper mother. Whereas Tyrell's abject Blackness led to Leticia's failure as a mother in *Monster's Ball*, Blackness becomes an asset to Bette's parenting rather than a disadvantage. Furthermore, Bette's claim implies that race trumps genetics. Furthermore, she sees her contribution as not just passing down her genes but as imparting lessons on living in a white-dominated society. Thus, it challenges Melvin's critique of racial essentialism. Similar to Halle Berry's own custody battle with Gabriel Aubry over their daughter, Nahla (see chapter 2), both Berry and Bette's character evoke a claim over their daughters because of their connection to a racial identity. Whereas Berry sees her daughter as Black according to the one-drop rule, Bette specifically describes her daughter as biracial and as nonwhite. Thus, unlike the Project RACE strands of the 1990s multiracial movement that sought a multiracial category to distance from Blackness, these claims foreground nonwhiteness in a white hegemonic society. Yet, as Hortense Spillers recalls, "If 'mulatto' originates etymologically in notions of 'sterile mule,' then mulatto-ness is not a genetically transfer-able trait."[60] Bette in fact has no genetic connection to Angelica. The connection between images of mulatta sterility and sexual deviance suggests that Bette occupies a racialized sexual difference and Otherness to the dominant culture.

The representation of Bette's sexual deviance also points to anxieties of racial difference. Bette is consistently portrayed as hypersexual and untrustworthy. After Bette cheats on Tina, her friends shun her, siding with Tina. While Bette assures Tina that she will never be unfaithful again, Tina is frequently suspicious of Bette. She accuses Bette of cheating on her again with Kelly. In fact, Kelly often flirts with Bette, but Bette rejects her. Jenny accuses Bette of cheating on Tina again with Kelly, and the burden of proving that she did not actually cheat falls on Bette. The implication is that Bette lacks the ability to be monogamous. While white characters on the show have also cheated, the main characters mention these incidents less frequently and do not label them as cheaters in the way that they label Bette. The treatment of Bette's infidelity reflects the idea that hypersexuality is essential to Bette's identity. Furthermore, while Shane, a white lesbian, also repeatedly cheats on multiple partners, her friends do not punish her with exclusion.

This differential treatment affirms white homonormativity while presenting racialized queer bodies as aberrant, exotic, and deviant. Proactive sexual aggression is key to the characterizations of Bette, Candace, and Papi, a Latina limo driver. Bette's friends eventually include her again, not because they recognize her loyalty to Tina but because they decide she can't help her inherent sexual promiscuity. As Alice says, Bette "just couldn't keep it in her pants" and is a "sex addict."[61] Thus, they pathologize Bette. Her other markers of belonging such as her class save her from abject Blackness. Homonormativity as related to the regulation of acceptable sexual monogamous activities, racial whiteness, and upper-class customs frame Bette's representation onscreen.

Bette's sexuality is also represented as potentially dangerous. After Tina confronts Bette for cheating on her with Candace, Bette forces Tina to have sex with her. Tina resists, then acquiesces, bringing herself to orgasm. While Bette represents the sensual and beautiful mulatta, she also represents the mulatta counterpart of danger and aggression. The scene marries presentations of the mulatta Bette as a hypersexual Jezebel with that of the feared hypersexual mulatto male evoked in films such as *The Birth of a Nation*. Bette enacts a sexual coercion that echoes a trauma of miscegenation from earlier colonial histories of sexual and racial exploitation that produced mulatta bodies such as Bette. However, the scene displaces violence onto Tina's white female body. The scene's violence and coercion combined with Tina's pleasuring herself thereby also evokes a seduction narrative that justifies sexual violence because of the victim's pleasure. While Bette functions here as the sexually devious temptress, her use of violence against Tina also evokes fears of Black rapists. Like correlations between sexual desire, hysteria, and the mulatto, Bette brings about these fears of a dangerous degenerate potential mulatto Blackness that has risen out of control, with Tina the white female victim. Furthermore, Tina's pleasure connects to colonial discourses of seduction ascribed to mulatta women and white men.

The position of the mulatta resembles the sexual deviant as formulated in sexological texts in the beginning of the twentieth century. Siobhan Somerville documents that "the figure of the mulatto was often seen, explicitly or implicitly, as analogous to the invert: the mixed-race body evoked the mixed-gender body." Eugenic sexologists associated nonwhite bodies with sexual abnormalities. As both lesbians and darker races were supposedly less sexually differentiated than the white norm, sexologists connected both groups together. Racialized bodies were linked with sexual abnormalities. In the 1920s, sexologists observed that clitoral enlargement, supposedly an indication of female homosexuality, was especially common in Black women. They therefore labeled mixed-race people as "sexual half-breeds."[62] While Bette is firm in her identity as a lesbian, this association between sexual and racial degeneracy points to Bette's body as flawed because of the combination of her lesbian and mulatta figure.

However, Bette can find redemption through Tina. While Bette is powerful, but deviant, Tina represents white female purity and virtue. In the beginning of the series, Bette and Tina's relationship is within a heteronormative model with fixed roles of wage earner and mother. When Tina goes back to work while pregnant, she starts at a nonprofit organization serving underprivileged children. With Tina's passion for children and talent as a development writer, she wins a major grant from the Peabody Foundation over Bette's grant application for the museum. Moved by Tina's grant proposal, Helena Peabody comes to visit the nonprofit and becomes smitten by Tina and her pregnant body. Tina is again idealized as honorable and virtuous. Rebecca Beirne describes the contrasts between Tina and Bette and how the show depicts them through "visual and narrative gendered and racial differences." Bette often wears business suits while Tina wears peasant blouses. Occasionally they both wear suits—one in white and one in black.[63] Most importantly, Tina's motherhood places her on a pedestal of purity and virtue associated with femininity and whiteness.

Despite numerous opportunities for relationships with other women, Bette continuously desires Tina. In season four, separated from Tina, Bette falls for Jodi, a deaf lesbian artist, but she questions if she and Jodi have the same values. An independent, outspoken character, Jodi challenges Bette's need for control. Jodi's deafness also forces Bette to confront her own privilege. Jodi is white, but she contrasts with the blonde virtuous docile Tina. When Tina and Bette get back together, they start renovating the house and begin steps to adopt a biracial Black-white child. Ultimately, The L Word suggests that a successful lesbian relationship is based on reproduction and kinship. Their story concludes as they plan a move to New York so that Tina can take advantage of a career opportunity there. Bette says that they should get married and that she will become a stay-at-home parent. Tina thus tames and domesticates Bette's hypersexuality. Bette's anchoring in domesticity, consumption, and hence respectability resembles Mônica of the telenovela Belíssima. Yet, accusations of infidelity with Kelly despite her devotion to Tina charge Bette as intrinsically incapable of monogamy. The L Word thus invokes the mulatta trope of lingering sexual promiscuity along with potential domestication and assimilation.

Alternate Forms of Kinship: Reconfiguring Race and Sexuality

While The L Word's kinship model refutes the primacy of the heteronormative family that undergirded the multiracial movement of the 1990s, the series nonetheless subscribes to normative ideas of the nuclear family with Bette and Tina as the two parents of Angelica.[64] However, the program also potentially points to alternate forms of kinship. It often reinforces the containment of kinship within a citizenship that is based on a nuclear-family model with an emphasis on the class privilege associated with Tina's insemination and Angelica's schooling. Therefore, Bette and Tina's relationship often conforms to an assimilationist politics rather than a restructuring of citizenship and kinship. Reproduction and childrearing are central to this affirmation of lesbian relationships, subject formation, and citizenship.

Depicting Bette as overly ambitious, sexually aggressive, and controlling, the show maintains Tina as a normalized white feminine mother. When Tina leaves Bette for Henry, a white heterosexual man, the program tames anxieties of racial mixing and lesbianism further, as Tina contends that Angelica should be reared in a "real" family, suggesting that a queer interracial family is illegitimate. Tina implies that white heterosexuality will bring normalcy to queered racially mixed disorder. Refusing Bette's request to legally adopt Angelica, Tina also reveals that she and Henry are thinking about having children together and want Angelica to be part of that family. Henry and Tina's refusal reinforces white heteronormativity and their threat attempts to discipline Bette's mixed-Black queer body as a means of control and assimilation. The potential that Tina and Henry can incorporate Angelica into a white heterosexual family points to the erasure of Black remnants through the removal of Bette. Eventually, Tina and Bette return to each other and resume their family unit. Nonetheless, Tina maintains her role as a normal ideal mother.

Tina's forgiveness, the presence of Angelica, and the hope for a new child help purge Bette's abject hypersexual Blackness so that she becomes a suitable citizen. The family formation through Tina and Angelica allows Bette to be represented as responsible, moral, and deserving of her citizenship. Aptly explaining the linkage between parenting, reproduction, and normative citizenship in his discussion of transnational adoption, David Eng states that "the possession of a child, whether biological or adopted, has today become the sign of guarantee not only for family but also for full and robust citizenship—for being a fully realized political, economic, and social subject in American life." However, various sections of *The L Word* attempt to disrupt this dominant narrative of citizenship and point to possible ways to "detach political belonging from (hetero)sexual reproduction."[65]

This detachment potentially undermines white heterosexual privilege. Tina and Bette's tight-knit group of friends and connection to Kit suggest an interracial kinship based on alliances rather than blood. Yet, the role of race as biology remains open. For example, in the last episode of the series, Angelica calls Kit's Black male boyfriend, who often performs in drag, "Daddy."[66] This suggests Angelica still sees a reflection of her own racial makeup in the boyfriend while

Bette (Jennifer Beals) holds her daughter, Angelica, in *The L Word* (2006). Courtesy of Showtime Networks.

also choosing to designate multiple parental figures. *The L Word* constructs an extended queer kinship network detached from biological reproduction, yet loosely ascribing to biological and affective notions of race.

The L Word reimagines the mulatta character by explicitly grappling with sexual agency, desire, class, and reproduction. Rather than the compulsory heterosexuality of mulatta figures such as *Monster's Ball*'s Leticia and mixed-race figures in Brazilian telenovelas, *The L Word* subverts the linkages between mulatta sexuality and white male sexuality. While *The L Word* plays with the idea of the sterile mulatta, who cannot physically reproduce her own form, Bette consciously procreates her own sense of racial self yet detaches her own body as the physical carrier. With Tina as Angelica's birth mother, the mulatta is not tied with sexuality for reproduction. Rather, Bette's sexuality is for pleasure and Tina's body is for reproduction. Such narratives and discourses of reproduction ask which kinds of racialized women's bodies deserve to reproduce, leaving Tina as the white female vessel of reproduction. However, rather than continuing a gradual whitening project, Bette encourages a Blackening of their future children. While Bette's wish points to a reification of race as biology, she also desires the survival of Blackness rather than the erasure of Blackness.

As a new mulatta, Angelica will grow up with a community of queer and straight women with multiple racial identities, suggesting the mulatta figure may be able to break free from heteronormative racial norms. In contrast to the normalizing multiracial model produced in the 1990s and early 2000s that emphasized heterosexual unions and middle-class values, Angelica offers a possible mode of resistance. Angelica represents a future trajectory, but without conditions or guarantees. Although mixed-race children continue to be invoked as the solution for racism, Angelica is neither offered as a promise or as a symbol of heterotopia. Thus, she is not asked to carry the burden of erasing or healing current racial legacies. Instead, her story remains subject to the imagination as to how the contours of the future will unfold.

By *The L Word*'s finale in 2009, media discourse around President Barack Obama's election marked a trajectory of racial progress, justice, and the fruition of the promise of democracy. From the iterations of multiculturalism and color blindness to the 2008 postracial rhetoric and imagery, the mixed-race Black male body served as a way to symbolize the obsoleteness of race. Meanwhile, the celebratory narrative surrounding Obama's election relied on racial progress within a masculine vision that cast aside the specificities of intersectional Black women's experiences. In contrast, the mulatta, as the haunting presence of fraught histories of racial and sexual violence and the embodiment of ambivalent racial and sexual desire, remained in the background. Her haunting, albeit reimagined in the millennial discourses of multiculturalism and post-race, served as a shadow reminder of these colonial histories that had yet to be reckoned with in the present. Instead of grappling with the persistence of racial and gender oppression, media texts manage her Blackness through a focus on her sexuality. The avoidance of interracial conflict through white saviors and the sexualization of the mulatta in *Monster's Ball* and *The L Word* preserved the path toward multicultural progress. Hence, this use of the mulatta figure largely erases the racial stratification in the early 2000s and helps move from color-blind ideology to the postracial visions of the mid-late 2000s around the time of Barack Obama's election and presidency. These mulatta figures do not move beyond Blackness, but rather their Blackness is managed through the regulation of sexuality that simultaneously uses this sexuality as racial capital. In the United States, the mulatta figure, already distilled in the cultural imaginary, presented the desires of placing race away while simultaneously occupying the shadows of colonial legacies. This enablement of postracial visions, weighted through mulatta figures, manages Blackness but does not subsume fears of Blackness. Even while the tenets of multiculturalism and later postracial rhetoric saddle mixed bodies with social and political desire, these same bodies, along with demographic shifts foreseeing the browning of the United States, kindle fears regarding the protection of whiteness. Rather than presented as exceptional, the mulatta represents the extension of persistent configurations of racialized and gendered marginalization.

Hemispherically, the anti-Blackness installed through the transatlantic slave trade to the models of Brazilian whitening and U.S. white purity maintenance transfer to neoliberal methods of Black management and containment. In the 2000s, popular media representations of the Brazilian morena and *mulata* and the U.S. mulatta largely act as mechanisms for maintaining this Black containment. While both U.S. and Brazilian cultural productions in the 2000s increased the visibility of mixed-race women of African descent, visibility does not equalize into progress for social equality. While these media texts do offer spaces of resistance countering whiteness as an ideal, these cultural productions, through tropes of mixed-race sexuality, also affirm white masculinity and white femininity.

In the 2000s, the mixed-race figure demonstrates the nexus of racial histories, contemporary racial politics, and future racial visions. Like Brazilian telenovelas, *Monster's Ball* and *The L Word* show how historical specters of the mixed-race figure come to bear on contemporary cultural productions, how understandings of mixed-race sexuality function as part of national racial narratives, and how a concern over the place of Blackness is inscribed on mixed-race characters. Yet, both Brazilian telenovelas and U.S. media offer spaces of resistance and agency alongside these narratives of Black containment. Despite different media genres, the mulatta figure across the hemisphere is presented in similar ways as a means to manage Blackness. Nonetheless, Brazil is often presented as the synecdoche of the ideal desirable and sensual mixed woman in the transnational imagination. The *mulata*, exemplifying Brazil, becomes the terrain through which historical intimacies and future visions are articulated. The following chapter examines how the U.S. media represents the idea of Brazil and the *mulata*. This U.S. media revisits notions of hemispheric mulatta sexual desirability and displaces U.S. desires and anxieties surrounding mixed race onto the idea of Brazil. Brazil's image projection also relies on revisiting discourses of the place of Blackness and racial mixing in a transnational frame.

5

Remixing Mixedness

U.S. Media Imaginings of Brazil and Brazil's Bid for Rio 2016

Close your eyes and imagine Brazil. You may envision an exotic locale, stretches of tropical beaches. Lining those shores are women in thong bikinis revealing taut brown buttocks, breasts, and luminous bronzed skin and lustrous flowing hair. Samba dancing and passionate sexual exuberance emanate from glistening bodies. In "I Got It From My Mama" (2007), will.i.am captures all of these images, summing up the transnational iconography of the *mulata* that enables the commodified illusion of Brazil as an erotic playground.

Not far from the fetishized *mulata* body on the beach, exotic sexual dangerous thrills can also be found in the form of the favela, wild parties, the passion of intermingling Black, brown, and white bodies embracing, the potential glamour of violence, and the promise of authenticity from poor and jubilant dark-skinned inhabitants. *Fast Five* (2011) and figures like Snoop Dogg and Pharrell also draw from the allure of this photogenic, exotic Brazil, while leaving unexamined the inequalities presented onscreen. With Brazilian national identity constructed through the transnational myths of Brazil, the Rio 2016 Olympic bidding process also branded Brazil as a multiracial paradise of passion, sensuality, and adventure. Samba, colorful dresses, and smiling Black and brown bodies contributed to Rio 2016's winning bid and hopes for future visions of Brazil.

For both Brazil and the United States, the mixed-race female figure serves a crucial role in holding these images together, along with a set of social, cultural, and political practices. Both countries view this figure through a lens of racialized sexual desire and fantasy. The mixed-race female figure elucidates how race, gender, and nation are not bound by a country's boundaries but are actually negotiated performances, existing in the in-between space of national exchange. The Brazilian *mulata* figure serves as an important site of mediation. By using the image of Brazil as it appears in dominant Hollywood, Brazilian-state sponsored, and African American cultural productions, racial mixing and the management of Blackness are translated across multiple audiences.

The *mulata* samba dancers who perform at Brazilian Carnival and appear in tourism marketing are intrinsically tied to the marketing of Brazil itself. The icon of the *mulata de exportação* (*mulata* for exportation) is specifically imagined with a foreign audience in mind. Mixed-race women are utilized as commodified domestic resources in these performances. Meanwhile, in the United States the *mulata* figure is a symbol of Brazilian sexual and racial exoticism. This image of Brazil acts as a site of mediation between the exotic and the familiar. Shaped by similar histories of colonization and slavery, discourses of anti-Blackness, and the postcolonial cultural imaginaries stemming from these legacies, Brazil and the United States engage with the mixed-race female figure to understand commonalities and explore racial management.

Furthermore, changing U.S. racial demographics, particularly an impending nonwhite majority, have led to recurring images and formations of politicized Blackness and anxieties about racial mixing in millennial hip-hop videos and film. Visual and narrative rhetoric of the United States as a future postracial nation circulate readily, and U.S. mixed-race and/or racially ambiguous actors are used to illustrate the idea that race will soon become meaningless in the United States. Like the Brazilian *mulata*, in the United States these mixed-race actors serve as proof of racial diversity, while simultaneously pointing the way toward racelessness.

Brazil stands in as a symbolic example of an already racially mixed and racially ambiguous nation. However, this image making must consider gender and sexuality along with race and nation. The hypersexualization of Brazilian female bodies in general, and the *mulata* body in particular, posits womanhood in service to a U.S. empire. Thus, women of color function largely as objects, not subjects, in this hemispheric imaginary. As we have seen in previous chapters, Brazil's national mythmaking projects the idea of a unified racially mixed nation that is on its way to gradual whiteness. It differs from the U.S. racial mixture, providing a familiar yet alien racialized national vision. However, U.S. cultural productions emphasize Brazilian sexuality and view Brazil as a form of escape and a site of sexual freedom through a reliance on the *mulata* figure.

U.S. cultural representations use Brazil to project an idea of Otherness that also encompasses sameness through popular culture images of the *mulata* and racial mixing.

U.S. music videos such as Snoop Dogg and Pharrell's "Beautiful" (2003), will.i.am's "I Got It From My Mama," and the Hollywood film *Fast Five* (2011) exploit Brazil's image as a racial paradise and a site of Black male independence, based on its reputation as a racial democracy with a large mixed-race population and the historical absence of legal segregation.[1] While the early 2000s emphasized mixed-Black women as the locus of sexual and racial fetishization, by the 2010s during the Obama era, the affirmation of a multicultural society flanked by mixed Black heroes such as Vin Diesel temporarily displaced the primacy of mixed-Black women. Easily commodified within global capitalism, racially mixed ambiguous bodies transform to meet differing ideologies of empire, racial democracy, neoliberal multiculturalism, and postrace. As this chapter reveals, these representations reflect U.S. desires and anxieties—and Brazil's participation as well, because the U.S. imagination of Brazil influences Brazil's self-understanding as a nation. The relationship between the national and the transnational is key in the production of an imaginary of Brazil.

Thus, as a participant in this production of self across borders, Brazil has cultivated an exotic image of itself. The Brazilian state partakes in the crafting of its national image to the West, creating a discourse of tropical abundance that has correlated with discourses of unbridled sexuality since Brazil's colonial period.[2] Presented itself on a global scale through the Rio 2016 Olympics bidding process and promotion of the Olympic Games, Brazil also temporarily discarded the sensual transnational *mulata* figure. Instead of the *mulata* whose body represented the racial fetishization of the nation, Brazil displayed other representations of mixture as a distinguishing feature that linked a sense of both national and global shared histories and futures. The United States' imagination of Brazil and Brazil's imagination of and presentation of itself to the world demonstrate a transnational dialogical process that shapes each country's identities and understandings of race.

Precursors to the Image of Brazil as Tropical Racial Paradise

Contemporary U.S. media's use of Brazil has its roots in 1940s cultural discourses including the films made under the Good Neighbor Policy in Hollywood as part of a strategic effort to advocate for Pan-American cooperation during World War II. These films represent Brazilian women as both sexual and consumable. With her wide smile and twinkling eyes, the Portuguese-born, Brazilian-raised Carmen Miranda helped propagate an exoticized and idealized image of Brazil's racial democracy. She allayed white anxieties about ethnic and racial differences and the potential threat these differences pose to U.S. national identity and citizenship.[3] Fashioning herself as an authentic emblem of brasilidade, she began to sing, dance, and perform samba and appropriated the Afro-Brazilian *baiana* (an iconic Afro-Brazilian woman from Bahia often associated with Afro-Brazilian street food markets and samba) figure through costumes and musical and dance performance. By the early 1900s, the baiana and *mulata* figure became collapsed within both Brazilian vaudeville theater and the collective Brazilian imagination. Played for laughs, white actresses dominated the baiana-*mulata* archetype in Brazilian theater until the 1920s when racially mixed actresses also began to take on this role.[4] By Hollywood standards, Miranda's phenotypical light skin and whiteness mixed with her performance and costuming allowed a mix of exoticism and assuring familiarity. Jubilant and sensual, Miranda represented a nominally white, yet Other representation for U.S. audiences. Significantly, the characters she portrayed in film could sing, dance, and flirt with white male characters, but they never married. The men in her movies ultimately tied themselves to U.S. actresses the audience would read as fully white. In this way, the narrative prevented Miranda's erotic characters from posing any threat to the U.S. racial order.

Carmen Miranda was the first major Brazilian celebrity in the United States, and her influence continues more than a half-century after her death, not only in the United States but also in Brazil. Positioned as exotic, friendly, and available, her image has shaped notions of Brazil and the exotic tropics in both countries. Miranda's exaggeration of accent, language, costuming, and body movement were all part of a performance of the Other. As a symbol of a racially mixed-Brazilian and a Pan-Latina, she represented tensions in the desire and fear of mestiçagem through her phenotypically white body. Her star persona familiarized and diminished the threat of the ethnic non-American Other, presenting the image of Brazil as primarily white. This allowed her to incorporate Afro-Brazilian culture, such as samba and Carnival, into an idea of Brazilian mestiçagem and racial harmony without disrupting the racial order in the United States and Brazil.

Contemporary U.S. images of Brazil as an exotic paradise draw on the legacies of Carmen Miranda. Portrayed in U.S. films as overtly sexual and desirous of white men, Miranda signified the *mulata* without actually being racially mixed. Thus, she displaced the desire for an exotic taboo mixed Blackness without a threat to U.S. racial boundaries. However, the light-skinned sensual and exotic

Miranda has been replaced by the darker-skinned sexually available *mulata* in the U.S. imaginary.

Carmen Miranda, as a white Brazilian playing an Afro-Brazilian baiana in Hollywood films stood at the nexus of transnational racial formations and notions of racial hybridity. Yet, her fame in Brazil and the United States did not budge white supremacy, but rather drew the racial regimes of the U.S. and Brazil closer together. President Getúlio Vargas sought to utilize Miranda to sell an image of Brazil as a nation of racial democracy, abundant coffee, and joy. The Brazilian state wished to project this image of racial democracy while diminishing the presence of Afro-Brazilians onscreen. By avoiding representing Brazil as a majority Black nation, the paradigm of whiteness for domestic and U.S. consumption prevailed.[5] Brazil's global image has been predicated on this fantasy of racial harmony. Following World War II, other countries began to regard Brazil as a model of racial harmony and tolerance, an image that has persisted in spite of racial inequalities.

Like *Paraíso Tropical*'s self-referential image of Brazil as a tropical paradise (see chapter 3), the Brazilian state has consistently adopted and promoted the idea of Brazil as a sensual utopia. While the Brazilian *mulata* is actually the product of colonial sexual violence rather than Gilberto Freyre's love allegory, the figure has functioned as a sign of racial harmony to Brazilian and international observers alike. Brazilian governmental tourism agencies began utilizing the image of the sexually available *mulata* for the promotion of Brazil as a tourist destination in the 1970s. Materials promoted the association of Brazil, especially Rio de Janeiro, with beautiful scantily clad *mulatas*, the beach, and samba.[6] These dominant images of the *mulata* reinforce the idea of a racial democracy and distort the historical legacies and contemporary practices of racism. The Olympic bidding process and the televising of the Rio Olympic handover from 2012's London Olympic Games illustrate the image of racial diversity that Brazil wants to project to the world.

Brazilian Racial Paradise and the *Mulata* in the African American Imagination

Until recently, the majority of U.S. media representations of Brazilian women pair them romantically or sexually with white men from the United States. Brazilian popular culture has presented racial mixing in gendered ways, pairing white men with women of African or Indigenous descent. These popular narratives exclude Indigenous and Afro-Brazilian men alike. However, U.S. cultural productions in the early 2000s, such as the "Beautiful" and "I Got It from My Mama" music videos, present African American men as the main sexual partners of Brazilian *mulata* women.

While U.S. audiences might deem light-skinned African American women more attractive than their darker-skinned counterparts, these videos, like earlier representations, present light-skinned Brazilian women as also reliably sexually available. Instead of contrasting the *mulata* with a U.S. white man, they contrast the essential femininity and sensuality of Brazilian women with images of U.S. Black virility and essential U.S. masculinity. Like earlier pairings, they articulate the essential masculinity and sexual prowess of the United States, extending those attending entitlements to African American men.

African American exploration of Brazil's racial system as a potential utopic imaginary is evident in both fictional and nonfictional African American cultural production. In *African-American Reflections on Brazil's Racial Paradise* (1992), David J. Hellwig anthologizes a number of accounts from African Americans who traveled to Brazil in the early twentieth century seeking a racial paradise that offered integration, economic opportunities, and social and political freedom. These primary sources of letters, essays, travel accounts, and newspaper articles demonstrate that for many African Americans, Brazil was an inspiring symbol. Also apparent in these pieces, however, is the eventual disillusionment many experienced later in Brazil. For example, set in Harlem in the 1920s, Nella Larsen's novel *Passing* (1929) describes the longing of Brian, an African American doctor, to leave the United States for perceived better racial and social conditions in Brazil. There, the reader understands, African Americans would have no need to pass for white. Brian envisions Brazil as a utopia, where African American men can have a place in national belonging and possess the Black male cultural citizenship the United States denied them. In 1965, a two-part series in *Ebony* magazine, "Does Amalgamation Work in Brazil?," used the example of Brazil to suggest that racial amalgamation was integral to racial integration and as such, racial mixing, could help solve racism.[7] In a later evocation of mixed races, passing, and the desire for an imagined racially free Brazil, Danzy Senna's *Caucasia* (1998), set in the 1970s, features Deck, a Black father who moves to Brazil with the darker of two mixed-race daughters in the hope that Brazil as a "mulatto nation" would offer better living conditions than the United States. Meanwhile, he leaves his lighter-skinned daughter, Birdie, behind in the United States. While Deck ultimately expresses his disillusionment with Brazil, which is not the "mulatto nation" he had imagined, saying that its racial inequalities resembled the ones he had left behind, the notion of racial utopia in Brazil persists in our culture. African Americans have imagined Brazil as a place without a color line where, alternatively, they might move and

be freed of racial discrimination, or that might provide a model for its elimination in the United States. However, these imaginations did not reflect the
conditions of Black people in the Americas under which Blacks lived under
exclusion and marginalization in both Brazil and the United States. While Brazil
sought to encourage European immigration as a means of branqueamento, and
restricted visitation to the country by U.S. citizens of African descent in the
late nineteenth and early twentieth centuries, the image of Brazil remained a
site of relative liberty.[8]

African American fascination with Brazil has, of late, transformed Brazil into
a tourist commodity. As Patricia Pinho observes, many African American tourists have begun to participate in "roots" tourism in the state of Bahia (known
as the most Afro-Brazilian state in terms of population and preservation of
heritage). While this roots tourism is important as a source of Black pride and
identity, the African Americans who can travel are usually those with the most
access to power and capital and may be far wealthier than the Afro-Brazilians
they visit.[9] Furthermore, with the rise of African American sex tourism, as Erica
Williams notes, African American men carry U.S. privileges exoticizing Brazilian women of African descent who fit into visual aesthetics of racial mixture.[10]

The legacies of African American ideas of Brazil remain very present in U.S.
hip-hop videos, where Brazil emerges as an eroticized space of adventure and
escape that capitalizes on Black hypersexuality. The relative racial freedom
that traveling to Brazil offers blends with sexual and political freedom as men
limited in the United States have their choice of women of various colors without consequences. The *mulata* figure in videos for songs like "Beautiful" and
"I Got It from My Mama" becomes reconfigured in U.S. imaginings of Brazil
as a site of racialized sexual paradise and freedom, and symbolically mediates
between the exotic and the familiar. This figure appears distinguishable from
the racial binaries of the United States and is, hence, exotic and desirable. Yet,
at the same time, she physically resonates with the often-silenced racial mixing
of the United States.

These videos present the *mulata* figure in a medium that permeates both national and transnational mediascapes through their dissemination via television
channels, the internet, and platform technologies such as Apple iTunes. Arjun
Appadurai uses the term "mediascape" to refer to the "global flow and distribution and dissemination of information and images."[11] These mediascapes are
particularly useful for considering the imagining of identity within and beyond
national boundaries. In these U.S. cultural productions, African American men
enact practices and discourses of U.S. masculinity and empire with the Brazilian *mulata* figure as a site of desire and conquest. Figuring Brazil as a place of

sexual freedom and male independence, they present African diasporic relationships between African Americans and Afro-Brazilians as sites of power imbalances and economic privilege rather than solidarity. In fact, many African Americans—not just successful pop stars—have more economic privilege than do Brazilian women of color. While focusing on their own racial and sexual freedom, African American men still have the capacity to enact patterns of oppression. By emulating the patriarchal white imperialist power structures, African American men in these U.S. cultural productions participate in U.S. heteropatriarchal empire.

Through the visual images in these music videos, Snoop Dogg, Pharrell, and will.i.am continue the descriptive rhetoric of European travel journals, narratives, and paintings and work within the racialized and sexualized ideologies of exoticism practiced during colonial and imperial periods.[12] With the transnational circulation of images of Brazilian women of African descent and the upsurge of globalization and tourism, Brazil emerges as a tropical sexually liberated paradise where brown female bodies are available for pleasure. As Joel Zito Araújo observes in his 2009 documentary, *Cinderelas, Lobos e um Príncipe Encantado* (Cinderellas, Wolves, and a Prince Charming), Afro-descendant women comprise 75 percent of foreign tourists' objects of desire. These African American musicians participate, along with white men, in the seeking of nonwhite eroticized female bodies as objects of sexual consumption with minimal financial costs or responsibilities. Their videos depict the United States within a heterosexual model of masculinity and Brazil within a context of erotic fantasy of feminized objects. Thereby, African American men in these hip-hop videos align themselves with white men in terms of an entitled Western masculine access to women. They hold African American male bodies and Brazilian female bodies of color as gendered and racialized ideals. However, they deny the women subjecthood at the expense of the development and privileging of heterosexual male subjects.[13]

Snoop Dogg and Pharrell are among the most famous hip-hop artists to use Brazil and its women in their videos and to use the Brazilian *mulata* figure as "the visual representation of the new *Black* feminine ideal in hip hop culture."[14] Their song "Beautiful" celebrates the beauty of Black women in the United States, and the accompanying video celebrates the beauty of Black women in Brazil. The song seems to present a diasporic pride and appreciation of Black female beauty. Yet the video's images focus on light-skinned Brazilian women, repeating the fetishization of light-skinned women that T. Denean Sharpley-Whiting notes in U.S. hip-hop videos set in the United States. This fascination with ascriptive mulattas combines Black sexual passion with white physical beauty.[15] The rise of African American sex tourism in search of these *mulatas* is a manifestation of the fantasy of the exotic, yet familiar. For example, Pharrell's DVD *Dude, We're Going to Rio* (2003) chronicles his search for a bronzed dripping-wet model he sees on a poster. While the women who appear in these videos may not literally identify as mixed-race women, the image of the light-skinned and hypersexual mulatta/*mulata* stands in for erotic desire. In the music video "Beautiful," which is set in Brazil, Pharrell and Snoop Dogg gaze at countless numbers of seminude Brazilian women of color as they smile seductively at Copacabana beach and the favela. While the song proclaims, "see I just want you to know that you are really special," it appears that such *mulata* beauty is actually quite commonplace rather than unique and deserving of individual attention. Emphasizing the centrality of the sexual desire of the video's protagonists, Snoop Dogg and Pharrell, Afro-Brazilian men only enter the video as samba drummers, performing as part of the *bateria* (percussion section) for the samba dancers and for Snoop Dogg and Pharrell to dance to at the party. Their role is to serve as backdrops that facilitate a sense of Brazilian authenticity.

The video focuses on hair and body parts, such as buttocks and hips, as Black signifiers. With lyrics that include "Long hair, wit'cha big fat booty" and "Black and beautiful, you the one I'm choosin' / Hair long and Black and curly like you're Cuban," Snoop Dogg and Pharrell enter into an existing discourse of the politics of hair in the African diaspora. As in the United States, in Brazil coarse hair is associated with Black phenotypes and therefore is often considered to be bad hair or "cabelo ruim."[16] Hair functions alongside skin color and phenotypical attributes, such as the nose and lips, to assign racial classification. Therefore, when Snoop Dogg presents long hair or curly hair as beautiful, he is also stating a preference for less Africanized features and working within a racialized and gendered hierarchal system of beauty. When the lyrics state "like you're Cuban," he is also making transnational references to an aesthetic of beauty that is not associated with the Blackness of the United States, but an exotic yet familiar Latinidad. Cuba, like Brazil, holds the *mulata* figure as central to national identity and sensuality.[17] Therefore, Cuba and Brazil become exchangeable symbols of *mulata* beauty within a narrative of hemispheric and diasporic racial mixing. Detailing the mid- to late-1990s rise of the Puerto Rican "butta pecan mami" in hip-hop culture, Raquel Rivera notes how these women are "represented as a tropical, exotic, and racially 'lighter' variation on ghetto Blackness and that is precisely why they are so coveted."[18] The commodification of racially ambiguous women feeds into the U.S. early 2000s multiracial chic and extends the mid-1990s fetishization of Latinas into a U.S. Black male entanglement with Brazil. Notions like Latinidad serve as conduits through which the figure of the *mulata* is "sold" to both U.S. and global audiences. In other words, the *mulata* might be Black in some eyes but Latina in others, yet she is hypersexualized in both through tropes of tropical bodies and other heterosexual fantasies that are polymorphous in terms of desire. Women of African descent are caught in these transnational ideological frameworks.

The reference to "like you're Cuban" also suggests that U.S. women have some of these same aesthetic attributes, and thus are also part of these hemispheric histories of racial mixing. The video views women through an exoticist heterosexist frame and imagines Brazilian women in relational terms to the United States. However, unambiguously Black female bodies are undesirable in a transnational paradigm. The song's lyrics referencing the United States and Cuba alongside the visual images of Brazil point to a conflation of national differences, yet also an understanding of Black women as connected through diaspora. Thus, it relies on notions of a shared Blackness while simultaneously casting Brazilian women of African descent as sensual exotic others.

The emphasis in both the lyrics and the video on body parts such as the buttocks invokes sexuality very directly. Hence, Snoop Dogg and Pharrell emphasize stereotypical exaggerations of Black female buttocks that are deemed desirable because they are also highly sexualized. When Snoop Dogg references "big fat booty" alongside "long hair," he suggests that only certain stereotypical Black physical attributes are desirable and only because they are considered to be sexually pleasurable. The camera at times focuses on the buttocks of women of African descent and, in a segment in which samba is performed at a party, the camera zooms in on the hips and buttocks of the women dancing.

In the "Beautiful" video, a young Black boy hears a phone ring and runs to find Snoop Dogg, who sits with a Brazilian *mulata* braiding his hair. He answers the phone with "E Ai" (an informal hello or "what's up?"). Thus, the opening associates local Blackness in Rio de Janeiro with a rawness or realness derived from urban Black culture. It constructs Black male authenticity as relational to street credibility and virility. The reliance on African American masculinity reinforces ideas of hypersexuality. However, the video also presents a racial narrative quite different from that of the United States, in that African American male sexuality is not feared or transgressive but rather is presented as powerful and authoritative in Brazil. Through the *mulata*, samba, Copacabana beach, and the favela, the video positions a foreign male gaze that invigorates images of Brazil as a sexual exotic paradise. "Beautiful" situates Snoop Dogg and Pharrell as masculine and virile through the objectification of brown female bodies—sexual commodities of transnational diasporic affiliations.

will.i.am's music video "I Got It from My Mama" offers another version of an alternative racial narrative, with African American men as the principal actors of power. It, too, relies on the sexual availability of Brazilian women and the evocation of Black heritage. The opening presents images of tourist brochures featuring beautiful bikini-clad Brazilian women of color on the beach. The tourist gaze in the initial part of the video, and in the last segment with will.i.am appearing in a postcard, reinforces the idea of sexual escape. After the opening, will.i.am is alone on the beach surrounded by Brazilian women of varying shades of brown. Like "Beautiful," the video's beach landscape reinforces conventional portable images of Brazil as an exotic tropical paradise of sexually available *mulatas*. In a musical refrain, he asks, "Where did you get that body from?" A light brown-skinned woman with tight curly hair responds, "I got it from my mama." In unison, a number of different women in the video, start singing the line "I got it from my mama." The statement invokes, by implication, Black mothers. These racially ambiguous women give a nod to their African descent as their bodies and genealogy are presumed to be from their Black mothers. Thus, the video incorporates the Brazilian narrative of whitening through racial mixing by presenting light-skinned brown bodies as desirable because of their supposed phenotypical combination of large Black buttocks with light skin and silky hair. Here again, European phenotypical traits, such as straight or wavy hair and lighter skin, represent beauty and Black phenotypical traits are constructed as sensual and sexual. Brazil has often presented itself as beautiful and sexually desirable precisely because of its racial mixing.

A number of times when will.i.am asks, "Where did you get that body from?," the camera answers with images of thong-clad Black and brown buttocks to represent racialized biological difference. As in the infamous case of Sara Baartman, known as the Hottentot Venus, the visual emphasis on the buttocks stands as a substitute for race.[19] However, when the women answer "I got it from my mama," their faces are brown, not Black. The video implies that Black female bodies supply sexually desirable body parts but that racial mixing perfects them phenotypically. At the same time, the oppositional Black maternal figure is evoked. While the Black maternal figure is not physically present in the video, "I got it from my mama" reminds the viewer of her role in the *mulata* figure's African ancestry and her supposed genetic gifts, including shapely buttocks and a curvaceous figure. Whereas the United States determines racial classification through hypodescent, Brazil uses phenotype, rather than ancestry, to determine classification. Therefore, the imagined Brazilian Black mother is only a contributor to some of the *mulata* figure's phenotypical traits but is not the determinant of the *mulata* figure's identity. The relational meanings between nation and race vis-à-vis the United States and Brazil allow the buttocks to signify racialized sexual difference.

In the videos, their buttocks carry the perceived nonwhiteness of women of varying shades of brown. The sexual objectification of women of African descent relegates women of varying shades to an imaginary of Black sexuality. This visual idea of Blackness displays their hypersexuality and availability for will.i.am. The focus on the buttocks in the music video connects Blackness and sexual pleasures. While U.S. hip-hop music videos such as Sir Mix-a-Lot's 1992 "Baby Got Back" could be read as subversive in its valuation of beauty standards, the emphasis on the buttocks also reduces Black women to a single body part, reinforces Black female hypersexuality, and links Black male "realness" with the objectification of Black women.[20]

This notion of Black authenticity relies on Black male heteronormativity stemming from white patriarchal objectifications of Black masculine hypersexuality and desire. Therefore, rather than rejecting white patriarchal origins, many Black male artists themselves embrace a strategy of hypersexuality and hypermasculinity as a marker of authentic Blackness or "keeping it real." The performance of authentic Blackness and self-representation is tied to notions of sexual prowess and sexual agency.[21] This supposed appreciation of the buttocks connects ideas of Black authenticity and African American masculinity. Hip-hop culture has often praised the buttocks, and will.i.am's focus on it further legitimizes him as racially authentic. Like Snoop Dogg and Pharrell, will.i.am reinforces linkages between virility and racialized masculinity, both within Black cultural politics and according to dominant white U.S. culture.

The "I Got It from My Mama" video uses the *mulata* figure as a mediation of white hegemonic beauty ideals and the spectacle of Black female sexuality. The light-skinned mulatta figure in the United States evokes histories of racialized sexual violence and chattel slavery. She also evokes the history of the U.S. fascination with the beauty of the mulatta, from antebellum novels to the tragic cinematic figure of Dorothy Dandridge. The mulatta exists in the African American cultural memory as proof of racial sexual transgressions, as victim, and/or as conspirator with white male hegemony. By desiring an aesthetically similar figure, namely, the *mulata*, outside U.S. borders, the video separates the mulatta from the racial and sexual tensions, desires, and taboos that she might invoke in the United States, allowing her, in Brazil, to be merely an object of sensual bliss.

The video's erasure of racial and sexual oppression in Brazil signifies a willful forgetting of U.S. empire and the entangled imperial histories between the

United States and Latin America. While most U.S. viewers are aware of the nation's histories of slavery, few recognize its imperial legacies, from economic and political exploitation to the systematic exportation of cultural values and ideologies. While both the Brazilian *mulata* and U.S. mulatta reflect hemispheric ideological legacies in which whiteness is privileged and Blackness is hypersexualized, the willful ignorance of entangled histories allows the Brazilian *mulata* figure to be a sign of sensuality relieved of troubled U.S. histories of Black slavery and sexual exploitation. The Brazilian *mulata* is, thus, removed from the African American cultural memory of the mulatta as proof of racial sexual transgressions, as victim, and/or as conspirator with white male hegemonies. Yet, she remains a specter of hemispheric and diasporic histories. Similar but not quite identical to the U.S. mulatta, the Brazilian *mulata* is thereby separate from the historical materiality of suffering in the United States, existing in a tropical landscape of pleasure. She can, through willful ignorance, be part of an African American male cosmopolitan imagination rather than a material reminder of hemispheric patterns of slavery and racialized sexual violence.

As in "Beautiful," "I Got It from My Mama" makes brown female bodies interchangeable and thus disposable. *Mulata* sexuality becomes an eroticized commodity. With will.i.am as the only male figure in the video, the women essentially become wallpaper for the set and their commodification emphasizes will.i.am's subjectivity, as the star of this cultural production. This video plays into male heterosexual fantasies of multiple sexual partners and male sexual insatiability. Thus, the masculine ideal is a subject, represented by a single Black man, while the feminine ideal is an object, represented by collective images of women that are in service to the individual man. Like the "Beautiful" video, "I Got It from My Mama" participates along with Carnival, advertising, telenovelas, and literature in the transnational cultural memory and production of the Brazilian erotic imaginary. These two videos reinforce centuries-old myths about *mulata* sensuality and sexual availability, while reconfiguring perspectives on hemispheric and diasporic relationships between African American men and women of color. Fast forwarding to 2011, Brazil and mixed Blackness take on new iterations in film format to meet the needs of shifting U.S. and Brazilian political racial orders.

Fast Five and Futuristic Racial Imaginings

Pushing past yellow police tape, Elena, a Brazilian police officer, gracefully walks to approach FBI agent Hobbs. The audience first encounters her surrounded by male officers at the late-night scene of a crime, backlit by the pulsing police lights. Hobbs admits that he recruited her because she is motivated, honest, and cannot be bought, making casual reference to Brazilian corruption and bribery. In subsequent scenes, Elena is continuously illuminated to give the illusion of glowing evanescence.

Elena's dirty blonde hair, green eyes, and tanned white skin allow her to transform into an ideal feminine whiteness associated with purity. This same purity allows for Elena to hold a strong moral compass as the darker-skinned Brazilians convey an implied lesson about comparative morality. Elena's whiteness is dissimilar from the *mulata* and dark Brazilian bodies on screen. Her whiteness combined with notions of Brazilian racial ambiguity stage a socially palatable aesthetic femininity that allows her to becomes a heroine in *Fast Five* (2011).

Played by Spanish actor Elsa Pataky, Elena appears as a liminal or off-whiteness. She is white by Brazilian standards, but to U.S. audiences she might still appear as mysterious or exotic. Spain, on the perimeters of Europe, Africa, and the Middle East, possesses a historically syncretic culture and population. While a Spanish identity is subsumed under Hispanic and thus implicitly othered from normative whiteness in the United States, white privilege tends to persist, especially in Latin America. Like the Spanish actor Penélope Cruz playing Isabella, a Brazilian woman in *Woman on Top* (2000), Elena, through Elsa Pataky, is also civilizable. She somatically fits into the idea of the new "multiculti" aesthetic with a tan hue.[22]

Differing from the morena and *mulata* women who are wild or needing to be cultivated into the white middle and upper classes, Elena does not blend into the scenery. She is exceptional. When Agent Hobbs specifically asks for Elena to be part of his team, he claims, "she is the one person in this country who cannot be bought."[23] The statement figures Brazil as corruptible, but it also puts the hope for honesty, justice, law, and order in the hands of a white woman with a slight ethnic difference for U.S. audiences.

Light-skinned and light-haired, Elena symbolically represents a point of purity in the corrupt Brazilian public sphere. She appears as superior to her male Brazilian police officers because of her integrity. Whereas the darker-skinned women in U.S. hip-hop videos and the assortment of Brazilian women accompanying offer inviting seductive smiles, Elena rarely smiles and instead glares intensely. Her face, rather than her body, is accentuated onscreen as she occupies a space of relative privilege in relation to darker-skinned Brazilian women. Yet, she is still an exotic figure onscreen. Her light features transition her to an exotic body within the space of the favela. Elena evokes familiarity, strangeness, and desire. Yet, unlike the *mulata* figure, she is neither a sexual threat nor a consumable sexual object.

Like U.S. hip-hop videos, the film *Fast Five* also relies on images of Brazil as a tropical, racially harmonious, sexualized, exotic paradise, but it also inserts a hypermasculine, multiracial U.S. hero and a white heroine to mediate between the United States and Brazil. Beginning in 2001, the earlier films in the *Fast and the Furious* franchise employed racially ambiguous protagonists to mediate concerns in regards to the changing racial landscape in the United States.[24] *Fast Five* extends these anxieties in 2011, in an era marked by U.S. postracial discourses, an increasing global audience base, and the emerging economic and political significance of Brazil. While the hip-hop videos emphasize multiracial Blackness, *Fast Five* uses an idea of racelessness that discards adherence to racial identities and bounded communities and, ultimately, recenters multiracial aesthetics as a process of becoming an ambiguous brown body that is closer to white than to Black.

By the time of *Fast Five's* release in 2011, the media framing of Barack Obama's presidential win had made a celebratory linear narrative of national masculine racial progress. Discussing Barack Obama, who became celebrated simultaneously as a postracial icon of "transcendent multiracial identity" and a symbol of Black advancement, Habiba Ibrahim argues that mixed male public figures become prominent to racial progress while Black mothers, as furthering Blackness itself, become antithetical to the national dream and to resolving racial divides.[25] By the 2010s, the U.S. mulatta could not function as a racial heroine—this task was now taken up by mixed Black public figures. Instead, the urgency of the 2010s required a break with previous racial narratives of multiraciality in which the mulatta is laden with memories of colonial sexual violence. That *Fast Five* coincided with Obama's presidency necessitated a forgetting of the past to conjure a social vision of multiracial utopia. Thus, the mulatta of the past and the futuristic mulatta reproducing the nation are displaced here by the urgent masculine mulatto present. It is here that Vin Diesel's star text as racially ambiguous, multiracial, and Black emerges as a key framing of *Fast Five's* tensions centering on the haunted histories of U.S. miscegenation with postracial desires.

While U.S. empire and notions of sexual availability restrain the Brazilian *mulata* figure, *Fast Five* demonstrates that the U.S. male mulatto figure can find freedom in Brazil. Dom, played by the racially ambiguous actor Vin Diesel, functions as an outlaw hero who can seamlessly cross national and ethnic boundaries in and between the United States and Brazil. Dom's ability to cross these borders is facilitated by Vin Diesel's persona. While Vin Diesel does not specify his ethnic background, rumors abound that he is of Italian, African American, and Afro-Dominican heritage.[26] He played an Italian American in *Saving Private Ryan* (1998), and he has played racially ambiguous characters in other films such as *Pitch Black* (2000), *XXX* (2002), and *The Chronicles of Riddick* (2004).

Viewers understand Vin Diesel as African American, multiracial, Italian, or Latino depending on marketing and context, unlike their understanding of Snoop Dogg, Pharrell, and will.i.am, which is independent of those factors. According to Rob Cohen, director of *The Fast and the Furious* (2001) and *XXX* (2002), "People can relate to his multiethnicity. Vin represents that big chunk of America that doesn't look at blond-haired, blue-eyed actors and think that could be them."[27] While the November 2002 *Ebony* and July 2002 *Jet* magazines and *BET* have featured Vin Diesel, and he has served as a presenter at the 2002 NAACP Image Awards, he does not outright claim his Blackness. However, unlike Jennifer Beals and Mariah Carey, who have been accused of passing, Vin Diesel has not met the same criticism. Rather, as an *Entertainment Weekly* article states, "Diesel isn't being coy, he's being clever. . . . By stripping away all identifying marks, presenting himself as a blank slate—particularly when it comes to his racial background—he's found a way to market himself to the broadest possible audience."[28] Indeed, in *Fast Five*, Vin Diesel stands in not only as a U.S. everyman, but as an everyman of the Americas due to his blurring of racial and national borders.

Just as the importance of celebrity mattered for reading the cultural texts of Camila Pitanga, Halle Berry, and Jennifer Beals in earlier chapters, Vin Diesel's star text is crucial to understanding his role as Dom and the connections to national identity and race. The actor's racially ambiguous star image allows for subversive potentialities in *Fast Five*. In contrast to the emphasis on hypersexuality or femininity for racially ambiguous female characters, Dom exhibits extreme masculinity in his large muscles, strength, authority, and attractiveness to women. These contrasting images of multiracial Blackness for female and male characters warrants further study; here I will emphasize that both images speak to racial anxieties and desires and read Vin Diesel as mixed and Black. However, unlike the mulatta and *mulata* characters in the United States and in Brazil, who must remain stationary in relation to correlations of national identity, status, and race, Vin Diesel's character in the *Fast and the Furious* film series, which includes *Fast Five*, transgresses the boundaries of race and nation, claiming subjectivity as the films' hero.

In *Fast Five*, Dom pursues economic and political freedom, rather than sexual freedom, in Brazil. As in *Narratives of the Life of Frederick Douglass, An American Slave* (1845), the mulatto hero highlights a masculinist fugitivity as a means of freedom. As Dom embodies national and racial hybridity, the slippages and tensions between race and nation are apparent. Through visual representation, the narrative, and the spatial logics of the film, Dom is constructed as a multiracial body that crosses racial and geographical spaces. Furthermore, Dom's dislodgement from the United States, its legal structures, and citizenship, places him in the role of an outlaw hero.

Throughout the franchise, the *Fast and the Furious* films have capitalized on a raceless aesthetic with broad audience bases. As Mary Beltrán argues, they present an urban multicultural and, seemingly, postracial world in which the film's heroes conduct cultural border crossings that are paramount to survival. The casting of mixed-race lead actors with light-tan skin hues suggests a potentially raceless aesthetic, but, in the process, the casting largely recenters whiteness.[29] While the relative racelessness of Dom offers ambiguous readings, what might it mean to see Dom not coded as raceless, as shorthand for white, but rather to see him explicitly as multiracial Black? As Mary Beltrán observes, the gradual Latinization of his character over the course of the films further facilitates Dom's racial fluidity. While their last name, Toretto, implies that Dom and his sister Mia (played by Jordana Brewster, who has Brazilian and European American heritage) are Italian, the scripts tell us they grew up among Latinos in Los Angeles. Dom's long-term girlfriend, Letty, in the previous *Fast and Furious* films (played by Michelle Rodriguez of mixed white, Black, and Indigenous Puerto Rican and Dominican heritage), speaks Spanish, and has traveled and lived in Latin America.[30] In an interview concerning his prequel film, *Los Bandoleros*, about Dom's life in the Dominican Republic, Vin Diesel says: "Growing up in Manhattan many of the brothers which I grew up with were Dominican. There is something very multicultural of the Dominican Republic and so I identify with [them] . . . 75% of the Dominican population is mulatto, which means, like me, are of European and African descent."[31] Dom manages to represent African American, Latino, and Latin American border crossings within a hemispheric context through Vin Diesel's persona.

In the opening of *Fast Five*, Dom is on his way to a maximum-security prison when Mia and her boyfriend, Brian, hijack the prisoner transport van. On the run, the three head to Rio de Janeiro. Once there, they contact Vince, a white U.S. friend living in Brazil. Uncovering corruption, money laundering, and a massive drug trade, Dom proposes organizing a group of friends to steal a large sum of money from Hernan Reyes (played by Portuguese actor Joaquim de Almeida), a dangerous, morally corrupt, but politically connected Brazilian drug lord. If Dom can accomplish this feat, known as his "last job," he will have enough economic resources to live anywhere he chooses. At stake is not just his economic freedom but his resistance to imprisonment after a team of FBI agents, led by Agent Hobbs (played by multiracial actor Dwayne "The Rock" Johnson), travel to Brazil to capture Dom. For Dom, political and economic freedom go hand in hand with Brazil.

Dom's freedom relies on his ability to assemble a diverse group skilled in racing, forgery, and auto mechanics. This multiracial team, which includes African American, Asian American, Latino, and white actors, must work together in harmony to succeed. Dom often calls this team his "family," reinforcing the idea of a multiracial nation that nullifies racial differences. His role is that of organizing leader, the racially ambiguous hero without whom the multiracial team would be impossible.[32]

The film's setting in Brazil reinforces images of the country as a racially harmonious site and fits in within Brazilian idealized discourses of racial democracy. Rather than the sensual paradise of the music videos, it functions as a harmonious racial paradise in which structures of racial inequality are invisible. Just as Gilberto Freyre thought of the Brazilian population as a new hybrid race with vigor for the tropics, the *Fast and Furious* franchise figures Brazil as a place where U.S. people of diverse racial identity can find success because of the country's racial diversity and mixture. Thus, as Mary Beltrán observes, "only the fast, furious, and multiethnic will survive"[33]—in a U.S. context *or* under increasingly globalized conditions.

Dom's ability to assimilate in Brazil also relies on notions of a multiracial Blackness that transcends racial and national borders. His supposed innate ability to fit into his new home in the favela and navigate obstacles from the Brazilian police to underground car gangs reflects notions of a masculine multiracial Blackness. With the favela capturing the international imagination in Brazilian films such as *Cidade de Deus* (2002), *Tropa de Elite* (2007), and *Tropa de Elite 2* (2010), the transnational circulation of favela images glamorize and capitalize on intertwined aesthetics of Blackness and poverty. Dom, like Snoop Dogg, appears not only comfortable in the *favela*, but already capable of ruling it. Like "Beautiful," the films present an idea of Blackness that allows a seamless fluid identity between the United States and Brazil. Meanwhile, the character of Elena, through Pataky's casting, places tensions between Spain, Brazil, and Latinidad yet nonetheless largely signs her embodiment as one of class, integrity, control, and the imaginary purity of whiteness. Elena's placement as closer to whiteness also has her stand in for social order and progress. Without explicitly articulating race, Elena's presence displaces Blackness. These racial differences, negated by discourses of postrace and racial democracy, are nonetheless evident when demarcating who is included as multicultural and global versus those persons excluded as Black, lawless, and deviant.

As mulatta depictions often rely on the hyper excesses of feminine sexuality, *Fast Five* also emphasizes Dom's hypermasculinity. His unmatched racing skills, physical strength, ability to escape, proficiency with firearms, leadership qualities, and position as a patriarch within his home and within his assembled "family" of street racers all position Dom as hypermasculine. Like the hyperfeminine and hypersexual mulatta and *mulata*, Dom's masculinity is excessive. However, unlike the mulatta, the hypermasculine mulatto figure is rewarded with agency and freedom. This becomes particularly clear in Dom's climatic fight scene with Agent Hobbs, which evokes a homoerotic tension between two multiracial characters rooted in divergent narratives of the mulatto man—representative of the multiracial outlaw mulatto figure and the multiracial figure who can be fully incorporated into civil society.

Dom and Hobbs provide counterpoints of multiraciality in the Obama era. While the two seem diametrically opposed, Dom and Hobbs both represent a desire to transcend racial structures—one with resistance to the state and the other as a leader and representative of the state. As an agent of state power, Hobbs represents civil society through his position as an FBI officer. Dom, reminiscent of the mulatto rebel of antislavery antebellum literature and slave narratives, is in tension with Hobbs, representing multiracial assimilation, an end to Blackness, and an end to racism. As Dom and Hobbs face off, their power struggle is over the direction of these multiracial paths. Dom's mulatto figure, like other literary mulatto heroes of nineteenth-century abolitionist literature, resists his place as a prisoner.[34] Unlike the tragic mulatta figure, who is often depicted as a martyr, Dom carves his own path to freedom even if that path is in opposition to legal and civil authorities.

A Brazilian party scene emphasizes the conflicting images of Brazil as a racialized sexual paradise and site of sensationalized violence. While scantily clad Brazilian women of color dance and grind against cars, Dom negotiates with an underground car racer. The women's sexual availability and the presence of loaded guns mix titillation with danger. When Agent Hobbs attempts to apprehend Dom in this setting, Dom asserts, "And your mistake: thinking you're in America. You're a long way from home. This is Brazil!" The multiracial Brazilian crowd wields their guns. Dom's ability to create an alliance that will protect him demonstrates not only his ability to gather respect but also

Dominic Toretto (Vin Diesel) and FBI agent Luke Hobbs (Dwayne Johnson) face off in Rio de Janeiro in *Fast Five* (2011). Courtesy of Universal Pictures.

his natural fit with a multiracial Brazil. Despite Dom's representation as a U.S. outlaw hero, this escape from the United States possibly alludes to separatist claims like the controversial ending of *Uncle Tom's Cabin*, when the mulatto George Harris writes a letter stating, "I want a country, a nation, of my own."[35]

The face-off scene in *Fast Five* offers two alternative readings: either Brazil is like the United States, or the United States is already like Brazil. Other *Fast and the Furious* films have emphasized the characters' tan, off-white hues, the car gathering party, the loud thumping music, and lots of scantily clad women. However, *Fast Five* is the only film in the franchise to place these elements in Brazil and surround them with Portuguese slang and funk brasileiro music. By situating the ensemble of Brazilians with their lightly tan skin tones as players in *Fast Five*'s multicultural aesthetic, the scene invokes hemispheric histories of racial mixing in both countries, the rapidly growing multiracial U.S. population, and debates about the future "Latin Americanization" of the United States. Thus, the image of a multiracial Brazil hints at the U.S. future.

The lens of Brazil provides a negotiation of visions of a multiracial United States in which racial ambiguity and whiteness are in tension with each other. As Dom manages to escape from the FBI and attain his hefty monetary prize, he achieves simultaneous bodily autonomy and economic freedom in Brazil.

While his hypermasculine cosmopolitan ambitions are not placed in tension with the daily realities of Brazilians, his success might also be read as part of a subversive pleasure in undermining class and racial barriers. The roles of affect and desire present a potential dismantling of hegemonic Black-white binaries in the United States. While Dom can no longer be a free citizen of the United States due to his status as an escaped felon, he is able to craft his own destiny and identity in defiance of the state and in opposition to Hernan, leader of a corrupt drug cartel. Agent Hobbs and Elena also temporarily side with Dom after Hernan's gang attacks Hobbs's convoy and his men are killed. Dom's team fights Hernan's gang, and Dom carries Agent Hobbs to safety. Hobbs helps Dom steal Hernan's money. At the end of the heist, Hobbs tells Dom that he must still arrest him but will give Dom a twenty-four-hour head start. Unbeknownst to Hobbs, Dom's team replaced the real ten-ton bank vault full of $100 million in cash with an empty one. The trickery pleases viewers who get to see Dom survive and defy the U.S. state, even to the point of making Hobbs an ally. The hero thus turns the oppression of the state into a victory for his team.

Dom's prize also includes Elena. When Dom later meets up with Mia and Brian on an unknown tropical beach, Elena is with him. Finding a woman becomes part of the package of his independence. By placing Dom and Elena against a backdrop of racial ambiguity and Latinidad that avoids placing Blackness and whiteness as opposites on a racial spectrum, the film obscures the idea of an interracial relationship. Elena evokes a position of privilege and the idea of an imaginary purity and stands in distinction from the majority of the scantily clad women in Brazil. Rosa, the partner of Dom's U.S. friend in Rio and mother of his son, is Afro-Brazilian, so their pairing does not interrupt white womanhood because it shows a white man with a Black woman. Their son is named after Dom. Therefore, Dom acts as a transnational mediator of racial mixing for both Brazil and the United States. The inclusion and use of a lightly tan cast, led by a racially ambiguous Vin Diesel, is palatable to white viewers while also appealing to audiences of color in and outside of the United States.

Fast Five primarily celebrates masculinity and focuses on the culture of male street racers. However, in addition to Elena, the film includes various female characters who play key roles. Gisele Yashar was formerly a liaison for a Mexican street-racing drug cartel and is one of the best drivers on the team. Mia, Dom's sister, drove the prison van and thus enabled his escape, and plays an important role in operating the backroom technology for the team's Brazil operation. Both Gisele and Mia pose a potential threat to racialized and gendered orders. Mia, played by Jordana Brewster of Brazilian and European-American heritage, and Gisele, played by Gal Gadot of Israeli heritage, still appear as exotic but are phenotypically white. This "off-whiteness" of their characters requires behavior within norms of white femininity, even as the characters are not fully included in mainstream whiteness. For both actors, these norms also require a distancing from Blackness to assert their own off-whiteness, yet within the parameters of multiculturalism and postrace, their characters also operate within close proximity to Black male characters without romantic engagement. When Mia becomes pregnant, she facilitates intelligence from the operation's home base and is at one point saved by another member of the crew from a kidnapping. Gisele, while possessing impressive driving skills, knowingly uses her body and sexual allure to attract the Brazilian drug lord, and has him place his hand on her buttocks in order to secure his handprint for later use in unlocking an important vault. Elena, Mia, and Gisele all act as links between underground worlds, and all are able to use their femininity and sexuality to give or extract key information. The female characters, then, are largely reduced to being damsels in distress or femme fatales. Yet, unlike, the silent Brazilian *mulata* of both U.S. and Brazilian media, who exists only for masculine sexual satisfaction, these characters demonstrate agency.

At the end of the film, Brian and Mia along with Dom and Elena peacefully reside on the beach; Gisele and Han (played by Korean American actor Sung Kang) are traveling in Europe together. Meanwhile, the other darker-skinned characters in the film, such as Tego (Puerto Rican reggaeton artist Tego Calderón) and Rico (played by Puerto Rican reggaeton artist Don Omar) continue to squabble playfully, and Roman (played by African American actor-model Tyrese) and Tej (played by African American actor-rapper Ludacris) compete and bicker, with dark-skinned Black women at their sides. These nonwhite characters traverse national borders, having succeeded in blending into Brazilian society and completing their mission. In *Fast Five*'s U.S. and global narrative, multicultural diversity is normalized and becomes an asset. The film presents a postracial and postnationalist vision that draws upon both U.S. and Brazilian notions of racial mixing.

The interracial relationships onscreen in *Fast Five* do not radically alter the social taboos on racial mixing in the United States. This is in part because the interracial relationships take place outside of U.S. borders and otherwise because relationships do not occur between Black men and women understood as unambiguously white in a U.S. context. *Fast Five*, then, celebrates the racially ambiguous aesthetic along with interracial alliances, but it primarily centers a racial mixing and mestiçagem that privileges whiteness. The main actresses in the film adhere to an aesthetic of "brown, but not too brown," and all the characters are heterosexual.[36] However, unlike the morena figure in Brazil, upward mobility in *Fast Five* does not rely on whiteness and, unlike the *mulata* figure, the central women in *Fast Five* are not sexually deviant.

In this film, Brazil acts as a canvas on which U.S. anxieties about its racial future and increasing nonwhite and multiracial demographic can be sketched out. Following Greg Carter's genealogy of the U.S. optimistic tradition of racial mixing that has persisted in a nonlinear fashion over three centuries, *Fast Five* reinvigorates a valorization of racial mixing but requires the heralding of the mixed Black hero, the expunging of mixed Black women, and the predominance of a browning and whitening rather than Blackness.[37] The celebration of racial subversion, racial hybridity, racial flexibility, and whitening are all presented in *Fast Five*. Dom, while racially ambiguous, can be presented with a phenotypically white woman onscreen precisely because this relationship does not occur in the United States. Within the distant tropics, interracial relationships between white women and racially ambiguous men of color can thrive and are not marked as illicit and threatening as they might be in the United States. In the film, Brazil allows for racial and sexual freedom. Dom's ambiguity allows for reassurance and subversion. His Italian last name assures viewers who might find an interracial relationship threatening that it is not actually happening. Furthermore, Elena's Brazilian national difference, as opposed to U.S. or European residency, allows some audiences to see her as nonwhite. While Elena is not represented as a *mulata*, her Brazilian citizenship and her European features allow audiences to see her as ambiguous and exotic, while nominally white. To viewers who see Dom as mixed-race Black, he is attaining the forbidden white woman unavailable to most African American characters in Hollywood. Unlike Carmen Miranda in Good Neighbor Policy films, Elena ends up with the male lead.

Dom and Elena together represent postracial visions in which racial ambiguity melds into whiteness. Elena, then, is a prop for the postracial male hero. Multiracial Brazil and the attainment of a phenotypically white woman makes Dom's path from racially ambiguous outlaw to independent cosmopolite possible. The ending with Dom and Elena on an idyllic lush tropical beach similarly evokes the idea of Brazil as a tropical racial paradise. With Elena, played by Spanish actor Elsa Pataky, standing in as an exotic yet phenotypically close to white figure and Dom via Vin Diesel as a heroic mulatto everyman who can cross national and racial boundaries, *Fast Five* stages a desire for alternate thinking around race and nation while simultaneously expressing ongoing anxieties of a postracial United States.

Elena's position in relation to Michelle Rodriguez's Letty in later *Fast and the Furious* films reveals the blurring of national, color, racial, gender, and class hierarchies in slippery U.S. articulations of Latinidad. Elsa Pataky as a Spanish actor playing a Brazilian woman reifies the signification of whiteness against the backdrop of tropical racially mixed Brazil in *Fast Five*. Once Elena works with Agent Hobbs in Los Angeles in later *Fast and the Furious* films, her whiteness and hence the impossibility of interracial mixing became contained. In *Fast and Furious 6* (2013), Letty, presumed to be dead, returns but suffers from amnesia. Elena encourages Dom's relationship with Letty. By *Furious 7* (2015), Letty regains her memory and resumes her marriage with Dom. Meanwhile, Elena did not disclose her pregnancy to Dom until after she and her son are kidnapped. Elena eventually dies during the kidnapping and their son is raised by Dom, Letty, and the *Fast and Furious* extended family. Elena, circulated as white, pure, respectable, and feminine, stands in contrast to the darker-skinned Letty, who is presented as tough, aggressive, criminal, and less feminine. As Latina celebrities often occupy an ambiguous racial status within U.S. racial systems, Michelle Rodriguez's body here becomes racially signified as nonwhite in relation to Elena.[38] As embodiments of U.S. and Latin American systems of racial mixing, mestizaje, and mestiçagem, the family of Dom, Letty, and Elena's son also requires the death of Elena to maintain this interracial image onscreen without a significant threat to whiteness. Yet, in *Fast Five*, the film's detachment from U.S. physical territories permits interracial relationships due to Brazil as fantasized as exotic, tropical, and racially mixed. With preoccupations surrounding racialized national identity and the browning of the United States, *Fast Five* functions as a site to negotiate the moment of the politics of difference in the 2010s.

In the context of demographic shifts, especially due to multiracial and Latino populations, *Fast Five* taps into competing narratives of racial diversity, racelessness as progress, and multiracial or multicultural utopias. Referring to the film's multiracial stars, Vin Diesel and Dwayne Johnson, Tim Cogshell, of *Box Office* magazine, published by the National Association of Theatre Owners, states that "both of whom are sort of postracial anyway, if you think about it. Like our President Obama. So the tensions that are existing in the film aren't around race."[39] If multiraciality can collapse into a postracial vision, one can conclude that, by adopting diversity in films and institutions, race will cease a relevant issue. The hype surrounding President Obama and *Fast Five* afforded the euphoria of racial diversity, an expectation that racial progress had been made, and a subsequent desire for racial transcendence. In 2011, the hopes of racial unity through multiraciality circulated in the United States amid increasing fears of racial polarization. Yet, again, this hope for postracial transcendence could only occur through a masculine body as the mulatta body is weighted by her histories in the cultural memory as a reminder of the aftermath of enslaved sexual exploitation, a symbol of the incestuous taboos of racial mixing, a constant sexual threat to racial boundaries, and an object of desire. Charismatic, strident, and creative, Dom vis-à-vis Vin Diesel, presents a race man model of leadership for a new era of racial uplift that can usher in a multiracial and eventually postracial order. Only a masculine subject such as Vin Diesel that is coded as a racially ambiguous, chameleonlike star could present this new vision of multiraciality and postrace together.

The construction of Brazil as a racial paradise and its reputation as a site of racial mixing and harmony emblematizes these postracial logics. In light of anxieties over the United States' racial future, *Fast Five* allows audiences to see a reflection of the United States in Brazil or deflect this racial mixing and ambiguity through reassurance that it has been contained abroad. At the same time, the potential for utopia associated with multiracial bodies such as Dom's, the multiracial spaces of Brazil, and the physical and financial freedom garnered from Dom's escape, depend on a fantasy of new beginnings, liberated from the racial histories of the United States. While set in Rio de Janeiro, *Fast Five* was actually filmed in Puerto Rico, showcasing that the ideal Brazil of strategic deployments of racial mixture is already well within the bounds of U.S. empire, yet still on the margins of a core U.S. national identity. Furthermore, the filming in Puerto Rico, a site known for its histories and ideologies of mestizaje, adds yet another layer of hemispheric racial mixing.

The notion of Brazilian racial paradise echoes across and through the United States and Brazil. As exemplified in the genealogy of the Brazilian *mulata* in chapter 1 and the star text and roles of Camila Pitanga in chapters 2 and 3, the Brazilian *mulata* functions to negotiate and re-create racial regimes that manage Blackness primarily for sexual pleasure or for the eventual containment of this Blackness. The uneven hemispheric circulation of the *mulata* also echoes in evocations of the U.S. mulatta as demonstrated in the star texts of Halle Berry and Jennifer Beals and *Monster's Ball* and *The L Word*. As such, these hip-hop videos, "Beautiful" and "I Got It from My Mama," utilize the Brazilian *mulata* to maintain desirous sensuality along with the possibilities of freedom for African American men. *Fast Five*, released after President Obama's election, also reclaims this Brazilian paradise with a U.S. mulatto rather than a mulatta figure to surpass rather than evoke histories of colonial violence. While Vin Diesel's body challenges binary logics of race, his possibility as a race leader also requires an investment in heterosexuality. Elena, as white but exotic in Brazil, and understood as white yet residing in the liminal space of whiteness in Spain for U.S. audiences, does dismantle these intertwined racial and sexual logics. Between consenting parties, Elena and Dom enact an embodied discourse of racial mixing that does not threaten U.S. whiteness but that has been evacuated of the trauma of colonial sexual violence represented by the mulatta. These representations of Brazil, then, function as the development of mixed and Black U.S. manhood through the bodies of Brazilian women.

U.S. representations of Brazil have often projected its own racial anxieties onto the country. However, the United States is not just one unified bloc of racial identities, so these racial anxieties depend on the particular group of U.S. residents and on particular racial desires. These images of Brazil are a way for U.S. cultural productions to project an idea of Otherness that also incorporates sameness. Furthermore, Brazil participates in a production of self across borders.

Rio 2016 Olympic Bid: Brazilian Mestiçagem as Ethos of the Olympics

Under a spotlight, a lone dark-skinned Black street sweeper in his orange uniform and hoisting a broom smiles infectiously and dances samba. Brazil's 2012 Olympic handover ceremony began not with the expected scantily clad brown *mulata* sambista, but with this Afro-Brazilian man. This shift spoke to the Brazilian state's efforts to deemphasize the sensationalized *mulata* figure as a site of sexual prostitution and exploitation. Yet although she is not explicitly highlighted in Brazil's run-up to the 2016 Rio Olympics, she structures the desires and performances of Brazilian eroticism and interracial sexual mixing. The reframing of national narratives to highlight multiculturalism and the centrality of Afro-Brazilian culture still utilized the rhetoric, language, and imagery related to the *mulata* as a racial and sexual commodity even without explicitly citing the *mulata* herself.

The bid and preparation for Rio 2016 acted as a platform on which notions of race could be enacted. The rhetoric and imagery of multicultural inclusion and racial mixing ran in tension with practices of racialized exclusion. The celebration of racial hybridity and plurality as unique markers of Brazilian identity elided continuing legacies of structural racism. In order to capture Brazilian aspirations and optimism during a period of economic growth and hopes of progress, this section largely focuses on the bidding process and the performance of the 2012 London handover ceremony during the period from 2009 to 2012 when Rio de Janeiro was selected by the International Olympic Committee and prior to the major 2013 street protests and political and economic crises.

In the 2000s, Brazil had increasingly become a powerful voice in global affairs and had attempted to position itself as a key spokesperson not only for South America but also for the Global South. The country's winning bids for the 2014 World Cup and the 2016 Olympic Games further positioned Brazil as a leader. With processes of national identity and globalization embedded in both the World Cup and the Olympics, the ceremony-like nature of these global mega-events have a long reach in the perception of the nation internally and abroad.[40] As a form of nation branding, these international sporting events were intended to reposition Brazil from a nation associated with past dictatorships, lawlessness, and poverty to one associated with modernity. These victories allowed Brazil, known as "the country of the future," to present itself as politically, economically, and socially modern, and Brazil's reputation as a multiracial nation, as well as the first nation with a majority Black population to host the Olympics, was to be on display. Hosting these events offered a potential global repositioning that defied histories of colonialism and imperialism. As President Lula da Silva said after winning the Olympics bid, "o Brasil sempre foi grande e importante, mas precisava dessas Olimpíadas como uma forma de desafio" (Brazil was always grand and important, but we needed the Olympics as a form of challenge).[41]

Interlinked with mestiçagem and racial democracy, the Rio 2016 slogan "Live Your Passion" expressed the image that Brazil wanted to project to the world. The slogan was intended to "express the open and democratic manner with which the country welcomes different cultures, races, customs and religions." The president of the Brazilian Olympic Commission, Carlos Nuzman, remarked: "The logo translates energy, happiness, and the characteristic of being welcoming without distinctions of race or culture, as is the Brazilian himself. These values translate what it means for the Rio de Janeiro candidature for the 2016 Olympic Games"[42] The slogan generates notions of the exoticized and erotic fantasies and desires of Latin American passion. Brazil engaged in a politics of self-exotification by extending its image of a peaceful sensual racial democracy. These sexualized terms such as embrace and passion were consistently associated with the Rio Olympics. Through the idea of the "carioca embrace," the warm welcome and passion of Brazil, governmental marketing situates Brazil as open and inclusive to the world while reincorporating Brazilian history and culture into those two defining features. Brazil thus participates in self-exotification that invokes racial mixing and racial harmony.

The bid images and the accompanying videos, such as "Live for Your Passion," showcased Rio de Janeiro as a city spilling over with happiness in everyday interactions. From soccer fans cheering for their team to samba dancing in bars and in the streets, the city presented itself as a joyful harmonious racial paradise in which Black and brown street sweepers and fishermen welcomed all. The candidature bid materials largely presented images of Brazil as white in relation to architecture, transportation, technology, and business, deploying images of mixed race and Blackness when passion, harmony, and diversity were emphasized.[43] Images linked to media communications, technology, and the political and economic climate all but omit Black people.[44] Thus, a vision of race and nation are predicated on an authentic Brazil as Black, the future of Brazil as young and mixed, and the present industries of progress and development as white.[45] These images use race to promote respective causes of multiculturalism and progress coded differently through images of Afro-Brazilians and white Brazilians. Meanwhile, in preparation for the games and for the 2014 World Cup, poor people of color in favelas were evicted as areas were razed to make room for new developments. Sparked by these global mega-events, the collapsing of business and political interests, rampant real estate speculation furthered segregation and justified racialized police brutality. Thus, in the run-up to the Olympics, conflicting ideas of Brazil competed with one another: as a nation of progress and near-whiteness; as a nation of joy, samba, and Afro-descendants; and as a country of racial and social inequalities.

The diverse and inclusive character of Brazil, coupled with its rising economic and political power, was key to Brazil's bid for the 2016 Olympics. Significantly, the award of hosting was granted in the wake of China's affirmation of its international prominence in the 2008 Beijing games. It also coincided with increasing economic power, as well as a time in which the country was nationally questioning the meaning of race and brasilidade amid debates concerning race-consciousness, Afro-Brazilian activism, and affirmative action policies. Through the 2016 Olympics bidding process and marketing, Brazilians negotiated Brazilian national identity in relation to the outside world.

To attract the Olympics Committee, President Lula employed the tropes of passion among the Brazilian population to attribute racial and cultural unity and harmony to the formation of a distinctively Brazilian people. The country capitalized on its reputation as a multiracial mixed society to present itself as already embodying the ethos of the Olympic Games. Brazil's project, then, was to continue to stress racial harmony and tolerance as part of its innate national identity, a project President Lula began immediately in his statement on Brazil's selection:

> We are a passionate people for sport, passionate for life . . . we are not only
> a mixed people, but a people that likes very much to be mixed and this is

what makes our identity . . . it is time to light the Olympic torch for a tropical country . . . for the Olympics to be an opportunity to feel the heat of our
people, the exuberance of our culture, and the sun of our happiness . . . the
gates of Brazil are open for the biggest celebration of humanity . . . the Rio
Olympic Games will be unforgettable, since it will be full of the passion, of
the joy, and of the creativity of the Brazilian people.[46]

Brazil's Olympic Committee and President Lula explicitly utilized the rhetoric of passion as part of Brazilian identity and as a theme of the 2016 Olympics.
This self-exotification imagined Brazil as a site of sexual and sensual possibilities ruled by emotion rather than reason—an identity constructed through
the idea of mestiçagem and racial tolerance. For example, the video "A paixão
nos une" that followed President Lula's remarks to the International Olympic
Committee in 2009 emphasized this idea of racial and ethnic comingling and
mixing.[47] The short film revolves around the circulation of various cultural
groups, marked by colored blazers, turbans, and headscarves, which stand in
for multiethnic and multinational diversity. It opens with the sun rising over
Brazil as a crowd of people of various nationalities and ethnicities gather near
the famous *Cristo Redentor* (*Christ the Redeemer*) statue. A young boy in front
of the statue, who appears as the epitome of the brown curly-haired racially
ambiguous Brazilian, speaks to the camera: "They come from countries, large
and small, arriving at the promising shore of a new land. They come as Olympians, carrying the dreams of nations, but when they gather in Rio, they unite
the world as never before." The selection of a young boy speaks to notions of
progress that are at once associated with masculinity and youth. While the
mulata is often an object of a sexualized gaze, here the boy opens up a vision of
Brazil that allows a detachment from colonial sexual violence and continuing
fetishizations of these colonial racial hierarchies in the domestic and international imagination. Furthermore, the youth allows for innocence and a hope
for the future, yet one that is not weighted by past imagery of the *mulata*.

This opening alluded to Brazil's colonial history as part of the "discovery
of the New World" as well as Brazil's place in a new world order, especially
because the Olympics had never taken place in South America before. As the
groups walk around the city, Brazilians greet them with enthusiastic welcomes,
and the visitors see capoeira and samba. The participants in the film affirm "a
paixão nos une" in various languages. Finally, they gather on the beach, with
their colorful blazers and form an image of the Olympic rings. The grafting of
different colors, through the bodies of the participants, into the Olympic Rings,
symbolically represents the ideals of the Olympic Games, and metaphorically
characterizes Brazil's rhetoric of passion.

Brazil's political discourse of passion sought to represent Brazil as a model of interracial and interethnic unity. This foundation for interracial and international harmony complements what Doris Sommer calls "an erotics of politics."[48] Like other Latin American countries, Brazil's use of passion is an important component of national discourses on national unity as it relates to processes of colonization and eroticization. With the *mulata's* body often celebrated as both a product and symbol of Brazilian passion embedded within the discourse of mestiçagem, her symbolism is evoked even when she is not physically present. The sensuality, passion, and exoticism aroused by the *mulata* body correspond to the mixing of bodies in the sexual manner at the basis of mestiçagem. The marketing of Brazilian passion draws on Brazilian racial democracy and Western notions of multiculturalism. By positioning itself as already comprising diverse races, ethnicities, and religions, Brazil represented the Olympic ideal.

While the film does not draw attention to the Indigenous and enslaved populations in Brazil, the image of various white groups coming to the country does evoke the encounter between the colonizing nations of Europe and Brazil, as well as European immigration to Brazil. The inclusion of sub-Saharan Africans in these same images invokes a different coming to the New World but displaces this colonial history, the legacies of slavery in particular, with the Olympic ideals of freedom. The film thereby produces an image of the diversity that created Brazil. It capitalizes on the utopian projections of the New World as an earthly paradise with the dreams of a new future. It also utilizes Brazilian conceptualizations of modernity as a new utopia with Brazil's desire for inclusion among the economies of the most powerful nations of the West. The images of the Olympians arriving in Brazil encapsulates the idea of former colonizing nations and postcolonial nations brought together to witness the establishment of a new world order with Brazil at its forefront. However, since a young brown boy narrates the video, it allows for a focus on the future that erases a painful history marked by colonization and enslavement. The video merges utopian images of the New World and utopian images of modern progress.

Amid these shifts in Brazil's self-presentation as modern, the *mulata* is at once celebrated and viewed as an objectification of women of African descent and of Brazil itself. At the handover from England to Brazil during the 2012 London Olympic Games, the state's emphasis on its Afro-Brazilian heritage became apparent as a way of presenting itself to the world. In the global stage of national performances, the perception of authenticity is a central resource for marketability. Both the *mulata* and samba have been heavily criticized within Brazil as a commodification of cultural resources. The handover ceremony did not feature the *mulata* sambista but instead a Black male figure to present notions of spontaneity and authenticity even as this same performance is also prone to the transnational forces that have enabled the *mulata* samba spectacle. From the opening, the ceremony featured Renato Sorriso, a street sweeper for Rio's Sambódromo who became an internet sensation after a YouTube video appeared of him dancing samba after a Rio de Janeiro Carnival samba parade. This Afro-Brazilian worker from the lower classes in his orange uniform presents an inclusive image of Brazil. A white British security guard dressed in a suit comes on stage and scolds him, then willingly succumbs to his offer of a samba lesson. With the security guard in a position of authority as allegorical to legacies of colonial dominance, Renato is also ascribed to an idealized Black jovial character of the hegemonic imagination. This populist imagery both elevates and debases a symbol of the working-class Afro-Brazilian population. Like the rhetoric of passion and carioca embrace, Renato's performance constructs a guise of authenticity and exoticism for the pleasure of the West. At the same time, the idea that Renato's smile and charisma win the security guard over represents a usurping of colonization from the periphery to former empire.

Significantly, Renato's lesson repeats a stereotypical notion of Black natural rhythm and dance ability. The Black male dancer teaching the white security guard how to samba is emblematic of a trope wherein dance is naturally and authentically Black. Dance ability becomes essentialized, not only as a national cultural ability but as a biological extension of race. Renato's samba performance yokes race and nationality together, even as it evokes Carmen Miranda, who taught the "Uncle Samba" in the Good Neighbor films. Just as Miranda's films became a mass-mediated entry point for Brazilian music and dance into the U.S. mainstream, Renato functions as a transnational mediation between Brazil and the rest of the world, particularly the West. While entry often happens through a female figure such as Miranda or Latin American actors such as Dolores del Río and Lupe Vélez, here Renato functions as a Black buddy in the tradition of interracial male buddy films.[49]

As a buddy who teaches the white security guard how to dance, Renato is an agent of multiracial and multicultural harmony. Thus, he performs the desired image of the Afro-Brazilian—friendly, docile, open, and distinctly nonthreatening. However, unlike the stereotypical image of the *mulata passista* (samba dancer) that is presented globally and marketed to tourists in Brazil, Renato takes the stage as a male dancer in his street-cleaning uniform. As samba is associated with a national cultural tradition, Renato thereby represents the nation as an Afro-Brazilian working-class male, instead of the *mulata*, representing a new Brazil that is perhaps responding to criticism of its own self-exotification and external marketing as a sexual paradise of *mulatas*.[50] Yet, this presentation does not challenge the sexual, political, or economic power of patriarchal systems.

A parade of Black female samba dancers in Afro hairstyles joins the ceremony later. Their hairstyles revise the presentation of the *mulata* figure, placing it within Black aesthetics and thereby compromising the dancers' sexual availability. Devoid of the typical skimpy bikini costuming and long often-chemically treated straight or wavy hair, the samba dancers refute the national and transnational images of the *mulata* sambista. With this nonconformity to the dominant embodiments and beauty standards of the *mulata*, the Black samba dancers perform in a space of potential resistance to discourses of sexualized mestiçagem while simultaneously projecting exotic Blackness as an enticing Olympic spectacle. This de-emphasis on the *mulata* figure as part of the marketing of Brazil raises questions about how Brazil wished to see and present itself to the world. The samba dancers, as part of an acceptable, palatable Blackness and representing Afro-Brazilian tradition, are a counterpoint to an abject Blackness as represented by favela inhabitants that the preparations for the Olympics have displaced. Nor do these samba dancers serve as a memory of slavery and inequality. This cultural moment points to a negotiation of national identity, race, class, gender, and sexuality with a look toward new representations of Blackness and mixedness.

Since the era of the telenovelas discussed in chapter 3 such as *Belíssima* (2005–2006) and *Paraíso Tropical* (2007), the range of acting roles for Afro-Brazilian women had increased by 2012. In September 2009, Globo launched *Viver a Vida* with Taís Araújo as the first Black female protagonist on a primetime television program. Araújo played the role of Helena, a Black fashion model. This character pointed to potential changes regarding the idea of beauty and the types of roles that are open to Afro-Brazilian actresses despite her reliance on white male romantic partners. Similarly, the Olympics presentation disrupted the hegemonic whiteness often broadcast in Brazil. Therefore, it indicated possible new directions for representations of women of color that did not rely on stereotypes of the *mulata*.

The image of the dancers points to an acknowledgment and celebration of Black politics and music stemming from Brazil's Black soul movement of the 1970s and Brazil's hip-hop movement beginning in the 1990s, as does the appearance of the rapper BNegão and the samba musician Seu Jorge in the ceremony. Seu Jorge and BNegão have openly criticized the racism and classism of the Brazilian state in debates over the place of Afro-Brazilians in Brazil. In the context of growing racial consciousness among Afro-Brazilians, and the advancement of affirmative action in universities, the inclusion of these Black power symbols and hip-hop musicians points to a validation of the Black experience in Brazil on national and international levels. The inclusion of Black soul and hip-hop along with samba presents Brazil within a changing cultural landscape. The inclusion of images of Afro-Brazilian figures such as musician Seu Jorge and soccer player Pelé points to a celebration of Afro-Brazilian figures within a pantheon of national heroes, but it is also notable that these inclusions confine the role of the Afro-Brazilian to entertainment and sports.

The Brazilian government had positioned Rio 2016 as a catalyst for Brazilian development. The vision manifested an obsession with progress and modernization, articulated in such language on rio2016.com as "All Brazilians uniting to deliver the greatest event on earth and proudly advancing through sport our national promise of progress."[51] This, the official website for Rio 2016, states that the winning bid "marked the summit of a path of accomplishments for the bid team, and the beginning of a journey of big opportunities and challenges for Rio, and for Brazil."[52] The executive summary on the website states that "all investments will yield substantial, tangible, and meaningful legacies for the people of Rio and Brazil and are consistent with our long-term development plans."[53] Marketing videos and hosting bid materials presented social inclusion as part of the nation's identity, implying that the Olympics will further this social inclusion with new development projects. According to the candidature file, the 2016 Rio Olympics promised programs for social inclusion such as youth sports programs, community outreach, education, and job development.[54]

Unfortunately, the urban renewal Brazil began in preparation for the 2014 World Cup and continued in preparation for the 2016 Olympic Games in Rio de Janeiro told a less optimistic story. As already mentioned, residents of favelas, the poorest areas of the city, where people of color predominate, were forcibly displaced and removed from their homes. In a process that repeats China's razing of areas populated with poor and unwanted citizens for the Beijing Olympic Games—which estimates say evicted over 1.5 million[55]—Brazil displaced some of its poorest populations as the games approached. As the state saw it, improving the international image of Brazil depended on staging images of favelas or eradicating them and the abject Blackness such communities represent. The shooting down of a police helicopter over a favela two weeks after the announcement of the 2016 Olympic winning bid and the international attention this received, as media questioned Brazil's ability to provide security for the games, supported this view. Police efforts to pacify the favelas in the wake of the incident also gained the attention of international media.[56] The UPP (Unidade de Polícia Pacificadora, Police Pacification Units) attempted to prevent violence and drug trafficking that did not align with Rio's attempts to present an image of a modern, secure city. Subsequent efforts have been marked by race and class, social segregation, social inequalities, and restricted citizenship for the poor Black underclass.[57] The state-sponsored efforts to modernize and transform Rio de Janeiro only furthered racial apartheid.

International human rights groups and the international media drew attention to forced evictions from favelas and have expressed concern over the right to housing and the displacement of the poor, mostly people of color.[58] These groups drew attention to poor townships in South Africa for the 2010 World Cup as well. Like the 2010 South Africa tournament, the Brazilian state's focus on disrupting favelas was key to the idea of an eventual modernity. The racial thought of the intertwinement of modernity, progress, and whiteness required the exclusion of poor people of color. The Rio 2016 bidding materials emphasized the inclusion and integration of not only visitors but of how the games would contribute to a transformative legacy for Rio. Yet, this transformation relied on a furthering of racial division and exclusion. The Olympics, then, justified violent projects in areas inhabited mostly by people of color while at the same time encouraging the consumption of people of color through cultural performances.

The Olympics bidding process and handover ceremony became a global stage for the image of multiculturalism that manifests in *Fast Five* and the music videos that accompany "Beautiful" and "I Got It from My Mama." Yet, the Rio Olympics' bidding process and the marketing of Black culture, like cultural productions in the United States, did not provide a model of racial harmony correlated to equality or opportunity. Instead, the marketing depicted a commodified and packaged Blackness for foreign eyes and a fetishization of Afro-Brazilian performance, culture, music, and bodies for domestic consumption.

Brazil is in the process of negotiating the contradictions inherent in multiculturalism amidst the reality of massive racial and class inequality. By June 2013, a year before the commencement of the 2014 World Cup, mass protests emerged in multiple cities in Brazil. These protests, sparked by a bus fare hike, revolted against corruption and the significant use of public funds for stadiums and World Cup infrastructure instead of public services, such as health care and education.[59] In this reclaiming of citizenship, protestors illuminated the contestation of official rhetoric of progress versus the practices of reinforcing social inequalities. The international media images of Brazil leading up to Rio 2016 were not of utopic inclusion but rather of a revolt against exclusion. Following the World Cup, Brazil continued to experience some of its largest social protests since the end of the military dictatorship. Yet, the tenor shifted to rally against the policies of Dilma Rousseff and an increasingly vocal white conservatism reemerged. Protests, failures, and frustrations with the direction of Brazil's future from the perspectives of the public sphere, the state, and international imaginings of Brazil pointed to competing visions of the nation and citizenship.

These contrasting images of a racially tolerant inclusive Brazil versus one of deprivation and inequalities presented a challenge in creating a new image for itself and the rest of the world. While the media have treated Brazil as a refuge from U.S. racial divisions, the two countries are both situated within changing panoramas of national and transnational thought and politics regarding racial discourses of harmony, inclusion, and difference. U.S. media images of Brazil present a reincorporation of the United States' exotic other and an image onto which it can project anxieties and desires surrounding its own racial future. The Olympics, along with the development of affirmative action and increased visibility of Afro-Brazilians on telenovelas, pointed to potential transformations in Brazilian ideologies of race and citizenship. Both Brazil and U.S. media demonstrated a negotiation of multiculturalism as racial difference or racelessness.

The mixed-race female figure and the specters of Blackness undergird processes of racialization in the United States and Brazil and circulate hemispherically within the body politic. Popular media images of the *mulata* evoke anxieties about Blackness and thus are tamed and managed through sexual logics and racialized and gendered hierarchies. While these states employ the rhetoric of multiculturalism and the protection of difference, the transnational discourses of whiteness prevail as racial mixing permits either the valuation of whiteness or the management of Blackness through the sexualization of the mulatta and *mulata* figures. This production of citizenship devalues women of African descent and also reproduces a virulent anti-Blackness that renders Blacks as abject. Thus, an imagining of Brazil and the United States as referential utopias or dystopias proves limiting. Rather, illuminating both the fractures and operations of these racial regimes together points to the possibilities of imagining new frameworks.

Epilogue

The Rio 2016 Olympic opening ceremonies recalled colonial trauma, demystifying romanticized narratives of harmonious erotic racial mixing. Yet U.S.-based NBC media coverage glossed over the depictions of clashes of Indigenous and Portuguese peoples and the slow somber march of Afro-Brazilians in shackles. Correspondent Meredith Vieira rejected this imagery of violence and oppression by reframing colonization and slavery as benign, voluntary immigration, noting "immigration has begun." Vieira later romanticized multiculturalism, describing each new immigrant group's arrival as "leaving their mark and creating the blended culture that is modern Brazil." This coverage ignored the ceremony's attempt to expose Brazil's hemispheric legacies of colonial violence on a global stage.

Notably, the Brazilian presentation of itself did not promote mythic visions of mestiçagem and the *mulata*. Featured performers included Elza Soares, Karol Conka, and MC Soffia, dark-skinned Afro-Brazilian female singers and rappers associated with Black feminist pride, in contrast to objectified scantily clad *mulata* samba dancers. The ceremony presented Afro-Brazilian female empowerment as an element of a potential new vision of Brazil. Yet, the idealized presence of white Brazilian Gisele Bündchen, which NBC correspondent Matt Lauer labeled as "Brazil's greatest export," demonstrates the continued association between modernity, beauty, capitalism, and whiteness.

While the 2016 Olympics bidding materials and the 2012 handover ceremony had presented a promise of passion, harmonious diversity, modernity, the Rio 2016 opening ceremonies grappled with transnationally mediated economic, political, and social struggles. Despite Brazil's attempt in the lead-up to the event to rebrand itself, the dominant U.S. media narrative at the time focused on crime, corruption, the Zika virus, pollution, and construction delays for stadiums and public transport. This focus complemented the reaffirmation of tropes of Brazil as a land of exotic, untamed pleasures for U.S. audiences alongside depictions of Brazil as a country of danger and insecurity. Both tropes reassert U.S. superiority in the media coverage, such as NBC's opening ceremony broadcast. Meredith Vieira assured viewers that the ceremonies would "push the headlines [about Brazil's problems and dangers] aside, hit the reset button, and throw one massive party." Hoda Kotb responded, "did somebody say party?," while pushing her hands up in the air in a raise-the-roof gesture, signifying the start of a celebration.[1] When featuring Afro-Brazilian performers during the ceremonies, the constant references to Brazil as joyful, vibrant, and celebratory helped construct tropicalized iconographies that reproduced and aestheticized a racializing logic of Black containment and Black pleasure. The mass spectacle of the Olympic ceremonies demonstrated the continuing management of Blackness and mixing in a neoliberal era.

The management of Blackness, cloaked as an embrace of Blackness, in the Americas that summer anticipated eruptions of white supremacy. A month after the Olympic Games in September 2016, I watched the U.S. presidential election debates between Hillary Clinton and Donald Trump in Rio de Janeiro. Brazil had impeached Dilma Rousseff, its first female president, on August 31. I had just returned from an organized session of the Inter-American Commission on Human Rights and Criola, a Black feminist organization; there I had met many Afro-Brazilian activists who described the impeachment as an attack on Black women. Expanding on her predecessor Lula da Silva's policies geared toward expanding opportunities for the poor, Afro-Brazilians, and women, Rousseff had sought to combat institutional racism and sexism within the state. Rousseff increased affirmative action for Afro-Brazilian and Indigenous groups, provided labor protections for domestic workers, the majority of whom are Afro-Brazilian women, expanded welfare programs directed toward women, and staffed her cabinet with more women than her predecessors, including prominent Afro-Brazilian women. Rousseff acknowledged that poverty has a face in Brazil and that face is Black and female.[2] Her trajectory, along with increased Black mobilization, widened spaces for Afro-Brazilians in the public sphere.

However, this widening of Afro-Brazilians in the public sphere—from television to universities to work settings to public social spaces—became a threat. Rousseff's successor, Michel Temer, formed an all-white and all-male cabinet and began his tenure by razing labor rights for domestic workers. He dismantled the Ministries of Women and Human Rights as well as the Ministry of Racial Equality, which had overseen affirmative action, Afro-Brazilian history education, and antiracism initiatives.

I had abandoned any illusion that Brazil is a racial democracy long before Rousseff's removal. The year before I had been visiting Brazil when the mass protests that led to Rousseff's impeachment erupted across the country. While protest demonstrations across Brazil in 2013 had expressed discontent at the state funding of the 2014 World Cup and 2016 Olympics, right-wing political groups co-opted this discontent, condemning Rousseff as a barrier to effective government services, accountability, reform, and anticorruption measures. It was immediately apparent to me when I observed anti-Rousseff protests on Avenida Paulista in São Paulo that there weren't any Afro-Brazilians in attendance, apart from Black domestic workers pushing strollers of white children as they walked behind their white employers. As demonstrations expanded to middle-class Brazilians, these protests coincided with "white participation and Black disidentification with the 2013 protests."[3]

The economic downturn, on the cusp of the World Cup, significantly impacted Afro-Brazilians, and while significant economic, social, and educational advances had been made, state-sanctioned violence against Black communities continued. While Rousseff was never found guilty of corruption charges and, in fact, led anticorruption probes, in contrast, Michel Temer and Rousseff's other political enemies have been mired in corruption charges. Despite her support of the largest corruption investigation in Brazilian history, Operação Lava Jato (Operation Car Wash), she was later accused of participating in these schemes. Notwithstanding a lack of evidence against her, mainstream media coverage such as *O Globo* helped launch a campaign against Rousseff and the Workers' Party that consisted from her inauguration to her eventual impeachment.[4] With right-wing political support and significant media bias, Rousseff's fall came not from corruption but from the dubious allegations of inappropriate budget management in which she borrowed funds from public banks to stabilize the national budget. While international media decried Rousseff's impeachment hearings as a threat to democracy, the mainstream Brazilian press refuted Brazilian and international critique of the impeachment as a coup.[5] Meanwhile, Temer faced his own corruption charges but Congress voted not to proceed with impeachment hearings. Furthermore, although Temer's allies were embroiled in corruption scandals, the media coverage depoliticized and deescalated the intensity of coverage. By 2018, former president Lula da Silva, Rousseff's predecessor, was sentenced to prison on thin evidence for accepting a beachside apartment. Due to Lula's immense popular support, his potential to win the election needed to be neutralized. The uneven selective legal application of corruption to Lula and Rousseff versus Temer and his political allies demonstrate the criminalization of the political left.[6] With Lula unable to run for president again and with Rousseff impeached, the far right promoted the Workers' Party as the party of corruption and used this myth to justify the suppression of race, gender, and class-based progressive social movements.

The April 2016 *Veja* magazine issue compared Rousseff unfavorably with the "beautiful, maiden-like, and housewife," thirty-three-year-old Marcela Temer, Michel Temer's wife. When casting his impeachment vote, Jair Bolsonaro, who would succeed Temer in 2019, dedicated it to Carlos Ustra, the colonel charged with directing the military unit responsible for torturing political dissidents during the dictatorship, including Rousseff herself. The segregation of a white elite minority in Brazil from the majority Black, mixed-race, and Indigenous population relies on white supremacy and the exclusion of citizenship to the majority. Rousseff's policies threatened that system—and she was punished. It was clear to me that the objective of her impeachment was the reestablishment of white patriarchy. The multiracial vision projected in relationship to the 2016 hosting in Rio had been an illusion.

In the fall of 2016, as I watched U.S. presidential candidate Donald Trump openly express racist and sexist views, I found myself succumbing to U.S. exceptionalism and narratives of racial progress, certain that he could not win. Despite my critiques of postracial narratives buttressed by racial mixing and a mixed-Black President Obama, I believed that white supremacy was in retreat. My shock at Donald Trump's election-night victory reminded me of my disappointment about Brazil on my first trip in 2001. The Trump, Temer, and Bolsonaro administrations were eerily parallel. The intersections ultimately revolved around anti-Blackness within waves of shifting race relations and identities.

Both Brazil and the United States are at a dangerous crossroads in which non-white bodies are continuously under threat of violence and death. The mixed-race female body is a reminder of these racial histories and potential futures as she continues to operate as a spectacle of the desire and disciplining of the Black body. In this era, it is worth asking: is the influence of the mulatta and *mulata* waning, or is she a retrograde harbinger of the past precluding satisfactory images of racial progress? I would argue that she continues to be mobilized to reinforce the social order. In fact, the necessity of the mulatta/*mulata* figure for neoliberal logic requires that she remains as exotically distinctive and consumable. As a conduit of global capitalism, her circulation manages race domestically and recasts Brazil and the United States as harboring multiculturalism In *Imagining the Mulatta*, I have demonstrated how this gendered racialized figure becomes an embodiment of national investments and hemispheric managements of Blackness. Tracing the genealogy of this figure and parsing out her historical contingencies, I illustrate how she coalesces to become emblematic of postracial success and racial democracy while buttressing whiteness.

Colonial histories stemming from slavery reassert themselves in the idealization of white femininity and the debasement of Black femininity. The mulatta/*mulata*, because of her connection to Black womanhood, is sexually available, potentially wild and dangerous, and in need of taming or containment. The mulatta/*mulata* threatens social order. Long histories of anti-Blackness in Brazil and the United States continuously manifest in popular media cultures. Drawing on historical constructions and experiences of mixed-race women within the racial hierarchies of the United States and Brazil and the tropes of mixed-race women in both countries, this book addresses racial anxieties manifested in the star texts of Jennifer Beals, Halle Berry, and Camila Pitanga ranging from the 1980s to the 2000s. Despite the premium placed on their symbolism, women of African descent have historically been excluded from participating in the discourses produced about them. In both U.S. and Brazilian media productions, the management of Blackness relies on disciplining and domesticating sexuality by eradicating Blackness through whitening or by extracting this Blackness for sexual pleasure and then containing it. Blackness is cultivated only for the *mulata*/mulatta's presumed sensuality and seductiveness and not to unsettle whiteness. The mixed-race figure remains entrenched in the reproduction of whitening through the intimate practices of domesticity and sexuality.

Mulatta and *mulata* bodies are writ with the discourse of racial imaginaries, a history of the Americas in which phenotypes resonate with a historical meaning not just within national contexts, but today as a global phenomenon. As we've seen throughout this book, mulatta and *mulata* figures reshape the hemispheric management of Blackness without rewriting hegemonic whiteness. Brazilian and U.S. popular media negotiate between desires and anxieties concerning the role of Blackness and mixedness. Popular media, with a few exceptions, attempted to contain Blackness either in the erasure of Blackness, the sexual regulation of Blackness, and/or the presentation of a palatable Blackness with the potential to whiten. Hence, presenting the uses of the mulatta and *mulata* in the 2000s become preconditions for understanding projects of postracialism and mestiçagem. Thus, the advancement of anti-Blackness occurs through the mixed-race female figure as the pinnacle of multiculturalism coinciding with systemic oppression.

The political events of 2016 are not aberrations but rather continuations of ongoing processes of the management of Blackness and the reification of whiteness. Even when framed through progressive liberal media framings with the hopes of a postracial future, forcing women's bodies toward actualizing whiteness is paramount. Indeed, the vision of mixed-race women's bodies as a tool to create a raceless future preceded the 2000s. For example, the 1993 *Time* magazine cover showing "the New Eve," a computer-generated image of a woman depicting the future of America through racial mixing, fueled the popular imagination of a raceless society through mixing and the role of women as the reproducer and symbol of the nation. Yet the image was essentially white. Thus, the celebration of the imagined future couched its tribute to racial mixing in management of nonwhiteness. This notion of the racial hybrid as the new future also erases the history of racial mixing and mixed-race people in the United States. African Americans have been embedded in histories of racial mixing from the beginnings of colonization in the Americas. Ignoring this history involves erasing a history of sexual violence and the racial oppression that accompanied it.

Renewed interest in genomics has spurred a reengagement of our racial past. Since about 2005 on U.S. television, *African American Lives* (PBS 2006) *African American Lives 2* (PBS 2008), *Faces of America* (PBS 2010), *Who Do You Think You Are?* (NBC 2010), and *Finding Your Roots with Henry Louis Gates, Jr.* (PBS 2012, 2014, 2016) have all profiled famous people's roots through genetic testing and DNA research and often highlighted histories of racial mixing. Brazil's entry into this lineup, *Raízes Afro-Brasileiras* (BBC Brasil 2007), emerged at the same time as debates about the racelesness of Brazil and the use of racial qualifiers for affirmative action. The resurgent interest in family history and genetic ancestry pointed to a renewed focus on familial histories of racial mixing and national roots. While these U.S. television shows revised understandings of racial and national histories and pointed to potential shifts in national imaginaries and popular culture representations, their acknowledgment of historical racial mixture has not necessarily furthered social justice. The historical reassessment of whiteness and a subsequent "browning" of the United States through this historical angle on family histories further justified a postracial ideology and affirmed an idealized legacy of U.S. multiculturalism. Meanwhile, in Brazil, the response to the 2007 BBC program helped justify the backlash against the implementation of affirmative action as it showed that many of the celebrities understood as Black in Brazil had high percentages of

European ancestry. The return to science helped remake race as biological while at the same time justifying institutional structural racism. The recognition of racial mixture and the upholding of Eurocentrism has worked in tandem in both societies. The reliance on linear narratives of racial progress and the use of the evidence of racial mixture as a shedding of racism both fail to address the hemispheric entrenchment of anti-Blackness.

In the United States, the second decade of the new century is also rife with contradictions. The fiftieth anniversary of the historic *Loving v. Virginia* case in 2017 coincided with increasing racial antagonisms evidenced by Donald Trump's rise and increased hate crimes.[7] The U.S. television hit *Scandal* marked the first Black female lead on network television in over forty years in 2012. By 2015, network television shows such as the drama *Empire* and the comedy *Black-ish* have featured all-Black casts and have engaged with issues of economic and social uplift and racial authenticity. Notably, the characters who are known to have mixed African and European descent constantly have their Blackness questioned. All are female. *Empire* presents various tropes of the U.S. mulatta— Anika is sexually promiscuous, untrustworthy, jealous, power-hungry, and mentally unstable. In *Black-ish*, Rainbow's biraciality is often played for laughs, yet she embraces her identity as part of a panorama of Blackness. In fall 2019, *Mixed-ish*, a spin-off of *Black-ish*, has been slated to focus on a young Rainbow's experiences growing up with an interracial family in the 1980s. *Queen Sugar* (2016–) on Oprah's OWN network sets the narrative and story of Charley, a mixed-Black woman, within Black communities and families. Notably, these television series purposefully have Black writers, directors, and production staff and thus, these mixed-Black figures are no longer enmeshed solely with white gazes. A younger generation of mixed-Black actors such as Zendaya Coleman, Tessa Thompson, and Amandla Stenberg has increasingly embraced Black activist identities in public while acknowledging colorism within the media industries. Their celebrity personas and corpus of media work illustrate an axis toward political Black identities to provoke social change rather than to rely on racial ambiguity.

In Brazil, contradictory shifts in the vision of Blackness and racial mixing reflect power struggles over who is valued in the nation. For example, the politics of women as national symbols crystallized in the Miss Brasil 2016 and the Globeleza of 2014, a Carnival queen contest organized by TV Globo. Merging the words *beleza* (beauty) and the name of the network, Globo, the competition embeds the icon of the *mulata* as essential to Carnival, sensuality, and samba. By popular vote, Afro-Brazilian Nayara Justino became Globeleza in 2014 and was posed to usher in Carnival. A public backlash ensued in which Brazilians took to social media taunting Justino as "ugly," "a monkey," and "too Black." Globo promptly replaced Justino with light-skinned Erika Moura, demonstrating the pervasive ideology of mestiçagem as an instrument of whitening rather than the darkening of the nation. The substitution suggests the colonial mentality that dark Black women are useful only for labor and that *mulatas* are suitable for sex. With the sexualization that fueled the Globeleza's rise, increasing activist pressure and discomfort with the fetishized spectacle of *mulata* bodies led to a break with tradition by 2017. Instead of appearing as a body-painted nude samba dancer, the 2017 Globeleza performed in a range of costumes and lesser-known Brazilian dance styles. Meanwhile, at the crowning of Miss Brasil 2016, Raissa Santana announced her pride in becoming the first Black woman to represent Brazil in over thirty years. Despite the increasing presence of Black women in the public sphere such as the crowning of Black women as Miss Brasil in 2016 and 2017, racial hierarchies are nonetheless present. Elsewhere on Brazilian television, notably with telenovelas, women of African descent still remain on the periphery: between 1984 and 2014, only 8 percent of telenovela protagonists were Black or brown. Taís Araújo and Camila Pitanga are the only two self-identified actresses of African descent who have played central roles.[8]

The 2012 pairing of Pitanga with another Black actor, Lázaro Ramos, in *Lado a Lado* indicates possible new directions in the representation of Afro-Brazilians. Set in post-abolition early twentieth-century Brazil, the telenovela illustrated the increased visibility of Afro-Brazilian and feminist politics onscreen. Instead of nostalgic myths of racial integration through interracial sex, soccer, and samba, the story presents the exclusion of mixed-race children and Afro-Brazilians from white elite sectors and the suppression of Black revolutionaries, and marks samba, capoeira, and candomblé as Afro-Brazilian traditions. One of the few telenovelas in which a light-skinned woman of African descent marries a dark-skinned Afro-Brazilian man, *Lado a Lado* reverses glorified narratives of mestiçagem and whitening to redefine ideas about the limits and possibilities of Black freedom. Rather than consistently inscribing mixed-race women's sexuality with white men, this series counters pairings of the hypersexual *mulata* or upwardly mobile morena with white men. At the same time, half of *Lado a Lado* focuses on white female upper-class struggles. This foregrounding of whiteness as well as the presentation of racism as in the past undermines radical racial-equality messages.

Shifting social, political, economic, and cultural factors have begun to crack white dominance in the media industries, but the vast majority of telenovelas still feature predominantly white casts. Following patterns such as that of telenovelas like *Porto dos Milagres* (2001), *Segundo Sol* (2018) initially cast only three

Black actors out of twenty-six in the cast, and not a single Black actor played a major character despite the program's setting in Bahia, the Blackest state in Brazil in which over 76 percent of the population identifies as preto (Black) or pardo (brown). When criticized for casting white actors in the main roles, Globo responded that neither Camila Pitanga nor Taís Araújo were available—implying that they were the only two nonwhite actors Globo was willing to hire. Significant Black activism, social media protests, and pressure from the Brazilian Public Ministry of Labor precipitated a small change with the inclusion of a few more Black actors with speaking parts.[9]

Calling attention to racial injustices and the necessity of representational visibility, Afro-Brazilian communities are reshaping the cultural conditions of Black recognition. Changing media industry laws, policies, and technologies are also shifting the terms of inclusion. In 2011, the passage of Lei da TV Paga (Law 12.485, the Pay Television Law) increased access to cable and foreign telecommunications companies. It required foreign channels to broadcast at least three and a half hours of Brazilian-produced programming and that Brazilian-owned companies must have produced at least 50 percent of the independently produced programs they broadcast. With the eighth largest pay television market in the world, Brazil now has a larger array of viewer choices outside of TV Globo than ever before, and these channels including Globo have begun experimenting with narrative formats outside of the telenovela, giving exposure to more independent producers.[10] Digital streaming platforms are also changing the structure, content, and production of televisual narratives. Brazil provides Netflix's largest market after the United States and the United Kingdom, and Netflix has been developing series in Brazil for release there and elsewhere since 2016.[11] Its Brazilian-produced series, 3% (2016–19), had the second highest global audience of any Netflix series.[12] In these shows Netflix presents diverse casts with major Black characters. This in turn has helped create demand for Afro-Brazilian writers and directors among all of the media producers that seek to capture Brazil's substantial audience.

Yet media imagery is not necessarily the sole symptom or cause of increased racial equality. The opening up of spaces for a few, such as Black actors, writers, and directors who have found success in the new media landscape, has prompted the reconstitution of racial hierarchies and structural inequalities in revised entrenched forms. In March 2019, Donald Trump and Jair Bolsonaro met in person for the first time. Bolsonaro presented Trump with a Brazilian soccer jersey, expressed his admiration for the man, and promised to fight against socialism, political correctness, and gender ideology. Both presidents have sought the increased uses of police violence, even as it overwhelmingly impacts Black citizens, the purging of left-leaning perspectives from universities and media industries, and the slashing of funds for education. Both present serious challenges to democracy and further disenfranchise people of African descent. With nostalgic views of a past based on white supremacy, the desire to manage, erase, and subordinate Blackness is at the bedrock of hemispheric narratives. The U.S. mulatta and Brazilian *mulata* are devices that can challenge or restore these racial frames.

Is it possible for the mulatta and *mulata* figures to enter into subjecthood rather than remaining suspended in the national and international imagination as a sexually available object of desire? Clearly this depends on Black empowerment, in both Brazil and the United States. Imagining a future in which racial difference would be eradicated has hinged on the containment of Blackness and the centrality of whiteness. The hope of this project is that media representations in the United States could portray mixed Blackness in a new way that represents multiplicities and subjectivities. The mixed-race body has been used to construct a racelessness that permits a liberal color blindness coded in white normativity, a tragic metaphor of racial division, and an eroticized exotic site of pleasure and deviance. I also hope that accounts of mixed Blackness in Brazil can avoid the tropes of upward mobility through branqueamento and the sexualized and desired Blackness that must be contained and does not bring about citizenship. Hemispherically, racial mixing is a political project. *Imagining the Mulatta* uses both Brazil and the United States to illustrate how the mixed female body becomes a battleground on which citizenship is shaped. This book demonstrates how media representations of the mulatta/*mulata* figures manage Blackness, which requires an examination of anti-Blackness. The illogic of mulatta/*mulata* representation—a strategic forgetting of colonial violence and the haunting of sexual racialized exploitation—have come to the fore in the 2000s.

Juxtaposing and tracing the mulatta/*mulata* in the 2000s highlights hemispheric managements of Blackness. These paradoxical racial orders deny and celebrate Blackness, othering Blackness while maintaining it as a key element of national identity. Keeping these racial hierarchies requires work, but they are not unchallenged. Black activists have made increasing efforts to push for not only more visibility, but also for more diversified representation. Valuing Black female bodies beyond the fetishization of light-skinned women and the mulatta/*mulata* figures requires an embrace of multiculturalism that does not ignore the systemic racism and sexism tracing roots back to slavery. This embracing of multiculturalism requires a new form of belonging that neither erases Blackness nor requires assimilation. At these crossroads, Black movements offer a hemispheric opening of resistance and collaboration. While popular media has often fueled ideologies of white supremacy, critical consciousness of how these narratives operate can also engender resistance to these colonial legacies. From this consciousness, media productions and audience engagement promise a hemispheric vision that links the interrelated struggles of people of African descent and their histories and solidarities against racism. As the *mulata* and mulatta both threaten and reinforce bodily racial and geographical orders, a radical resistance that challenges the invisibility of whiteness, the prevailing conforming whitening practices, and the marginalization of Blackness opens possibilities for disruptions of white supremacy.

Notes

Introduction

1. "The Race Issue," special issue, *National Geographic*, April 2018, www.nationalgeographic .com/magazine/2018/04/.

2. "The New Face of America," special issue, *Time*, November 18, 1993, 2. Jon Meacham, "The New Face of Race," *Newsweek*, September 17, 2000, www.newsweek.com.

3. Lisa Funderburg, "The Changing Face of America," *National Geographic*, October 2013, www.ngm.nationalgeographic.com.

4. *Veja*, June 2007.

5. Silvia Salek, "BBC Delves into Brazilians' Roots," *BBC News*, July 10, 2007, http:// news.bbc.co.uk/2/hi/6284806.stm.

6. See for example George Reid Andrews, "Racial Equality in Brazil and the United States: A Statistical Comparison," *Journal of Social History* 26, no. 2 (1992): 229–63; Pierre Bourdieu and Loïc Wacquant, "On the Cunning of Imperialist Reason," *Theory, Culture & Society* 16, no. 1 (1999): 41–57; Carl Degler, *Neither Black nor White: Slavery and Race Relations in Brazil and the United States* (Madison: University of Wisconsin Press, 1971); Gilberto Freyre, *Casa Grande e Senzala: Formação da Familia Brasiliera sob o Regime da Economia Patriarcal* (Rio de Janeiro: José Olimpio, 1933); Antonio Sérgio Guimarães, *Racismo e Anti-Racismo no Brasil* (Rio de Janeiro: Editora 34, 1999); John D. French, "Translation, Diasporic Dialogue, and the Errors of Pierre Bourdieu and Loic Wacquant," *Nepantla: Views from South* 4 (2003): 375–89; Michael Hanchard, *Orpheus and Power: The Movimento Negro of Rio de Janeiro and São Paulo, Brazil, 1945–1988* (Princeton, N.J.: Princeton University Press, 1994); Thomas E. Skidmore, "Bi-Racial USA vs. Multi-Racial

Brazil: Is the Contrast Still Valid?," *Journal of Latin American Studies* 25, no. 2 (1993): 373–86; Frank Tannenbaum, *Slave and Citizen* (New York: A. Knopf, 1946); Edward Telles, *Race in Another America: The Significance of Skin Color in Brazil* (Princeton, N.J.: Princeton University Press, 2004).

7. Micol Seigel, "Beyond Compare: Historical Method after the Transnational Turn," *Radical History Review* 91, no. 1 (2005): 62–90.

8. Denise Ferreira da Silva, *Toward a Global Idea of Race* (Minneapolis: University of Minnesota Press, 2010).

9. Celine Parreñas Shimizu, *The Hypersexuality of Race: Performing Asian/American Women on Screen and Scene* (Durham, N.C.: Duke University Press, 2007).

10. Carl N. Degler, *Neither Black nor White: Slavery and Race Relations in Brazil and the United States* (Madison: University of Wisconsin Press, 1971).

11. Christen Smith, *Afro-Paradise: Blackness, Violence, and Performance in Brazil* (Urbana: University of Illinois Press, 2016).

12. Early twentieth-century Latin American intellectual thought ranging from Gilberto Freyre's racial democracy in Brazil to José Vasconcelos's cosmic race in Mexico and Fernando Ortiz in Cuba mobilized notions of racial mixing such as *mestiçagem, mestizaje,* and *mulataje.*

13. See Micol Seigel, *Uneven Encounters: Making Race and Nation in Brazil and the United States* (Durham, N.C.: Duke University Press, 2009); Frank Andre Guridy, *Forging Diaspora: Afro-Cubans and Black Americans in a World of Empire and Jim Crow* (Chapel Hill: University of North Carolina Press, 2010).

14. Ann Laura Stoler, "Intimidations of Empire: Predicaments of the Tactile and Unseen," in *Haunted by Empire: Geographies of Intimacy in North American History,* ed. Ann Laura Stoler (Durham, N.C.: Duke University Press, 2006), 1–22.

15. Jennifer C. Nash, *The Black Body in Ecstasy: Reading Race Reading Pornography* (Durham, N.C.: Duke University Press, 2014).

16. Sharon Patricia Holland. *The Erotic Life of Racism* (Durham, N.C.: Duke University Press, 2012), 9.

17. Néstor García Canclini, *Consumers and Citizens: Globalization and Multicultural Conflicts* (Minneapolis: University of Minnesota Press, 2001).

18. Pew Research Center, "Multiracial in America: Proud, Diverse and Growing in Numbers," June 11, 2015, www.pewsocialtrends.org/2015/06/11/multiracial-in-america/.

19. Jennifer Lee and Frank Bean, *Reinventing the Color Line: Immigration and America's New Racial/Ethnic Divide. Social Forces,* 86, no. 2 (2007): 572–74; Jennifer Lee and Frank Bean, "A Postracial Society or a Diversity Paradox?," *Du Bois Review* 9, no. 2 (2012): 422–23.

20. Ruth La Ferla, "Generation E.A.: Ethnically Ambiguous," *New York Times,* December 28, 2003, www.nytimes.com.

21. Jodi Melamed, *Represent and Destroy: Rationalizing Violence in the New Racial Capitalism* (Minneapolis: University of Minnesota Press, 2011).

22. Chris Smith, "In Conversation: Michael Bloomberg," *New York* magazine, September 7, 2013, http://nymag.com.

23. Henry Louis Gates Jr. quoted in Salek, "BBC Delves into Brazilians' Roots." Stephen Stearns quoted in Natalie Wolchover, "Future Humans Will All Look Brazilian," *Business Insider*, September 19, 2012, www.businessinsider.com.

24. Eduardo Bonilla-Silva, "We Are All Americans! The Latin Americanization of Racial Stratification in the USA," *Race and Society* 5 (2002):3–16; Eduardo Bonilla-Silva, "From Bi-Racial to Tri-Racial: Towards a New System of Racial Stratification in the USA," *Ethnic and Racial Studies* 27 (2004): 931–50.

25. "Monteiro Lobato era Racista?," *Bravo!*, May 2011, http://bravonline.abril.com.br/ materia/monteiro-lobato-era-racista#image=carta-lobato-extra3–1–p. For more on the curriculum implementation, see Alexandre Emboaba da Costa, "Afro-Brazilian Ancestralidade: Critical Perspectives on Knowledge and Development," *Third World Quarterly* 31, no. 4 (2010): 655–74.

26. Telles, *Race in Another America*, 81.

27. Melissa Nobles, *Shades of Citizenship: Race and the Census in Modern Politics* (Stanford, Calif.: Stanford University Press, 2000), 146–62.

28. Laura Capriglione, "Cor de celebridades revela critérios 'raciais' do Brasil," *Folha de São Paulo*, November 23, 2008, www1.folha.uol.com.br/fsp/especial/fj2311200827.htm.

29. The terms "preto" and "negro" have different meanings depending on historical context. "Preto" has usually referred to skin color, while "negro" usually has a political significance or consciousness. On the shifting meanings of these terms, see Livio Sansone, *Blackness without Ethnicity: Constructing Race in Brazil* (New York: Palgrave Macmillan, 2003).

30. Secretaria de Políticas de Promoção da Igualdade Racial (SEPPIR), "Campanha Censo 2010 de incentivo à declaração da raça," posted October 14, 2010.

31. Alessanda Duarte, "Censo 2010: população do Brasil deixa de ser predominantemente branca," *O Globo*, April 29, 2011, http://oglobo.globo.com/politica/censo-2010 -populacao-do-brasil-deixa-de-ser-predominantemente-branca-2789597.

32. See Christen Smith, *Afro-Paradise: Blackness, Violence, and Performance in Brazil* (Urbana: University of Illinois Press, 2016).

33. Ranier Bragon, "Bolsonaro defendeu esterilização de pobres para combater miséria e crime," *Folha de São Paulo*, June 11, 2018, www1.folha.uol.com.br/poder/2018/06/ bolsonaro-defendeu-esterilizacao-de-pobres-para-combater-miseria-e-crime.shtml.

34. Gladys Mitchell-Walthour, *The Politics of Blackness: Racial Identity and Political Behavior* (New York: Cambridge University Press), 216.

35. Jair Bolsonaro, interview by Preta Gil, *CQC O Povo Quer Saber*, Rede Bandeirantes, March 28, 2011.

36. Jair Bolsonaro, interview by Luciana Gimenez, *Luciana by Night*, Rede TV, May 7, 2019.

37. See Nobles, *Shades of Citizenship*; Anthony Marx, *Making Race and Nation: A Comparison of South Africa, the United States, and Brazil* (New York: Cambridge University Press, 1998); G. Reginald Daniel, *Race and Multiraciality in Brazil and the United States: Converging Paths?* (University Park: Pennsylvania State University Press, 2006); Chinyere

K. Osuji, *Boundaries of Love: Interracial Marriage and the Meaning of Race* (New York: New York University Press, 2019).

38. See Seigel, *Uneven Encounter*; Zita Nunes, *Cannibal Democracy: Race and Representation in the Literature of the Americas* (Minneapolis: University of Minnesota Press, 2008); Tiffany Joseph, *Race on the Move: Brazilian Migrants and the Global Reconstruction of Race* (Stanford, Calif.: Stanford University Press, 2015), Paulina Alberto, *Terms of Inclusion: Black Intellectuals in Twentieth Century Brazil* (Chapel Hill: University of North Carolina Press, 2011); Amilcar Pereira, *O mundo negro: Relações raciais e a constituição do movimento negro contemporâneo no Brasil* (Rio de Janeiro: Universidade Federal Fluminense, 2013).

39. See Mary Beltrán and Camilla Fojas, eds., *Mixed Race Hollywood* (New York: New York University Press, 2008); Caroline A. Streeter, *Tragic No More: Mixed-Race Women and the Nexus of Sex and Celebrity* (Amherst: University of Massachusetts Press, 2013); Ralina Joseph, *Transcending Blackness: From the New Millennium Mulatta to the Exceptional Multiracial* (Durham, N.C.: Duke University Press, 2012); Michele Elam, *The Souls of Mixed Folk: Race, Politics, and Aesthetics in the New Millennium* (Stanford, Calif.: Stanford University Press, 2011).

40. Daniel, *Race and Multiraciality in Brazil and the United States.*

Chapter 1. Foundations of the *Mulata* and Mulatta in the United States and Brazil

1. Edward Telles, *Race in Another America: The Significance of Skin Color in Brazil* (Princeton, N.J.: Princeton University Press, 2004), 14–15.

2. Kathleen Brown, *Good Wives, Nasty Wenches, and Anxious Patriarchs: Gender, Race, and Power in Colonial Virginia* (Chapel Hill: University of North Carolina Press, 1996), 132–35, 196; Joel Williamson, *New People: Miscegenation and Mulattoes in the United States* (Baton Rouge: Louisiana State University Press, 1995), 10.

3. George M. Fredrickson, *White Supremacy: A Comparative Study in American and South African History* (New York: Oxford University Press, 1981), 99–108.

4. On free Black communities, see Williamson, *New People.* These cities' economic and colonial relationships to the Caribbean, France, and Spain also evidenced hemispheric circuits of race-making.

5. Emily Clark, *The Strange History of the American Quadroon: Free Women of Color in the Revolutionary Atlantic World* (Chapel Hill: University of North Carolina Press, 2013), 159–64.

6. For example, Frank Tannenbaum claimed that the large mixed-race population in Brazil was an indicator of the less harsh conditions of slavery in comparison to the United States. Frank Tannenbaum, *Slave and Citizen* (New York: Knopf, 1946); Carl N. Degler, *Neither Black nor White: Slavery and Race Relations in Brazil and the United States* (Madison: University of Wisconsin Press, 1971), 67–75.

7. Degler, *Neither Black nor White*, 67–75.

8. Melissa Nobles, *Shades of Citizenship: Race and the Census in Modern Politics* (Stanford, Calif.: Stanford University Press, 2000), 36–37, 46.

9. Maria Helena Machado and Sasha Huber, (*T*)*races of Louis Agassiz: Photography, Body and Science, Yesterday and Today / Rastros e raças de Louis Agassiz: fotografia, corpo e ciência ontem e hoje* (São Paulo: Capacete, 2010), 30–33.

10. For example, Cirilo Villaverde's canonical abolitionist novel *Cecilia Valdés* (1839) focuses on the beautiful *mulata* protagonist Cecilia, who is obsessed with social mobility through white men and inevitably meets a tragic end.

11. Alfredo Bosi, *História concisa da literatura brasileira* (São Paulo: Cultrix, 1998), 143–44. Bosi notes that *A escrava Isaura* is Brazil's *Uncle Tom's Cabin*. Furthermore, he suggests that the escape of Stowe's light-skinned slave heroine Eliza inspired the depiction of Isaura's escape.

12. Peggy Pascoe, *What Comes Naturally: Miscegenation Law and the Making of Race in America* (New York: Oxford University Press, 2009).

13. U.S. Bureau of the Census, *Measuring America: The Decennial Censuses from 1790 to 2000* (Washington, DC: Government Printing Office, 2002), 27.

14. Daylanne K. English, *Unnatural Selections: Eugenics in American Modernism and the Harlem Renaissance* (Chapel Hill: University of North Carolina Press, 2004), 22–34.

15. See Matthew Frye Jacobson, *Whiteness of a Different Color* (Chicago: University of Chicago Press, 1998); David R. Roediger, *The Wages of Whiteness: Race and the Making of the American Working Class* (New York: Verso, 1999).

16. Angela Onwuachi-Willig, "A Beautiful Lie: Exploring *Rhinelander v. Rhinelander* as a Formative Lesson on Race, Identity, Marriage and Family," *California Law Review* 95 (2007): 7–27.

17. Arthur de Gobineau, quoted in Kim Butler, *Freedoms Given, Freedoms Won: Afro-Brazilians in Post-Abolition São Paulo and Salvador* (New Brunswick, N.J.: Rutgers University Press, 1998), 34.

18. See Lilia Moritz Schwarcz, *O Espetáculo das Raças: Cientistas, Instituições e Questão Racial no Brasil, 1870–1930* (São Paulo: Companhia das Letras, 1993).

19. Lilia Moritz Schwarcz, *As Barbas do Imperador: D. Pedro II, um monarca nos trópicos* (São Paulo: Companhia das Letras, 1998), 103, 393.

20. Zita Nunes, *Cannibal Democracy: Race and Representation in Literature of the Americas* (Minneapolis: University of Minnesota Press, 2008), 126–27.

21. Butler, *Freedoms Given, Freedoms Won*, 28–36.

22. Augusto Sales dos Santos and Laurence Hallewell, "Historical Roots of the 'Whitening' of Brazil," *Latin American Perspectives* 29, no. 1 (2002): 74–75.

23. João Batista de Lacerda, "The Metis, or Half-Breeds, of Brazil," in *Papers on Inter-Racial Problems Communicated to the First Universal Races Congress*, ed. Gustav Spiller, 337–82 (London: P. S. King & Son, 1911), https://archive.org/stream/papersoninterracoouniviala#page/376/mode/2up/search/Lacerda.

24. Thomas E. Skidmore, *Black into White: Race and Nationality in Brazilian Thought* (Durham, N.C.: Duke University Press, 1993), 200.

25. P. Gabrielle Foreman, "'Who's Your Mama?' 'White' Mulatta Genealogies, Early Photography, and Anti-Passing Narratives of Slavery and Freedom," *American Literary History* 14, no. 3 (2002): 505–39.

26. Giralda Seyferth, "A Antropologia e a teoria do branqueamento da raça no Brasil: A tese de João Batista de Lacerda," *Revista do Museu Paulista*, n.s., 30 (1985): 81–92.

27. See Claudia Tate, *Allegories of Political Desire: The Black Heroine's Text at the Turn of the Century* (New York: Oxford University Press, 1992).

28. Hollywood occasionally evaded the racial censorship of the Hays Code. See Susan Courtney, *Hollywood Fantasies of Miscegenation: Spectacular Narratives of Gender and Race* (Princeton, N.J.: Princeton University Press, 2004).

29. David J. Hellwig, ed., *African-American Reflections on Brazil's Racial Paradise* (Philadelphia: Temple University Press, 1992), 32.

30. Denise Ferreira da Silva, "Facts of Blackness: Brazil Is Not (Quite) the United States . . . And Racial Politics in Brazil?," *Social Identities* 4 (1998): 201–34.

31. Gilberto Freyre, *Casa Grande e Senzala*, 19th ed. (Rio de Janeiro: José Olympio, 1978; originally published 1933).

32. Lilia Moritz Schwarcz, "Gilberto Freyre: adaptação, mestiçagem, trópicos e privacidade em *Novo Mundos nos trópicos*," in *Gilberto Freyre e os estudos latino-americanos*, ed. Joshua Lund and Malcolm McNee (Pittsburgh, Pa.: Instituto Internacional de Literatura Iberoamericana, 2006), 305–34.

33. Saidiya Hartman, "Seduction and the Ruses of Power," *Callaloo* 19, no. 2 (1996), 538.

34. Gilberto Freyre, *The Masters and The Slaves*, [*Casa Grande e senzala*]: *A Study in the Development of Brazilian Civilization*, 2d ed. (New York: Alfred A. Knopf, 1956; originally published 1933), 278.

35. Sonia Maria Giacomini, *Mulher e escrava: uma introdução histórica ao estudo de mulher negra no Brasil* (Petrópolis: Vozes, 1988), 66.

36. George Reid Andrews, *Blacks and Whites in São Paulo, Brazil 1888–1988* (Madison: University of Wisconsin Press, 1991), 147.

37. See Bryan McCann, *Hello, Hello Brazil: Popular Music in the Making of Modern Brazil* (Durham, N.C.: Duke University Press, 2004), 60–76.

38. The government also forbade the speaking of foreign languages in public, banned Brazilian children of foreign residents from international travel, and closed foreign-language newspapers. Jeffrey Lesser, *Immigration, Ethnicity, and National Identity in Brazil, 1808 to the Present* (Cambridge: Cambridge University Press, 2013), 165–67.

39. Kim Butler, *Freedoms Given, Freedoms Won*, 127–30.

40. Miriam Petty, *Stealing the Show: African American Performers and Audiences in 1930s Hollywood* (Oakland: University of California Press, 2016), 218.

41. See Richard Dyer, "Singing Prettily: Lena Horne in Hollywood," in *In the Space of a Song: The Uses of Song in Film* (New York: Routledge, 2011), 114–44.

42. Donald Bogle, *Toms, Coons, Mulattoes, Mammies, and Bucks: An Interpretive History of Blacks in American Films*, 2d ed. (New York: Continuum, 1991), 143–58.

43. Natasha Pravaz, "Imagining Brazil: Seduction, Samba, and the *Mulata's* Body," *Canadian Women Studies: National Identity and Gender Politics* 20, no. 2 (2000): 48–55.

44. Kia Caldwell, *Negras in Brazil: Re-Envisioning Black Women, Citizenship, and the Politics of Identity* (New Brunswick, N.J.: Rutgers University Press, 2007), 88–90.

45. Pravaz, "Imagining Brazil," 50.

46. James T. Patterson, *Brown v. Board of Education: A Civil Rights Milestone and Its Troubled Legacy* (New York: Oxford University Press, 2001), 86–117.

47. Mary Dudziak, *Cold War Civil Rights: Race and the Image of American Democracy* (Princeton, N.J.: Princeton University Press, 2011), 115–36.

48. Marcos Chor Maio, "The UNESCO Project: Social Sciences and Race Studies in Brazil in the 1950s," *Portuguese Literary and Cultural Studies 2000* (spring/fall 2001): 51–63.

49. Skidmore, *Black into White*, 209.

50. Jerry Dávila, "Challenging Racism in Brazil. Legal Suits in the Context of the 1951 Anti-Discrimination Law," *Varia Historia* 33, no. 61 (2017): 167.

51. Lourdes Bandeira and Analía Soria Batista, "Preconceito e discriminação como reconceito e discriminação como expressões de violência," *Estudos Feministas* 119 (2002): 127–28.

52. Charles Wood and José Alberto Magno de Carvalho, *The Demography of Inequality in Brazil* (New York: Cambridge University Press, 1988), 135–53.

53. Ashley Farmer, *Remaking Black Power: How Black Women Transformed an Era* (Chapel Hill: University of North Carolina Press, 2017).

54. See the Combahee River Collective, "A Black Feminist Statement," in *All the Women Are White, All the Blacks Are Men, But Some of Us Are Brave*, ed. Gloria T. Hull, Patricia Bell Scott, and Barbara Smith (New York: Feminist Press at the City University of New York, 1982), 13–22.

55. Andrews, *Blacks and Whites in São Paulo*, 7.

56. Nobles, *Shades of Citizenship*, 117.

57. See Michael Hanchard, *Orpheus and Power: The Movimento Negro of Rio de Janeiro and São Paulo, Brazil, 1945–1988* (Princeton, N.J.: Princeton University Press, 1994).

58. Sueli Carneiro, "Black Women's Identity in Brazil," in *Race in Contemporary Brazil: From Indifference to Inequality*, ed. Rebecca Reichmann (University Park: Pennsylvania State University Press, 1999), 217–38.

59. Cláudia Pons Cardoso, "Feminisms from the Perspective of Afro-Brazilian Women," *Meridians: Feminism, Race, Transnationalism* 14, no. 1 (2016): 1–29; Lélia Gonzalez, "For an Afro-Latin Feminism," in *Confronting the Crisis in Latin America: Women Organizing for Change* (Santiago: Isis International, 1988) 95–101.

60. Luiza Bairros, "Nossos feminismos revisitados," *Revista Estudos Feministas* 3, no. 2 (1995): 458–63; Sueli Carneiro, "Mulheres em Movimento." *Estudos Avançados* 17, no. 49 (2003): 117–32.

61. Robert Stam, *Tropical Multiculturalism: A Comparative History of Race in Brazilian Cinema and Culture* (Durham, N.C.: Duke University Press, 1997), 342.

62. Walter Avancini quoted in *A negação do Brasil* (Denying Brazil), written and directed by Joel Zito Araújo (2000).

63. Ibid.

64. Gilberto Freyre, *Modos de Homem e Modas de Mulher* (São Paulo: Record, 1987), 24.

65. Natasha Pravaz, "Performing *Mulata*-ness: The Politics of Cultural Authenticity and Sexuality among Carioca Samba Dancers," *Latin American Perspectives* 39, no. 2 (2012): 113–33.

Chapter 2. Framing Blackness and Mixedness

1. Josh Robertson, "The 50 Hottest Biracial Women," *Complex*, June 12, 2012, http://www
.complex.com/pop-culture/2012/06/the-50-hottest-biracial-women/

2. *VIP* 189 (January 2001): 80–81.

3. Caroline Streeter, *Tragic No More: Mixed Race Women and the Nexus of Sex and Celebrity* (Amherst: University of Massachusetts Press, 2012).

4. bell hooks, "Eating the Other," in *Black Looks: Race and Representation* (Cambridge, Ma.: South End Press, 1992), 21–41; Richard Dyer, *Heavenly Bodies: Film Stars and Society*, 2d ed. (New York: Routledge, 2003), 70–71, 115–16, 138–39.

5. José Muñoz, *Disidentifications: Queers of Color and the Performance of Politics* (Minneapolis: University of Minnesota Press, 1999), 5.

6. See Kim Williams, *Mark One or More: Civil Rights on Multicultural America* (Ann Arbor: University of Michigan Press, 2006).

7. Jesse Jackson quoted in Jerelyn Eddings and Kenneth T. Walsh, "Counting a 'New' Type of American," *U.S. News and World Report*, July 14, 1997, A22, www.usnews.com.

8. Lynn Norment, "Am I Black, White, or in Between?," *Ebony*, August 1995, 108–12.

9. Williams, *Mark One or More*, 73, 121–28.

10. *Federal Measures of Race and Ethnicity and the Implications for the 2000 Census, Hearings Before the Subcommittee on Government Management, Information, and Technology of the Committee on Government Reform and Oversight, House of Representatives*, 105th Congr., (Washington, D.C.: U.S. Government Printing Office, 1997) (Testimony of Newt Gingrich, Speaker, U.S. House of Representatives), 662.

11. Williams, *Mark One or More*, 112–26.

12. *Abigail Fisher v. University of Texas Austin*, 133 S. Ct. 99 (2013), oral arguments, 33–35, https://www.supremecourt.gov/oral_arguments/argument_transcripts/11-345.pdf.

13. *Abigail Fisher v. University of Texas Austin* (Fisher II), 136 S. Ct 2198 (2016), 27–28.

14. Edward Telles, *Race in Another America* (Princeton, N.J.: Princeton University Press, 2004), 76–92.

15. Sérgio da Silva Martins, Carlos Alberto Medeiros, and Elisa Larkin Nascimento, "Paving Paradise: The Road from 'Racial Democracy' to Affirmative Action in Brazil," *Journal of Black Studies* 34 (2004): 787–816.

16. Ediane Merola, "Não Haverá Distorções," *O Globo*, September 9, 2003, 3.

17. Marcos Chor Maio and Ricardo Ventura Santos, "Política de cotas raciais, os 'olhos da sociedade' e os usos da antropologia: O caso de vestibular da Universidade de Brasília (UnB)," *Horizontes antropológicos* 11 (2005): 181–214.

18. The Universidade Federal do Paraná (UFPR) also incorporated outside evaluation of an applicant's claim to racial identity. Ciméa Barbato Bevilaqua, "The Institutional Life of Rules and Regulations: Ten Years of Affirmative Action Policies at the Federal University of Paraná, Brazil," *Vibrant: Virtual Brazilian Anthropology* 12 (2015): 193–232.

19. Fernanda Bassetes, "Cotas na UnB: gêmeo idêntico é barrado," *O Globo*, May 29, 2007, G1. A PBS *Wide Angle* series also documented the case in "Brazil in Black and White." Adam Stepan, producer (Washington, D.C., PBS, 2007).

20. Fernanda Bassetes, "UnB volta atrás e aceita gêmeo barrado em cotas," *O Globo*, June 6, 2007, G1.

21. Luiz Augusto Campos, João Feres Júnior, and Verônica Toste Daflon, "Administrando o debate público: O Globo e a controvérsia em torno das cotas raciais." *Revista Brasileira de Ciência Política* 11 (2013): 7–31.

22. ADPF 186 (Arguição de Descumprimento de Preceito Fundamental n. 186), Federal Supreme Court of Brazil, www.stf.jus.br.

23. Isabel Fleck, "Caso de cotista com autodeclaração rejeitada acende debate no Itamaraty," *Folha de São Paulo*, August 20, 2016, http://www1.folha.uol.com.br/.

24. Rachel Abramowitz, *Is That a Gun in Your Pocket? Women's Experience of Power in Hollywood* (New York: Random House, 2000), 245.

25. Aisha D. Bastiaans, "Detecting Difference in *Devil in a Blue Dress*: The Mulatta Figure, Noir, and the Cinematic Reification of Race," in *Mixed Race Hollywood*, ed. Mary Beltrán and Camilla Fojas (New York: New York University Press, 2008), 235.

26. Melissa Blanco Borelli, "A Taste of Honey: Choreographing Mulatta in the Hollywood Dance Film." *International Journal of Performance Arts and Digital Media* 5, no. 2–3 (2009): 148.

27. Joan Morgan, "Regarding Jennifer: Mystery and Mistaken Identity Follow Beals Everywhere. The Star of the Upcoming Thriller *Devil in a Blue Dress* Sets the Record Straight," *Vibe*, August 1995, 52–60.

28. Mark Morrison, "The Two Faces of Jennifer," *US Weekly*, September 9 1985, 26; "Jennifer Beals: Dazzling Looks and a Ripped Wardrobe Turn a Dancing Yalie into a Flashy Star," *People*, December 26, 1983,www.people.com.

29. Morrison, "Two Faces of Jennifer." "Jennifer Beals: Dazzling Looks and a Ripped Wardrobe Turn a Dancing Yalie into a Flashy Star," *People*; Michael London, "Flashdance Star Taps Her Own Beat," *Los Angeles Times*, May 8, 1983, U21; Gene Siskel, "Two Years After 'Flashdance,' Beals Is Back as 'The Bride,'" *Chicago Tribune*, August 11, 1985, section 13, 5.

30. Michael London, "Flashdance Star Taps Her Own Beat," *Los Angeles Times*, May 8, 1983, U21.

31. Ibid.

32. Bill O'Reilly, "What President Obama Can Teach America's Kids," *Parade Magazine*, August 9 2009, www.parade.com; Julie Bosman, "Obama Sharply Assails Absent Fathers," *New York Times*, June 16, 2008, www.nytimes.com.

33. Morrison, "Two Faces of Jennifer."

34. Siskel, "Two Years After 'Flashdance.'"

35. Kimberly DaCosta, *Making Multiracials: State, Family, and Market in the Redrawing of the Color Line* (Palo Alto, Calif.: Stanford University Press), 30–50.

36. "Celebrity Lookout," *Los Angeles Sentinel*, November 21, 1985, 4.

37. "Rae Dawn Chong: Black Actresses Star in Non-racial Movie Roles," *Jet*, September 9, 1985, 26.

38. Kobena Mercer, *Welcome to the Jungle: New Positions in Black Cultural Studies* (London: Routledge, 1994), 233–58.

39. Lynn Norment, "Who's Black and Who's Not: New Ethnicity Raises Provocative Questions About Racial Identity," *Ebony*, March 1990, 136; Lynn Norment, "Are the Children of Mixed Marriage Black or White?," *Jet*, May 21 1990, 53. See also letters, *Ebony*, July 1990, 140–41.

40. Caroline Streeter, "Faking the Funk? Mariah Carey, Alicia Keys, and (Hybrid) Black Celebrity," in *Black Cultural Traffic: Crossroads in Global Performance and Popular Culture*, ed. Harry J. Elam Jr. and Kennell Jackson (Ann Arbor: University of Michigan Press, 2005), 185–207.

41. Catherine Squires, *Dispatches from the Color Line: The Press and Multiracial America* (Albany: State University of New York Press, 2007), 74–94.

42. Caroline Streeter, "Ambiguous Bodies: Locating Black/White Women in Cultural Representations," in *The Multiracial Experience: Racial Borders as the New Frontier*, ed. Maria Root (Thousand Oaks, Calif.: Sage, 1996), 317.

43. Norment, "Who's Black and Who's Not?"

44. Squires, *Dispatches from the Color Line*, 7.

45. Morgan, "Regarding Jennifer."

46. Jennifer Beals, interview by Tavis Smiley, *The Tavis Smiley Show*, PBS, February 7, 2011.

47. Jennifer Beals, POWER UP Gala, November 7, 2004, http://www.power-up.net/pages/newsevents2.html, www.youtube.com/watch?v=nD3FTUsTBPM.

48. Adam Sternbergh, "Black in a Flash, " *New York Magazine*, May 21 2005, http://nymag.com.

49. Sonia Saraiya, "Jennifer Beals on Playing the Secretly Biracial Star Margo Taft in 'The Last Tycoon'," August 31, 2017, http://variety.com.

50. Lisa Liebman, "The Fascinating Old Hollywood Story that Inspired *The Last Tycoon*'s Best Plotline," *Vanity Fair*, July 28, 2017, www.vanityfair.com.

51. Lisa Nakamura, "Mixedfolks.com: Ethnic Ambiguity, Celebrity Outing, and the Internet," in *Mixed Race Hollywood*, ed. Mary Beltrán and Camilla Fojas (New York: New York University Press, 2008), 64–87.

52. Liebman, "Fascinating Old Hollywood Story."

53. Halle Berry, "Acceptance Speech," March 24, 2002, *Academy Awards Acceptance Speech Database*, http://aaspeechesdb.oscars.org.

54. Streeter, *Tragic No More*, 94–97.

55. Donald Bogle, *Dorothy Dandridge: A Biography* (New York: Amistad Press, 1997), 267–74.

56. Ibid, 400.

57. Streeter, *Tragic No More*, 94–97.

58. Sika A. Dagbovie-Mullins, *Crossing B(l)ack: Mixed Race in Modern American Literature and Culture* (Knoxville: University of Tennessee Press, 2013), 118–19.

59. Lisa Jones, *Bulletproof Diva: Tales of Race, Sex, and Hair* (New York: Doubleday, 1994), 50.

60. Dana Kennedy, "Halle Berry, Bruised, and Beautiful, Is On a Mission," *New York Times*, March 10, 2002, www.nytimes.com.

61. Lisa Jones, "The Blacker the Berry," *Essence*, June 1994, 60.

62. Mireya Navarro, "Going Beyond Black and White, Hispanics in Census Pick Other," *New York Times*, November 9, 2003, www.nytimes.com.

63. "How Census Results Could Redefine America's Definition of Black," *Jet*, April 6, 2001, 5–10.

64. Streeter, *Tragic No More*, 88–103.

65. "Who Should Play the Tragic Star?," *Ebony*, August 1997, 66. Laura Randolph, "Halle Berry: On How She Found Dorothy Dandridge's Spirit and Healed Her Own," *Ebony*, August 1999, 90–98.

66. Dagbovie-Mullins, *Crossing B(l)ack*, 116. Lynn Hirschberg, "The Beautiful and Damned," *New York Times Magazine*, December 23, 2001, 26. Kennedy, "Halle Berry, Bruised, and Beautiful." Frank Senello, *Halle Berry: A Stormy Life* (London: Virgin Books, 2003). Halle Berry, interview by Alina Choa, *American Morning*, "Big Stars, Big Giving," *CNN*, December 14, 2010.

67. Michael Arceneaux, "Halle Berry on Breaking Cycle of Violence. The Oscar Winner Talks History of Domestic Abuse at Fundraiser," BET, June 20, 2011, www.bet.com.

68. "Justice Is Served," *People*, October 21, 1996, www.people.com.

69. Vincent Coppola, "Beauty and the Brave," *Redbook*, July 1994, 46–50. Karen S. Schneider, "Enough Is Enough: After Struggling to Rebuild Her Marriage, Halle Berry Leaves Her Cheating Husband, Eric Benét—the Latest in a Line of Men Who've Failed Her. So Why Can't One of the World's Most Beautiful Women Find a Half-Decent Guy?," *People*, October 20, 2003, 64–66.

70. Lonnae O'Neal Parker, "Halle Berry, in Character: For the Actress, Dorothy Dandridge Is a Star Worth Shooting For," *Washington Post*, August 20 1999, C8.

71. Kennedy, "Halle Berry, Bruised, and Beautiful."

72. Laura Randolph, "Halle Berry, on Her Roles, Her Regrets, and Her Real Life Nightmare," *Ebony*, December 1994, 120.

73. Leo Ebersole and Curt Wagner, "Sealed with a Kiss," *Chicago Tribune*, March 25, 2003, www.chicagotribune.com.

74. Robert Hanashiro, "A Kiss Isn't Just a Kiss," *USA Today*, March 30, 2003, www.usatoday.com.

75. "Halle Berry's Baby Daddy Hurled 'N' Word at Her," *TMZ*, February 2, 2011, www.tmz.com.

76. Amy DuBois Barnett, "On the Very Solid, Fantastically Full Life of Halle Berry," *Ebony*, March 2011, 78.

77. Joyce Maynard, "Roles of a Lifetime-Halle Berry," *New York Times Magazine*, October 18, 2012, http://tmagazine.blogs.nytimes.com.

78. Dana Oliver, "Halle Berry on How She Went Short, Advice for Her Daughter Nahla, and Owning a Whole Lot of Flip-Flops," *Huffington Post*, May 29, 2012.

79. Iyana Robertson, "Halle Berry Takes Ex-Boyfriend to Court Over Their Daughter's Hair," *Vibe*, November 26, 2014, www.vibe.com.

80. Marjon Carlos, "Team Natural: Why Halle Berry's Lawsuit over Her Daughter's Hair Matters," *Vogue*, November 25, 2014, https://www.vogue.com/article/halle-berry -gabriel-aubrey-lawsuit-natural-hair. "Halle and Nahla's Hair Can Both Relax," *TMZ*, December 5, 2014, www.tmz.com.

81. All translations of quotations in this book are mine unless otherwise noted. Sionei Ricardo Leão, "Hallewood," *Raça,* June 2006, 33.

82. Anistia Internacional, "Jovem Negro Vivo," https://anistia.org.br/campanhas/jovem negrovivo.

83. *Raça Brasil*, October 1996.

84. Leyde Moraes, "Camila Pitanga," *Raça,* October 1996, 13.

85. Regina Rita, "Porque Não Foi Gabriela," *Revista Amiga*, May 1975, 14.

86. Joel Zito Araújo, A *negação do Brasil: O negro na telenovela brasileira* (São Paulo: Senac, 2000).

87. Rodrigo Cardoso and Laura Capriglione, "Da cor do sucesso: Ídolos negros contam como estão ajudando a romper a barreira do preconceito," *Veja*, June 24, 1998, 100.

88. Vera Gudin, "Pitanga em Flor," *Claudia*, April 2010, 34.

89. Cardoso and Capriglione, "Da cor do sucesso."

90. Laura Capriglione, "Cor de celebridades revela critérios 'raciais' do Brasil," *Folha de São Paulo*, November 23, 2008, Racismo, Caderno Especial 12.

91. *RG Vogue Brazil* 42, 2005. *Claudia*, March 2006. *VIP*, July 2000.

92. Dora De Lima Bertulio, "Enfrentamento do Racismo em um Projeto Democrático," in *Multiculturalismo e Racismo: Uma Comparação Brasil-Estados Unidos*, ed. Jesse Souza (Brasilia: Paralelo 15, 1996), 189–208.

93. Kim D. Butler, *Freedoms Given, Freedoms Won: Afro-Brazilians in Post-Abolition São Paulo and Salvador* (New Brunswick, N.J.: Rutgers University Press, 1998); Michael George Hanchard, *Orpheus and Power: The Movimento Negro of Rio de Janeiro and São Paulo, Brazil, 1945–1998* (Princeton, N.J.: Princeton University Press, 1998); Abdias do Nascimento, "Teatro experimental do negro: trajetória e reflexões," *Estudos Avançados* 18, no. 50 (2004): 209–24.

94. Eliane Martins, "Mulher, Mãe, e Militante," *Raça*, November 2009, 62.

95. Muñoz, *Disidentifications*, 31.

96. Luísa Brito, "UFPR vai recorrer da decisão judicial que obrigou matrícula de aluna cotista," *Globo*, March 3, 2007, http://g1.globo.com/Noticias/Vestibular/0,,MUL9696- 5604,00-UFPR+VAI+RECORRER+DA+DECISAO+JUDICIAL+QUE+OBRIGOU +MATRICULA+DE+ALUNA.html.

97. Luísa Brito, "'Ela é a cor de Camila Pitanga,' diz advogado de aluna cotista," *Globo*, March 7, 2007, http://g1.globo.com/Noticias/Vestibular/0,,MUL9708-5604,00-ELA+ E+DA+COR+DA+CAMILA+PITANGA+DIZ+ADVOGADO+DE+ALUNA+COT ISTA.html.

98. Degler, *Neither Black nor White*.

99. Telles, *Race in Another America*, 115.

100. Eliane Martins, "Mulher, mãe, e militante," *Raça Brasil* 138 (2009) 63.

101. Alberto Pereira Jr., "Acerto de Cotas," *Folha de São Paulo*, October 21, 2012, /www1 .folha.uol.com.br.

102. "Camila Pitanga é a rainha dos comercias," *Folha de São Paulo*, June 5, 2012, www1 .folha.uol.com.br.

103. Dolores Orosco and Mayra Stachuk, "Protagonista de 'Babilônia,' Camila Pitanga diz que já morou em morro e viu a violência do tráfico," *Marie Claire*, March 2015, http:// revistamarieclaire.globo.com/Celebridades/noticia/2015/03/protagonista-de-babilonia -camila-pitanga-diz-que-ja-morou-em-morro-e-viu-violencia-do-trafico.html.

104. ONU Mulheres Brasil, "Camila Pitanga-ElesPorElas HeForShe," Youtube video, posted November 21, 2016, https://www.youtube.com/watch?v=fB1-QzEB _5g&feature=youtu.be.

105. "Chapter One," *Dear White People*, Netflix, dir. by Justin Simien, aired April 28, 2017.

106. Dagbovie, *Crossing Black*, 126.

107. Brantley Bardin, "Meet Karen from *The Office*: Interview with Rashida Jones," *Women's Health*, March 5, 2008, www.womenshealthmag.com/relationships/rashida -jones-interview. Rashida Jones, interview by Andy Cohen, *Watch What Happens Live with Andy Cohen*, Bravo, New York, April 6, 2014.

108. Tracee Ellis Ross, interview by Trevor Noah, *The Daily Show with Trevor Noah*, Comedy Central, New York, February 8, 2017.

Chapter 3. The Morena and the *Mulata* in Brazilian Telenovelas

1. Joseph Straubhaar, "The Development of the Telenovela as the Paramount Form of Popular Culture in Brazil," *Studies in Latin American Popular Culture* 1 (1982): 138–50.

2. Roberto Amaral and Cesar Guimarães, "Media Monopoly in Brazil," *Journal of Communication* 44, no. 4 (1994): 26–38.

3. Maria Immacolata Vassallo de Lopes and Guillermo Orozco Gómez, coordinators, "Qualidade na ficção televisiva e participação transmidiática das audiências"—Anuário OBITEL 2011 (Rio de Janeiro: Editora Globo, 2011).

4. Maria Immacolata Vassallo de Lopes, "Telenovela como recurso comunicativo," *Matrizes* 3, no. 1 (2010): 4.

5. Adriana Estill, "The Mexican Telenovela and Its Foundational Fictions," in *Latin American Literature and Mass Media*, ed. Deborah Castillo and Edmundo Paz Soldán (New York: Garland, 1991), 169–71.

6. Doris Sommer, *Foundational Fictions: The National Romances of Latin America* (Berkeley: University of California Press, 1991), 5–6.

7. Jesús Martín-Barbero, "Matrices culturales de la telenovela," *Estudios sobre las culturas contemporáneas* 2, no. 5 (1988): 137–64.

8. Samantha Nogueira Joyce, *Brazilian Telenovelas and the Myth of Racial Democracy* (Lanham, Md.: Lexington Books, 2012), 9.

9. Thomas Tufte, *Living with the Rubbish Queen: Telenovelas, Culture and Modernity in Brazil* (Luton, U.K.: University of Luton Press, 2000), 227–31.

10. Ana López, "Our Welcomed Guests: Telenovelas in Latin America," in *To be Continued: Soap Operas Around the World*, ed. Robert Clyde Allen (London: Routledge, 1995), 260–62.

11. Esther Hamburger, *O Brasil antenado: a sociedade da novela* (Rio de Janeiro: Jorge Zahar, 2005), 131; Armand Mattelart and Michèle Mattelart, *The Carnival of Images: Brazilian Television Fiction* (New York: Bergin and Garvey, 1990), 15.

12. "Globo in the World," Rede Globo, http://redeglobo.globo.com/Portal/institucional/foldereletronico/ingles/g_globo_mundo.html.

13. Joel Zito Araújo, *A negação do Brasil: o negro na telenovela brasileira* (São Paulo: SENAC, 2000), 58–60.

14. Herman Gray, *Watching Race: Television and the Struggle for "Blackness"* (Minneapolis: University of Minnesota Press, 1995), 84–88.

15. Araújo, *A negação do Brasil.*

16. Reighan Gillam, "Resistance Televised: The TV da Gente Television Network and Brazilian Racial Politics," in *Watching While Black: Centering the Television of Black Audiences*, ed. Beretta Smith-Shomade (New Brunswick, N.J.: Rutgers University Press, 2012), 211.

17. On the Black model quota, see "Marcas ignoram cota de modelos negros na SPFW," *Folha de São Paulo*, June 15, 2011, www1.folha.uol.com.br/ilustrada/929994-marcas-ignoraram-cota-de-modelos-negros-na-spfw.shtml.

18. Tufte, *Living with the Rubbish Queen*, 228–31.

19. Kia Caldwell, *Negras in Brazil: Re-envisioning Black Women, Citizenship, and the Politics of Identity* (New Brunswick, N.J.: Rutgers University Press, 2007), 55.

20. John Burdick, *Blessed Anastácia: Women, Race, and Popular Christianity in Brazil* (New York: Routledge, 2013), 31.

21. Luisa Farah Schwartzman, "Does Money Whiten? Intergenerational Changes in Racial Classification in Brazil," *American Sociological Review* 72 (2007): 940–63.

22. A notable exception is *Duas Caras* (2007–8).

23. Silvia Helena Simões Borelli, "Telenovelas brasileiras: territórios de ficcionalidade, universalidades, segmentação," in *Desafios da comunicação*, ed. Octávio Ianni, Paulo Edgar A. Resende, and Hélio Silva. (Petrópolis: Vozes, 2001), 131–32.

24. France Winddance Twine, *Racism in a Racial Democracy: The Maintenance of White Supremacy in Brazil* (New Brunswick, N.J.: Rutgers University Press, 1998), 89–93.

25. Nancy Leys Stepan, *The Hour of Eugenics: Race, Gender, and Nation in Latin America* (Ithaca, N.Y.: Cornell University Press, 1991)

26. Lilia Moritz Schwarcz, *O Espetáculo das Raças—cientistas, instituições e questão racial no Brasil 1870–1930* (São Paulo: Companhia das Letras, 1993).

27. George Reid Andrews, *Blacks and Whites in São Paulo, Brazil, 1888–1988* (Madison: University of Wisconsin Press, 1991), 69.

28. Thaïs Machado-Borges, *Only for You!: Brazilians and the Telenovela Flow* (Stockholm: Dept. of Social Anthropology, Stockholm University, 2003), 203–4.

29. Hamburger, *O Brasil Antenado*.

30. Heloísa Buarque de Almeida, "Consumidoras e heroínas: gênero na telenovela," *Revista Estudos Feministas* 15, no. 1 (2007): 180–81.

31. Néstor García Canclini, *Consumidores y Ciudadanos: Conflictos Multiculturales de la Globalización* (México City: Grijalbo, 1995).

32. Brazilians are divided into five social classes: classe A has the highest amount of consumer potential; classes B and C comprise the middle- and lower-middle classes; classes C and D are the highest telenovela audience members. See Almeida, "Consumidoras e heroínas," 180–84.

33. Patricia Pinho and Elizabeth Silva, "Domestic Relations in Brazil: Legacies and Horizons," *Latin American Research Review* 45, no.2 (2010): 90–113.

34. Morris Kachani, "A santa mais brasileira, Branca ou negra? Festa de Nossa Senhora Aparecida, Padroeira do Brasil, traz de volta debate sobre sua cor," *Folha de São Paulo*, October 12, 2011, www1.folha.uol.com.br/fsp/poder/po121020111112.html.

35. Many Middle Eastern immigrants, whether Muslim, Jewish, or Christian, came to Brazil under the category of *turco* (Turk). Jeffrey Lesser, *Immigration, Ethnicity, and National Identity in Brazil, 1808 to the Present* (Cambridge: Cambridge University Press, 2013), 119.

36. See Antonio La Pastina, Dhaval S. Patel, and Marcio Schiavo, "Social Merchandizing in Brazilian Telenovelas," in *Entertainment Education and Social Change*, eds. Arvind Singhal, Michael J. Cody, Everett M. Rogers, and Miguel Sabido (Mahwah: N.J.: Lawrence Erlbaum Associates, 2004), 261–77.

37. Episode 209, *Belíssima*, July 7, 2006, TV Globo.

38. Oliveira Vianna quoted in Mara Loveman, *National Colors: Racial Classification and the State in Latin America* (New York: Oxford University Press, 2014), 149.

39. The economic success of many Middle Eastern, Arab, and Jewish immigrant groups as well as the changing of surnames facilitated placement into a broader white category. Yet at the same time, the *foreigner* label is continually applied to Brazilians of Arab or Japanese heritage. However, unlike the United States, hyphenated ethnic identities are rare. Jeffrey Lesser, *Negotiating National Identity: Immigrants, Minorities, and the Struggle for Ethnicity in Brazil* (Durham, N.C.: Duke University Press, 1999), 46–68, 89–150.

40. Elizabeth Hordge-Freeman, "What's Love Got to Do with It?: Racial Features, Stigma, and Socialization in Afro-Brazilian Families," *Ethnic and Racial Studies* 36, no. 10 (2013): 1507–23.

41. From the 1970s to 1990s, Embratur distributed images of scantily clad women on Brazilian beaches in tourism brochures. The government's promotion of Brazil's women as a natural asset for international tourism heightened the market for sex work. See Louise

Prado Alfonso, "Embratur: Formadora de imagens da nação brasileira" (master's thesis, Universidade Estadual de Campinas, São Paulo, 2005).

42. In response to criticism in the 1990s, Embratur presented an awareness campaign, "Beware. Brazil is watching you," to discourage prostitution and ceased creating sexually suggestive promotional materials. In 2003, President Lula da Silva replaced Embratur with the Ministry of Tourism to reposition Brazil on the international market. See Ana Paula Felizardo and Vitória Vergas Andrade, *Compartilhando experiências: O progresso das iniciativas brasileiras—equilibrando a responsabilidade social no enfrentamento à exploração sexual de crianças e adolescentes no turismo* (Natal: Resposta, 2005).

43. Anadelia A. Romo, *Brazil's Living Museum: Race, Reform, and Tradition in Bahia* (Chapel Hill: University of North Carolina Press, 2010).

44. Caldwell, *Negras in Brazil*, 60.

45. "'Paraíso Tropical' chega ao fim e Bebel entra para história da TV," September 22, 2007, http://noticiasco.terra.com.co/tecnologia/interna/0,OI1928199-EI7811,00.html. As scripts are written during the airing of the telenovela, the writers were able to adapt the script to include Pitanga as a *mulata* type.

46. E. Patrick Johnson, *Appropriating Blackness: Performance and the Politics of Authenticity* (Durham, N.C.: Duke University Press, 2003), 29.

47. Mireille Miller-Young, "Putting Hypersexuality to Work: Black Women and Illicit Eroticism in Pornography," *Sexualities* 13, no.2 (2010): 219–35.

48. Belly dancing in Brazil was popularized by another telenovela, *O Clone* (2001–2002). While Karam explores how non–Middle Eastern women of primarily European descent appropriate belly dancing, I argue that in Bebel's performance the exotic brown body serves as a rendering of Otherness that emphasizes sensuality and desire for a male gaze. See John Tofik Karam, "Bellydancing and the (En)Gendering of Ethnic Sexuality in the 'Mixed' Brazilian Nation," *Journal of Middle East Women's Studies* 6, no. 2 (2010): 86–114.

49. Natasha Pravaz, "Brazilian Mulatice: Performing Race, Gender, and the Nation." *Journal of Latin American Anthropology* 8, no. 1 (2003): 116–46.

50. Laura Mulvey, "Visual Pleasure and Narrative Cinema." *Screen* 16, no. 4 (1975): 6–18.

51. bell hooks, *Black Looks: Race and Representation* (Boston: South End, 1992), 55.

52. Pierre Bourdieu, *Distinction: A Social Critique of the Judgment of Taste* (Cambridge, Mass.: Harvard University Press, 1984).

53. Heloísa Buarque de Almeida, *Telenovela, consumo e gênero: "muitas mais coisas"* (Bauru: Anpocs/EDUSC, 2003).

54. Néstor García Canclini, *Consumidores y ciudadanos*.

55. Teresa Pires do Rio Caldeira, *City of Walls: Crime, Segregration, and Citizenship in São Paulo* (Berkeley: University of California Press, 2000), 70–72.

56. Almeida, *Telenovela, consumo e gênero*.

57. Donna M. Goldstein, *Laughter Out of Place: Race, Class, Violence, and Sexuality in a Rio Shantytown* (Berkeley: University of California Press, 2003), 120–27.

58. Ibid., 124.

59. "Bebel, a queridinha do Brasil," http://paraisotropical.globo.com/Novela/Paraisotropical/0,AA1642119–8295,00.html.

60. Almeida, *Telenovela, consumo e gênero*, 168–69.

61. Cláudia Sarmento, "Bebel não veste Prada," *O Globo*, May 20, 2007, 12–13.

62. Episode 27, *Paraíso Tropical*, aired April 4, 2007, on TV Globo.

63. Alvaro Jarrín, *The Biopolitics of Beauty: Cosmetic Citizenship and Affective Capital in Brazil* (Berkeley: University of California Press, 2017), 184, 197–98.

64. Episode 136, *Paraíso Tropical*, aired August 9, 2007, on TV Globo.65. "Bebel vai ter final feliz em Paraíso Tropical," *O Globo*, September 19, 2007, www.gazetadopovo.com .br/caderno-g/bebel-vai-ter-final-feliz-em-paraiso-tropical-aneokks2oofpmnd899zxsrrda.

66. Liv Sovik, "We Are Family: Whiteness in the Brazilian Media," *Journal of Latin American Cultural Studies* 13, no. 3 (2004): 318.

67. Natasha Pravaz, "Where Is the Carnivalesque in Rio's Carnaval? Samba, *Mulatas*, and Modernity," *Visual Anthropology* 21, no. 2 (2008): 95–111.

Chapter 4. Reinventing the Mulatta in the United States for the 2000s

1. Martin Kasindorf and Haya El Nasser, "Impact of Census' Race Data Debated," *USA Today*, March 12, 2001, www.usatoday.com.

2. Orlando Patterson, "Race Over," *New Republic*, January 10, 2000, 6.

3. Herman Gray, "Subject(ed) to Recognition," *American Quarterly* 65, no. 4 (2013): 771–98.

4. See Geoff King, *Indiewood USA . . . Where Hollywood Meets Independent Cinema* (London: I. B. Tauris, 2009).

5. Janet Wasko, "Show Me the Money: Challenging Hollywood Economics," in *Toward a Political Economy of Culture: Capitalism and Communication in the Twenty-First Century*, ed. Andrew Calabrese and Colin Starks (Boulder, Colo.: Rowman & Littlefield, 2004), 144.

6. *Recession and Regression: The 2011 Hollywood Writers Report*, Writers Guild of America-West, www.wga.org/uploadedFiles/who_we_are/hwr11execsum.pdf; Stacy L. Smith and Marc Choueiti, *Black Characters in Popular Film: Is the Key to Diversifying Cinematic Content Held in the Hand of the Black Director?* (Los Angeles: Annenberg School for Communication and Journalism, 2011).

7. Sasha Torres, "Television and Race," in *A Companion to Television*, ed. Janet Wasko (Malden, Mass.: Blackwell, 2005), 399.

8. Jane Arthurs, "*Sex and the City* and Consumer Culture: Remediating Postfeminist Drama," *Feminist Media Studies* 3, no. 1 (2003): 83.

9. Candace Moore, "Having It All Ways: The Tourist, the Traveler, and the Local in *The L Word*," *Cinema Journal* 46, no. 4 (2007): 5.

10. Richard Huff, "The Final Frontier: Lesbians: Showtime Teases 'L-Word,'" *New York Daily News*, October 24, 2003, www.nydailynews.com/archives/entertainment/final -frontier-lesbians-showtime-teases-l-word-article-1.513832.

11. Allison Glock, "She Likes to Watch," *New York Times*, Television, February 6, 2005, www.nytimes.com.

12. Herman Gray, *Watching Race: Television and the Struggle for "Blackness"* (Minneapolis: University of Minnesota Press, 1995), 86.

13. Joseph, *Transcending Blackness*; Catherine R. Squires, *The Post-racial Mystique: Media and Race in the Twenty-First Century* (New York: New York University Press, 2014); Caroline Streeter, *Tragic No More: Mixed Race Women and the Nexus of Sex and Celebrity* (Amherst, Mass.: University of Massachusetts Press, 2012).

14. Patricia Hill Collins, *Black Sexual Politics: African Americans, Gender, and the New Racism* (New York: Routledge, 2004), 102.

15. *Monster's Ball*, directed by Marc Forster (2001; Lionsgate; DVD released 2002), 111 min.

16. Saidiya Hartman, *Scenes of Subjection: Terror, Slavery, and Self-Making in Nineteenth Century America* (Oxford: Oxford University Press, 1997), 88–89.

17. For a description of "scientific" mulatto traits, see Edward Byron Reuter, *The Mulatto in the United States: Including a Study of the Role of Mixed-Blood Races Throughout the World* (Boston: Badger, 1918), 87–91.

18. Laura Briggs, "The Race of Hysteria: Overcivilization and the 'Savage' Woman in Late Nineteenth-Century Obstetrics and Gynecology," *American Quarterly* 52, no. 2 (2000): 246–73; Joel Williamson, *New People: Miscegenation and Mulattoes in the United States* (Baton Rouge: Louisiana State University Press, 1995) 95–96.

19. Elin Diamond, *Unmaking Mimesis: Essays on Feminism and Theatre* (New York: Routledge, 2004), 5.

20. See Khalil Gibran Muhammad, *The Condemnation of Blackness: Race, Crime, and the Making of Modern America* (Cambridge, Mass.: Harvard University Press, 2010).

21. Mia Mask, "Monster's Ball," *Film Quarterly* 58, no. 1 (2004): 52.

22. I use social death here as a metaphorical condition deriving from the legacies of slavery and contemporary racial oppression. See Orlando Patterson, *Slavery and Social Death: A Comparative Study* (Cambridge, Mass.: Harvard University Press, 1982), 13.

23. Mask, "Monster's Ball," 54.

24. bell hooks, "Eating the Other: Desire and Resistance," in *Black Looks: Race and Representation* (Boston: South End Press, 1992),23.

25. Aimee Carrillo Rowe, "Feeling in the Dark: Empathy, Whiteness, and Miscege-nation in Monster's Ball," *Hypatia* 22, no. 2 (2007): 122–42.

26. W. E. B. Du Bois, *The Souls of Black Folk*, introduced by Donald B. Gibson, and with notes by Monica M. Elbert (New York: Penguin, 1991 [1903]); Alain Locke, *The New Negro: Voices of the Harlem Renaissance* (New York: Albert & Charles Boni, 1925).

27. Joseph, *Transcending Blackness*, 63–65.

28. Kevin K. Gaines, *Uplifting the Race: Black Leadership, Politics, and Culture in the Twentieth Century* (Chapel Hill: University of North Carolina Press, 2012), 1–2.

29. *The L Word*, season 1, episode 1, "Pilot," directed by Rose Troche, written by Ilene Chaiken, Kathy Greenberg, and Michele Abbott, aired January 18, 2004, on Showtime.

30. Kellie Burns and Cristyn Davies, "Producing Cosmopolitan Sexual Citizens on *The L Word*," *Journal of Lesbian Studies* 13 (2009): 182.

31. See Siobhan Somerville, *Queering the Color Line: Race and the Invention of Homosexuality in American Culture* (Durham, N.C.: Duke University Press, 2000), 77–110.

32. *The L Word*, season 6, episode 3, "LMFAO," directed by Angela Robinson, written by Alexandra Kondracke, aired February 1, 2009, on Showtime.

33. *The L Word*, season 2, episode 1, "Life, Loss, Leaving," directed by Daniel Minahan, written by Ilene Chaiken, aired February 20, 2005, on Showtime.

34. *The L Word*, season 1, episode 10, "Liberally," directed by Mary Harron, written by Ilene Chaiken, aired March 21, 2004, on Showtime.

35. David Eng, *The Feeling of Kinship: Queer Liberalism and The Racialization of Intimacy* (Durham, N.C.: Duke University Press, 2010), 5–17.

36. Ibid., 45.

37. José Esteban Muñoz, "Queer Minstrels for the Straight Eye: Race as Surplus in Gay TV," *GLQ: A Journal of Lesbian and Gay Studies* 11, no. 1 (2005): 102.

38. LeiLani Nishime, "Queer Keanu: The Politics of Bad Acting," in *Undercover Asian: Multiracial Asian Americans in Visual Culture*, 21–40 (Urbana: University of Illinois Press, 2014).

39. Adrian Piper, "Passing for White, Passing for Black," *Transition* 58 (1992): 6–10.

40. Joseph, *Transcending Blackness*, 59.

41. *The L Word*, season 1, episode 8, "Listen Up," directed by Kari Skogland, written by Mark Zakarin, aired March 7, 2004, on Showtime.

42. Ibid.

43. Michele Elam, *Souls of Mixed Folk: Race, Politics, and Aesthetics in the New Millennium* (Palo Alto: Stanford University Press, 2011), 96.

44. Joseph, *Transcending Blackness*, 60. *The L Word*, "Listen Up."

45. See Deborah E. McDowell, "The 'Nameless . . . Shameful Impulse': Sexuality in Nella Larsen's *Quicksand* and *Passing*," in *"The Changing Same": Black Women's Literature, Criticism, and Theory*, 78–97 (Bloomington: Indiana University Press, 1995).

46. Maurice O. Wallace, *Constructing the Black Masculine: Identity and Ideality in African American Men's Literature and Culture, 1775–1995* (Durham, N.C.: Duke University Press, 2002), 153.

47. Quoted in Joseph, *Transcending Blackness*, 60.

48. Habiba Ibrahim, *Troubling the Family: The Promise of Personhood and the Rise of Multiracialism* (Minneapolis: University of Minnesota Press, 2012), vii.

49. *The L Word*, "Pilot."

50. Dorothy Roberts, "Race, Gender, and Genetic Technologies: A New Reproductive Dystopia," *Signs: Journal of Women in Culture and Society* 34 (2009): 783–804.

51. *The L Word*, "Pilot."

52. Ibid.

53. Pam Grier, *Foxy: My Life in Three Acts* (New York: Grand Central, 2010).

54. Lawrence Otis Graham, *Our Kind of People: Inside America's Black Upper Class* (New York: Harper Perennial, 1999), 377.

55. Patricia Williams, *The Alchemy of Race and Rights* (Cambridge, Mass.: Harvard University, 1991), 186–87.

56. Patricia Williams, "Babies, Bodies, and Buyers," *Columbia Journal of Gender and the Law* 33, no. 1 (2016): 1–49.

57. *The L Word*, season 1, episode 5, "Lawfully," directed by Daniel Minahan, written by Rose Troche, aired February 15, 2004, on Showtime.

58. Joseph, *Transcending Blackness*, 54.

59. *The L Word*, season 3, episode 11, "Last Dance," directed by Allison Anders, written by Ilene Chaiken, aired March 19, 2006, on Showtime.

60. Hortense J. Spillers, "Notes on an Alternative Model—Neither/Nor," in *Black, White, and in Color: Essays on American Literature and Culture* (Chicago: University of Chicago Press, 2003), 310.

61. *The L Word*, "Life, Loss, Leaving."

62. Somerville, *Queering the Color Line*, 80, 25–33.

63. Rebecca Beirne, "Fashioning *The L Word*," *Nebula* 3, no. 4 (2006): 17.

64. On the 1990s multiracial movement, see Ibrahim, *Troubling the Family*.

65. Eng, *Feeling of Kinship*, 101. Siobhan Somerville, "Notes Toward a Queer History of Naturalization," *American Quarterly* 57, no. 3 (2005): 672.

66. *The L Word*, season 6, episode 8, "Last Word," directed and written by Ilene Chaiken, aired March 8, 2009, on Showtime.

Chapter 5. Remixing Mixedness

1. "Beautiful," written by Snoop Dogg (Calvin Broadus), Pharrell Williams, and Chad Hugo, vocals by Snoop Dogg, Pharrell Williams, and Charlie Wilson, released January 21, 2003, https://www.youtube.com/watch?v=_FE194VN6c4; "I Got It from My Mama," written by will.i.am (William Adams), vocals by will.i.am., released August 2, 2007, https://www.youtube.com/watch?v=XomQLhjCYYk. All subsequent quotations to these songs are to this source.

2. Laura de Mello e Souza, "O padre e as feiticeiras—notas sobre sexualidade no Brasil Colonial," in *História e sexualidade no Brasil*, ed. Ronaldo Vainfas (Rio de Janeiro: Graal, 1986), 9–18.

3. See Ana López, "Are All Latins from Manhattan? Hollywood, Ethnography and Cultural Colonialism," in *Mediating Two Worlds: Cinematic Encounters in the Americas*, ed. John King, Ana M. López, and Manuel Alvarado (London: British Film Institute, 1993), 78; Shari Roberts, "The Lady in the Tutti-Frutti Hat: Carmen Miranda, a Spectacle of Ethnicity" *Cinema Journal* 32, no. 3 (1993): 3–23.

4. See Tiago de Melo Gomes and Micol Seigel, "Sabina's Oranges: The Colours of Cultural Politics in Rio de Janeiro, 1889–1930," *Journal of Latin American Cultural Studies* 11, no. 1 (2002): 13–20.

5. Ana Rita Mendonça, *Carmen Miranda Foi a Washington* (Rio de Janeiro: Record, 1999), 30–45.

6. Angela Gilliam, "The Brazilian *Mulata*: Images in the Global Economy," *Race and Class* 40, no. 1 (1998): 66–67.

7. Era Bell Thompson, "Does Amalgamation Work in Brazil? Part I," *Ebony* 20 (July 1965): 27–30; and Era Bell Thompson, "Does Amalgamation Work in Brazil? Part II," *Ebony* 20 (September 1965): 33–41.

8. The Brazilian Constitution in 1934 prohibited Black and Asian immigration and limited immigration to whites. Jeffrey Lesser, "Immigration and Shifting Concepts of National Identity in Brazil During the Vargas Era," *Luso-Brazilian Review* 31 (1994): 23–44.

9. Patricia de Santana Pinho, "African-American Roots Tourism in Brazil," *Latin American Perspectives* 35, no. 3 (2008): 76.

10. Erica Williams, *Sex Tourism in Bahia: Ambiguous Entanglements* (Urbana: University of Illinois Press, 2013), 90–94.

11. Arjun Appadurai, *Modernity at Large: Cultural Dimensions of Globalization* (Minneapolis: University of Minnesota Press, 1996), 33–36.

12. Mary Louise Pratt, *Imperial Eyes: Studies in Travel Writing and Transculturation* (New York: Routledge, 2007), 221–24.

13. Laura Mulvey, "Visual Pleasure and Narrative Cinema," *Screen* 16, no. 3 (1977): 11.

14. T. Denean Sharpley-Whiting, *Pimps Up, Ho's Down: Hip-Hop's Hold on Young Black Women* (New York: New York University Press, 2008), 42.

15. Ibid., 27.

16. See Kia Lilly Caldwell, "'Look at Her Hair': The Body Politics of Black Womanhood in Brazil," *Transforming Anthropology* 11, no. 2 (2004): 18–29.

17. See Vera Kutzinski, *Sugar's Secrets: Race and the Erotics of Cuban Nationalism* (Charlottesville: University Press of Virginia, 1993).

18. Raquel Rivera, *New York Ricans from the Hip Hop Zone* (New York: Palgrave Macmillan, 2003), 148.

19. See Sander Gilman, *Making the Body Beautiful: A Cultural History of Aesthetic Surgery* (Princeton, N.J.: Princeton University Press, 2000), 212.

20. Janell Hobson, "The 'Batty' Politic: Towards an Aesthetic of the Black Female Body," *Hypatia* 18, no. 4 (2003): 96.

21. See bell hooks, *We Real Cool: Black Men and Masculinity* (New York: Routledge, 2004); Imani Perry, *Prophets of the Hood, Politics and Poetics in Hip Hop* (Durham, N.C.: Duke University Press, 2004); Miles White, *From Jim Crow to Jay-Z: Race, Rap, and the Performance of Masculinity* (Champaign: University of Illinois Press, 2011); Mark Anthony Neal, *Looking for Leroy: Illegible Black Masculinities* (New York: New York University Press, 2013).

22. See Mary C. Beltrán, "The New Hollywood Racelessness: Only the Fast, Furious, (and Multiracial) Will Survive," *Cinema Journal* 44, no. 2 (winter 2005): 50–67.

23. *Fast Five*, directed by Justin Lin, written by Chris Morgan (Universal Pictures, 2011), 130 min.

24. Beltrán, "New Hollywood Racelessness."

25. Ibrahim, *Troubling the Family*, 167–75.

26. Mary Beltrán, "Fast and Bilingual: *Fast & Furious* and the Latinization of 'Racelessness,'" *Cinema Journal* 53, no. 1 (fall 2012): 75–96.

27. Rob Cohen quoted in "Men of Action," *People*, December 12, 2002, 156.

28. "Benjamin Svetkey, "At All Costs," *Entertainment Weekly*, August 2, 2002, www.ew.com/ew/article/0,331535,00.html.

29. Beltrán, "New Hollywood Racelessness."

30. Beltrán, "Fast and Bilingual." Beltrán notes that the character Dominic speaks fluent Spanish in *Los Bandoleros*, the prequel to *Fast & Furious*.

31. Vin Diesel quoted in "Vin Diesel 'Adores' Dominicans, Presents 'Los Bandoleros,'" *Dominican Today*, July 30, 2009, www.dominicantoday.com.

32. See Beltrán, "New Hollywood Racelessness."

33. Ibid., 59.

34. The mulatto is often a double figure. See Werner Sollors, *Neither Black nor White yet Both: Thematic Explorations of Interracial Literature* (New York: Oxford University Press, 1997), 240. Mulatto heroes in nineteenth-century abolitionist literature such as Archy Moore in Richard Hildreth's *The Slave* (1836) and *The White Slave* (1852), George Harris in *Uncle Tom's Cabin* (1852), often rebelled or resisted white dominance with violence. See Barbara Christian, *Black Women Novelists: The Development of a Tradition, 1892–1976* (Westport, Conn.: Greenwood, 1980), 21–22; Nancy Bentley, "White Slaves: The Mulatto Hero in Antebellum Fiction," *American Literature* 65, no. 2 (1993): 507, 508.

35. Harriet Beecher Stowe, *Uncle Tom's Cabin, The Minister's Wooing and Oldtown Folks*, ed. Kathryn Kish Sklar (New York: Library of America, 1982), 610.

36. Angharad N. Valdivia, "Geographies of Latinidad: Deployments of Racial Hybridity in the Mainstream," in *Race, Identity, and Representation in Education*, ed. Warren Crichlow, Greg Dimitriadis, Nadine Dolby, and Cameron McCarthy (New York: Routledge, 2005), 313.

37. See Greg Carter, *The United States of the United Races: A Utopian History of Racial Mixing* (New York: New York University Press, 2013).

38. Mary C. Beltrán, *Latina/o Stars in U.S. Eyes: The Making and Meanings of Film and TV Stardom* (Urbana: University of Illinois Press, 2009).

39. Tim Cogshell quoted in Ted Chen and Julie Brayton, "*Fast Five*'s Diverse Cast Is a Hit," *NBC Los Angeles*, May 3, 2011, www.nbclosangeles.com.

40. Alan Tomlinson and Christopher Young, *National Identity and Global Sports Events: Culture, Politics, and Spectacle in the Olympics and the Football World Cup* (Albany: State University of New York Press, 2006).

41. Lula da Silva Speech to International Olympic Committee in Copenhagen, www.youtube.com/watch?v=R3rO8xhHxMs.

42. "Rio 2016 Launches 'Live Your Passion' at New Year Celebrations," Rio 2016, December 30, 2008, www.rio2016.org.br/en/Noticias/Noticia.aspx?idConteudo=706. "COB lanca logomarca da candidatura do Rio aos Jogos 2016," *Estadão*, December 18, 2007, http://esportes.estadao.com.br/noticias/geral,cob-lanca-logomarca-da-candidatura-do-rio-aos-jogos-2016,97773.

43. Rio 2016 Candidate City 2009: Rio de Janeiro 2016, Candidature File for Rio de Janeiro to Host the 2016 Olympic and Paralympic Games, vols. 1–3. http://rio2016.com/ sites/default/files/parceiros/candidature_file_v1.pdf, http://rio2016.com/ sites/default/ files/parceiros/volume2, http://rio2016.com/ sites/default/files/parceiros/volume_3.

44. Ibid., vol. 1, 29, 39, 40, 82, 83.

45. Ibid., 14–15.

46. Rafael Maranhão, "Com reforço de Lula, 'seleção' brasileira usa a emoção na cartada final por 2016," *O Globo*, February 10, 2009, http://globoesporte.globo.com/Esportes/Noticias/ Olimpiadas/0,MUL1326806–17698,00-COM+REFORCO+DE+LULA+SELECAO +BRASILEIRA+USA+A+EMOCAO+NA+CARTADA+FINAL+POR.html.

47. Maranhão, "Com reforço de Lula." For the video of the announcement, see http://article .wn.com/view/2012/06/06/IOC_Rio_has_made_great_strides_for_2016_Olympics _but_warns_0/#/video. Quotations in text are to this video.

48. Doris Sommer, *Foundational Fictions: The National Romances of Latin America* (Berkeley: University of California Press, 1991), 6.

49. U.S. Black buddies are characterized as friendly, deferential and non-threatening. See Edward Guerrero, "The Black Image in Protective Custody: Hollywood's Biracial Buddy Films of the Eighties," in *Black American Cinema*, ed. Manthia Diawara (New York: Routledge, 1993), 237–46.

50. Natasha Pravaz, "Performing *Mulata*-ness: The Politics of Cultural Authenticity and Sexuality among Carioca Samba Dancers," *Latin American Perspectives* 39, no. 2 (2012): 113–33.

51. Rio 2016 presents strategic pillars to IOC in Durban: Vision and Mission of Rio 2016 Olympic and Paralympic Games were also unveiled, http://www.rio2016.org/en/news/ news/rio-2016-presents-strategic-pillars-to-ioc-members-in-durban, updated Jul 22, 2011.

52. Rio 2016: The Event, http://www.rio2016.org/en/the-games/olympic/event.

53. Rio 2016: Live Your Passion, http://www.rio2016.org.br/sumarioexecutivo/default _en.asp.

54. Rio de Janeiro Candidature File, vol. 1.

55. *Fair Play for Housing Rights: Mega-events, Olympic Games and Housing Rights* (Geneva: Centre on Housing Rights and Evictions [COHRE], 2007), 154.

56. Alexei Barrionuevo, "Violence in the Newest Olympic City Rattles Brazil," *New York Times*, October 20, 2009, ; Alexei Barrionuevo, "With World Watching, Rio Focuses on Security," *New York Times*, January 17, 2010, A1.

57. See Teresa Caldeira, *City of Walls: Crime, Segregation, and Citizenship in São Paulo* (Berkeley: University of California Press, 2000).

58. Simon Romero, "Slum Dwellers Are Defying Brazil's Grand Design for Olympics," *New York Times*, March 4, 2012, www.nytimes.com; "Brazil: Forced Evictions Must Not Mar Rio Olympics," Amnesty International News, November 14, 2011,; "Brazil Off Course for World Cup and Olympics-Un Housing Expert," United Nations Human Rights, April 26, 2011, www.ohchr.org/en/NewsEvents/Pages/DisplayNews .aspx?NewsID=10960&LangID=E.

59. *O Globo* and *Folha de São Paulo* websites had special dedicated sections of the protests with daily coverage. See http://www1.folha.uol.com.br/especial/2013/paisem protesto/ and http://g1.globo.com/protestos-no-brasil/2013/cobertura/.

Epilogue

1. "2016 Rio Olympics opening ceremony coverage," NBC, August 5, 2016.

2. Agência Brasil, "Dilma diz que 'pobreza no Brasil tem face negra e feminina,'" November 19, 2011, www.ocarcara.com/2011/11/presidenta-dilma-rousseff-disse-hoje-19.html.

3. João H. Costa Vargas, "Black Disidentification: The 2013 Protests, Rolezinhos, and Racial Antagonism in Post-Lula Brazil," *Critical Sociology* 42, nos. 4–5 (2016): 551–65.

4. Mads Damgaard, "Cascading Corruption News: Explaining the Bias of Media Attention to Brazil's Political Scandals," *Opinião Pública* 24, no. 1 (2018): 114–43; João Feres Júnior and Luna de Oliveira Sassara, "Failed Honeymoon: Dilma Rousseff's Third Election Round," *Latin American Perspectives* 45, no. 3 (2018): 224–35.

5. Liziane Guazina, Hélder Prior, and Bruno Araújo, "Framing of a Brazilian Crisis: Dilma Rousseff's Impeachment in National and International Editorials," *Journalism Practice* 13, no. 5 (2019): 620–37.

6. Aaron Ansell, "Impeaching Dilma Rousseff: The Double Life of Corruption Allegations on Brazil's Political Right," *Culture, Theory and Critique* 59, no. 4 (2018): 312–31.

7. Southern Poverty Law Center, "The Year in Hate and Extremism," special issue of *Intelligence Report*, February 15, 2017, www.splcenter.org/fighting-hate/intelligence-report/2017/year-hate-and-extremism.

8. Luiz Augusto Campos and João Feres Júnior, "'Globo, a gente se vê por aqui?' Diversidade racial nas telenovelas das últimas três décadas (1985–2014)." *Plural-Revista de Ciências Sociais* 23, no. 1 (2016): 43.

9. "Após críticas à Bahia branca da Globo, '2º Sol' tem um negro para cada nova participação," *Folha de São Paulo*, September 4, 2018, https://telepadi.folha.uol.com.br/apos-criticas-bahia-branca-2o-sol-tem-um-negro-para-cada-participacao/.

10. María Immacolata Vassallo de Lopes and Guillermo Orozco, eds., *Ibero-American Observatory on Television Fiction OBITEL Yearbook 2018* (São Paulo: Globo Universidade, Editora Sulina, 2018); Eli Carter, "Entering through the *Porta Dos Fondos*: The Changing Landscape of Brazilian Television Fiction," *Television and New Media* 18, no. 5 (2017): 410–26.

11. Lucas Shaw, "Netflix Wants the World to Binge-Watch," *Bloomberg*, January 12, 2017, www.bloomberg.com.

12. "2017 in Netflix—A Year in Bingeing," Netflix Media Center, December 11, 2017, https://media.netflix.com/en/press-releases/2017-on-netflix-a-year-in-bingeing.

Index

The letter *f* following a page number denotes a figure.

JASMINE MITCHELL is an assistant professor of American studies and media and communication at SUNY Old Westbury.

The University of Illinois Press
is a founding member of the
Association of University Presses.

_____

Composed in 10.75/13 Arno Pro
with Adrianna Extended Pro display
by Lisa Connery
at the University of Illinois Press
Cover designed by Cynthia Liu
Cover images: Background television pattern
(The7Dew.Shutterstock.com).
Silhouette (photo by Suad Kamardeen on Unsplash).

University of Illinois Press
1325 South Oak Street
Champaign, IL 61820-6903
www.press.uillinois.edu